KT-440-444

GM Crops

PAGE 2

Stem cell research

PAGE 28

Contents

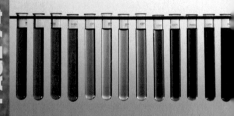

Acid rainbow

PAGE 74

Hard water

PAGE 91

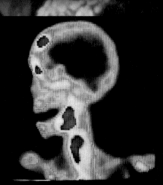

X-ray vision

PAGE 138

Welcome to Collins GCSE Science!

This book aims to give you a fascinating insight into contemporary science that is relevant and useful to you, right now today. We have written it to convey the excitement of Biology, Chemistry and Physics, and hope it will help you to carry a knowledge and understanding of science and scientific thinking with you throughout life.

USING THIS BOOK

What you should know

It is amazing how much knowledge you gain each year in your studies. Hopefully you can then build on this in the following years. In science there are many key ideas that are continually revisited and developed. To remind you of these, there are summaries for each of the main sections: biology, chemistry and physics.

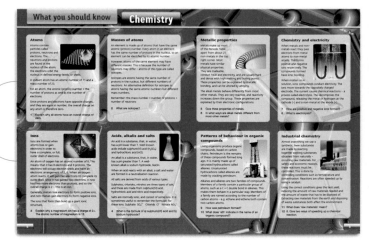

Unit opener

Altogether there are six topics, two biology, two chemistry and two physics. At the start of each topic there is an introductory spread, showing just some of the exciting science you will learn about. Also listed on this page are the spreads you will work through in the topic.

Main content

Most topics have 10 double page spreads. An introductory paragraph at the start of each spread puts the material in an everyday context. Separate sections then look at progressively more demanding ideas and applications.

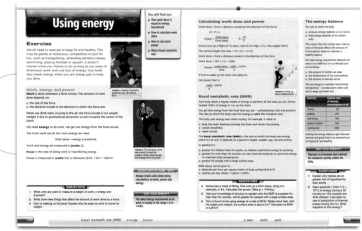

Collins

EDEXCEL 360

SCIENCE

FOR EDEXCEL
GCSE BIOLOGY
CHEMISTRY
PHYSICS

WAVE ENERGY TESTING

HEIGHT 6 METRES
SPEED 20 M/S

Brian Arnold SERIES EDITOR
Gareth Price
Phil Routledge
Rob King
Mike Tingle
Jane Cartwright
Sandra Mitchell
Edmund Walsh

S104079

William Collins' dream of knowledge for all began with the publication of his first book in 1819. A self-educated mill worker, he not only enriched millions of lives, but also founded a flourishing publishing house. Today, staying true to this spirit, Collins books are packed with inspiration, innovation and practical expertise. They place you at the centre of a world of possibility and give you exactly what you need to explore it.

Collins. Do more.

Published by Collins
An imprint of HarperCollins*Publishers*
77–85 Fulham Palace Road
Hammersmith
London
W6 8JB

> Browse the complete Collins catalogue at
> **www.collinseducation.com**

© HarperCollins*Publishers* Limited 2006

10 9 8 7 6 5 4 3 2 1

ISBN 0-00-721641-6
ISBN 978-0-00-721641-3

The authors assert their moral right to be identified as the authors of this work.

All rights reserved. No part of this publication may be reproduced, stored in a retrieval system, or transmitted in any form or by any means, electronic, mechanical, photocopying, recording or otherwise, without the prior written permission of the Publisher or a licence permitting restricted copying in the United Kingdom issued by the Copyright Licensing Agency Ltd., 90 Tottenham Court Road, London W1T 4LP.

British Library Cataloguing in Publication Data. A Catalogue record for this publication is available from the British Library.

Commissioned by Cassandra Birmingham

Publishing manager: Melanie Hoffman

Project management: Sue Gardner

Editor: Ros Woodward

Cover design by John Fordham and Starfish Design

Cover artwork by Bob Lea

Prepared by Starfish Design, Editorial and Project Management Ltd.

Internal design by JPD

Illustrations by Rory Walker and Peters and Zabransky Ltd.

Exam questions by John Marill, Lesley Owen and Nicky Thomas

Glossary by Gareth Price

Production by Natasha Buckland

Printed and bound by Printing Express, Hong Kong

Acknowledgements

The authors and publisher are grateful to the following for permission to reproduce copyright material: www.pewagbiotech.org/resources/factsheets (p. 23, Figure 2); Ian Heap (www.WeedSmart.com) (p. 26, Figure 2); Safety Office, University of Waterloo (page 130, Figure 2); www.egglescliffe.org.uk/physics (p.167, Figure 3).

Whilst every effort has been made to trace the copyright holders, in cases where this has been unsuccessful or if any have been inadvertently overlooked, the publisher will be pleased to make the necessary arrangements at the first opportunity.

EG32497

EHWLC
LEARNING CENTRE EALING GREEN

500
PRI

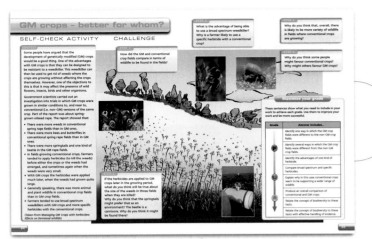

Mid-unit assessment

The mid-unit assessment questions enable you to recap on several weeks' work and assess your own level of understanding. Achieving good marks in these will confirm your progress and highlight any areas of weakness that need to be addressed.

Unit summary

Unit summaries offer the opportunity to visualise links between key ideas through the use of spider diagrams. Constructing your own versions of these would be a useful way to begin your revision. The unit finishes with a number of questions designed to sharpen up your skills in these areas.

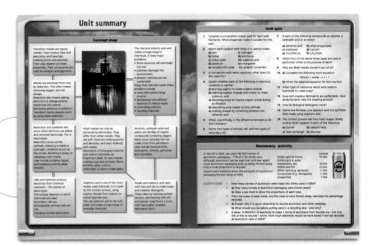

Exam practice

Developing a good exam technique will ensure that you take full advantage of the skills and knowledge you have gained. You need to give clear answers with working out and reasoning shown, in order to earn top marks. To help you achieve this we have included some practice questions. Try your best with these and don't rush them. Tackle one or two, see where you went wrong and then try some more, ensuring that you don't make the same mistakes. Remember: practice makes perfect – so use the questions well.

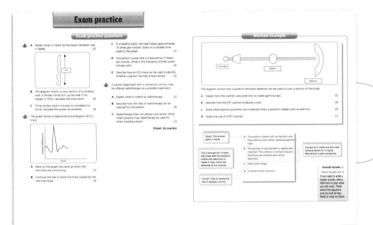

Genetics

Genetics is the study of the genes that control how organisms develop. A gene is a length of DNA found in the chromosomes of cells in the nucleus. Every organism has a unique set of genes called its genotype.  These work with the environment to produce the new organism. Diseases can be passed through the genes from parent to offspring. Clones are unusual because they all share the same genes. Animal clones are rare but many vegetables are clones, e.g. some types of potato.

1 Where are the genes in a human cell?

2 Why might a doctor be interested in the genes you have?

Biotechnology

Biotechnologists are interested in the genes in an organism because by manipulating or transferring them they can control how an  organism develops. Genetic engineers have developed tomatoes with fish genes, bacteria that produce human insulin and pigs that have human immunity proteins. It is a recent science but is moving very rapidly. It generates considerable debate about the rights and wrongs of scientific research. Some types of biotechnological research are already banned, for example human cloning or the development of biological weapons.

3 What do genetic engineers do?

4 Give one example of a biotechnology research area that you think is unethical.

Food and farming

As our population rises can we guarantee that everyone will have enough to eat? Biotechnologists work hard to develop improved crops to produce  more food. They also look at ways of improving the quality of food and even find ways to stop it going off so quickly. But many people think this is dangerous because it changes our food and farming methods. They insist on organic food grown in the same way as a hundred years ago. Is this sensible or an irrational fear of what might be?

5 What is the main reason for developing biotechnology in agriculture?

6 Why do some people prefer organic foods?

DNA data

Deoxyribonucleic acid (DNA) is the chemical that genes are made from. It is a complex double-helix shape carrying a code consisting of four bases. The  sequence of these bases contains the information needed to create new organisms. Genetic engineers can recognise parts of the molecule by looking for particular sequences of bases. This allows them to cut out particular genes. The Human Genome Project has plotted the sequence of all of the bases for the human body's 20 000 separate genes.

7 What does DNA stand for?

8 How many genes does a human being contain?

Evolution

Over generations, the effects of natural selection lead to the evolution of new species from variants that are better adapted to their environment.

Genes are parts of chromosomes which are found within the nucleus and control a cell's activity. Genes are made of DNA and carry the code to make a specific protein. Alternative forms of a gene (alleles) cause variation in a characteristic.

9 Explain how vertebrates are classified into different groups.

10 A mule is a hybrid. What is meant by a hybrid?

11 How is sexual reproduction different from asexual reproduction?

Chemicals and cells

The central nervous system is made up of the brain and the spinal cord. It links sensory organs to muscles. Receptors in sense organs detect internal and external changes, called stimuli. Muscles and other effectors allow the body to respond to these stimuli. Some responses are voluntary while others are involuntary and are called reflex responses. Reflex responses are often designed to protect the body.

12 Write out the sequence of a reflex action, starting with a stimulus and ending with a response.

13 List three reasons for and three reasons against testing drugs on animals.

Genes

DNA controls the joining together of amino acids to make a specific protein in a cell and the order of bases in a section of DNA decides the order of amino acids in the protein.

Selective breeding (artificial selection) can be used in many ways including improving the quality of milk from cattle and increasing the number of offspring in sheep.

Scientists often have to debate ethical questions that arise from their work.

14 Domestic cattle have been selectively bred. Describe the features that are desirable in cattle bred for milk production and compare them with features in cattle bred for meat production.

Animals and the environment

Factors such as interdependence, adaptation, competition and predation influence the distribution and population sizes of organisms in a particular habitat. Humans influence changes in these habitats and can have a disproportionate effect on populations living within a habitat. Most people consider that humans have a duty to protect natural populations.

15 Name a predator and describe three features that are important in making it successful.

16 Name a prey animal and describe three features that are important in preventing it from being eaten.

Atoms

Atoms contain particles called protons, neutrons and electrons. The neutrons and protons are found in the nucleus of the atom; the electrons orbit the nucleus in defined energy levels, or shells.

A sodium atom has an atomic number of 11 and a mass number of 23.

For an atom, the atomic (proton) number = the number of protons as well as the number of electrons.

Since protons and electrons have opposite charges, and they are equal in number, the overall charge on any atom is therefore zero.

1 Explain why all atoms have an overall charge of zero.

Masses of atoms

An element is made up of atoms that have the same atomic (proton) number. Every atom in an element has the same number of protons in the nucleus, so an element can be identified by its atomic number.

However, atoms of the same element may have different masses. This is because the number of neutrons may differ – atoms of this type are called isotopes.

Isotopes are atoms having the same number of protons in the nucleus, but different numbers of neutrons. An alternative definition for isotopes is: atoms having the same atomic numbers but different mass numbers.

Remember: the mass number = number of protons + number of neutrons

2 What are isotopes?

Ions

Ions are formed when atoms lose or gain electrons in order to have a complete, or full, outer shell of electrons.

An atom of oxygen has an atomic number of 8. This means that it has 8 electrons and 8 protons. The electrons will occupy electron shells and have an electronic arrangement of 2, 6. When an oxygen atom reacts, it will gain two electrons to complete its outer shell. Since it has gained two electrons, it now has two more electrons than protons, and so the overall charge is 2–. This is an ion.

Generally, metals lose electrons to form positive ions, and non-metals gain electrons to form negative ions.

The ions that form then build up a giant ionic structure.

3 Explain why a magnesium ion has a charge of 2+. The atomic number of magnesium is 12.

Acids, alkalis and salts

An acid is a substance, that, in water, has a pH lower than 7. Well-known acids include sulphuric(VI) acid (H_2SO_4) and hydrochloric acid (HCl).

An alkali is a substance, that, in water, has a pH greater than 7. A well-known alkali is sodium hydroxide, NaOH.

When an acid reacts with an alkali, a salt and water are formed in a neutralisation reaction.

All salts are derived from acids of various types.

Sulphates, chlorides, nitrates are three types of salt, and these are made from sulphuric(VI) acid, hydrochloric acid and nitric acid respectively.

Salts are normally ionic, and consist of some ions. It is sometimes useful to remember the formulae for these ions: Sulphate SO_4^{2-} Chloride Cl^- Nitrate NO_3^-

4 What is the formula of a) sulphuric(VI) acid and b) sodium hydroxide?

Metallic properties

Metals make up most of the Periodic Table, apart from about 25 non-metals in the top right corner. Most metals have similar physical properties. They are malleable, conduct heat and electricity, and are usually hard and dense with high melting and boiling points. These properties can be explained by metallic bonding, and can be altered by alloying.

The alkali metals behave differently from most other metals. They are very reactive, and reactivity increases down the group. These properties are explained by their electronic configurations.

5 Give three properties of metals.

6 In what ways are alkali metals different from most other metals?

Chemistry and electricity

When metals and non-metals react they pass electrons from metal atoms to non-metal atoms. This forms positive and negative ions respectively. The compounds formed have ionic bonding.

When molten or in solution, ionic compounds conduct electricity. The ions move towards the oppositely charged electrode. The current causes chemical reactions – a process called electrolysis. This decomposes the compound, releasing the metal or hydrogen at the cathode (–) and a non-metal at the anode (+).

7 How are positive and negative ions formed?

8 What is electrolysis?

Patterns of behaviour in organic compounds

Living organisms produce organic compounds, based on carbon chains. Petroleum is the remains of these compounds formed long ago. It is mainly made up of saturated hydrocarbons called alkanes. Unsaturated hydrocarbons called alkenes are made by cracking petroleum.

Alkanes and alkenes are two families of compounds. Members of a family contain a particular group of atoms, such as a C = C double bond in alkenes. This makes them behave in a particular way. Members of a family are named according to the number of carbon atoms – e.g. ethane and ethene both contain two carbon atoms.

9 How was petroleum formed?

10 What does 'eth' indicate in the name of an organic compound?

Industrial chemistry

Almost everything we use is synthetic. New substances are made by reacting together existing substances obtained from naturally occurring raw materials. For safety and economic reasons, these reactions must be controlled. This is done by controlling conditions such as temperature and concentration. Reactions are often speeded up by using a catalyst.

Using the correct conditions gives the best yield, reducing the amount of raw materials needed and the amount of waste that has to be disposed of. Extracting raw materials from the earth and disposing of waste substances both affect the environment.

11 What does 'raw materials' mean?

12 Give two ways of speeding up a chemical reaction.

Energy

There are several types of energy including kinetic energy and heat.

Energy is never created or destroyed, but may be transferred between objects or transformed into different types of energy.

Kinetic energy is calculated using the equation

$$KE = \frac{1}{2} mv^2$$

1   Name three other types of energy.

2   What type of energy is stored in a battery?

Particles

All substances are made up of particles.

Particles are arranged differently in solids, liquids and gases.

In a gas, particles move very quickly and interact only through collisions.

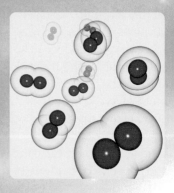

3   List three differences between the arrangements of particles in a solid and in a gas.

4   Why can gases be compressed when solids and liquids cannot?

Heating up

When a material is heated, the particles vibrate faster or move faster.

If enough heat energy is put in, the material may change state.

Materials expand when heated.

5   What happens to the particles when a solid turns to a liquid?

6   Explain, using the idea of particles, why a material expands when heated.

Inside the atom

Atoms consist of negatively charrged electrons surrounding a very small positively charged nucleus.

The nucleus contains protons and neutrons.

Objects can be uncharged, negatively charged or positively charged.

Some atoms spontaneously emit nuclear radiation and are said to be radioactive.

7   What happens if two objects with the same (like) charge are brought close together?

8   What happens if two objects with different (opposite) charges are brought close together?

Light

Refraction is the change in direction of a ray of light when it enters or leaves a material of different density. If light passes into a less dense medium (e.g. glass to air), it is possible for the angle of refraction to be a right angle (90°). When this happens, the angle of incidence is called the critical angle.

If the angle of incidence is greater than the critical angle, *all* the light is reflected inside the denser material; this is total internal reflection.

9 Why cannot total internal reflection occur when light goes from a less dense to a more dense medium?

10 Draw a diagram to show a ray of light passing through a prism periscope.

Radiation

Radiation is the name given to any sort of energy that spreads out from a source.

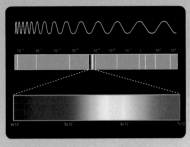

The electromagnetic spectrum includes waves from long wavelength (low-frequency) radio waves to very short wavelength (high-frequency) gamma rays.

Wave speed = frequency × wavelength

Radiation can be useful, but sometimes it can be harmful.

11 What forms of radiation do we receive from the Sun?

12 Find the frequency of Radio 4, broadcasting waves with a wavelength of 1500 m and a speed of 3×10^8 m/s.

Work, power and energy

Work is done when a force moves an object through its point of application.

$W = F \times d$

Work is measured in joules (J). Energy is needed to do work. Energy is also measured in joules.

Power is a measure of how quickly work is done.

$P = W/t$

Power is measured in watts (W).

13 How much work does Sam do when he lifts a 20 N box from the ground to a shelf 2 m high?

14 Jane weighs 500 N. She climbs the Eiffel Tower, which is 300 m high, in 15 minutes.

   a   How much work does she do?

   b   Calculate her average power.

Using radioactivity

A Geiger counter measures radioactivity. Radioactive sources emit ionising radiation. There are three types of ionising radiation – alpha (α), beta (β) and gamma (γ).

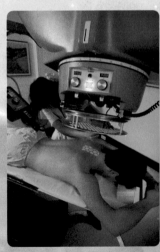

Medical uses include sterilising equipment, treating cancers and as tracers for diagnosis.

15 Which type of ionising radiation is most penetrating?

16 What is 'background radiation'?

17 Which type of radiation is positively charged?

BIOTECHNOLOGY

Does this gene show that you may have a higher probability of heart disease? Would you like a future employer to know about this? Do you think it would make you less likely to get that high-stress job?

And this gene might be one you shared with Margaret Thatcher. Or the queen of England. Or a criminal serving time for murder. What might that say about you? Are you just a product of your genes?

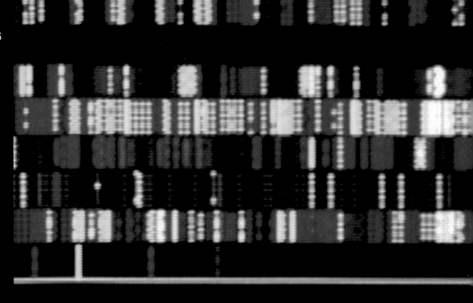

You're looking at human genes! This pattern shows different bands of DNA from a human being. The whole picture would take up all of the pages in this book – and more! In the future you might even be able to get a picture like this of your own genes. Your doctor could check it to see how you will respond to different medicines. These coloured bands could save your life.

This gene codes for a protein that can kill cancer cells. Maybe a genetic engineer could copy it and make a new treatment for lung cancer. But who owns the drug? And the profits from the sale? You? Or the researcher?

What is biotechnology?

You will find out:
- What we mean by biotechnology
- How biotechnology has changed over the last 10 000 years
- How biotechnology might change over the next 100 years

Who's the daddy?

Biotechnology is the most modern science, right? Well, in a way. It is also one of the oldest – the first cooks were changing biological organisms to make them more useful to humans. The most important change for humans was also a biological technology – the invention of agriculture. Maybe biotech is the daddy of all science?

FIGURE 1: Date palm trees, with dates ready to eat!

The biotech timeline

8000 BC Humans begin to control **breeding** of animals. Potatoes are planted for food. Agriculture is invented and world food supply rises dramatically.

4000–2000 BC **Yeast** is used to make bread rise and brew alcoholic drinks (Egypt). The Chinese, Sumerians and Egyptians learn how to make cheese and ferment fruit juice to make wine. Babylonians know enough about flower pollination to control date palm breeding.

500 BC The Chinese use mouldy soy bean curd (tofu) to treat boils – this is the first **antibiotic**!

AD 100 The Chinese use powdered chrysanthemums to kill insect pests on crops – the first insecticide.

1322 An Arab chieftain uses artificial insemination to produce better horses.

1797 Edward Jenner inoculates a child against smallpox.

1857 Pasteur shows that microorganisms are needed for **fermentation**.

1914 **Bacteria** are used to clean sewage in Manchester. There are more bacteria digesting faeces in one sewage farm than there are stars in our galaxy!

FIGURE 2: Jenner inoculating a baby.

QUESTIONS

1 When was the first insecticide produced?
2 When was the Human Genome project launched?
3 Who discovered how to make bread rise using yeast?

...*antibiotic* ...*bacteria* ...*biotechnology* ...*breeding* ...*fermentation* ...*genetic engineering*

1928	Fleming discovers penicillin. It was not until 1944 that it could be mass produced – but it saved hundreds of thousands of lives in the Second World War and millions since.
1953	The journal *Nature* publishes Watson and Crick's paper about DNA. This proposed the now-famous double-helix structure.
1963/4	The organisations CYMMIT in Mexico and IRRI in the Philippines produce new breeds of wheat and rice that increase yields by up to 70%. The **green revolution** begins and scientists and politicians talk of banishing hunger through scientific progress.
1978	Human insulin is produced through the use of **genetic engineering**. The hormone was produced when a human gene was inserted into a **microorganism** called *E. coli*.
1984	Genetic fingerprinting is developed by Prof. Alec Jeffries at Leicester University. It is later used to track down murderers and rapists.
1986	First genetically modified plant crop is planted. It is a variety of tobacco plant that is resistant to some diseases.
1990	The **Human Genome Project** is launched. This is an attempt to map every gene in the human body.
1992	Scientists find a way to test human embryos for certain genetic diseases such as cystic fibrosis and haemophilia.
1997	Dolly the sheep is produced at the Roslin Institute in Scotland. This is the first cloned mammal produced from a single adult cell.
1998	Human embryonic **stem cells** grown in culture.
2000	Genetically modified 'golden rice' launched in developing countries in an attempt to prevent certain types of blindness.
2004	The first cloned pet, a kitten, is delivered to its owner.

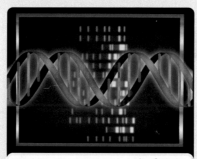
FIGURE 3: Computer artwork of DNA and genetic code.

DID YOU KNOW?
Global biotechnology companies made over $63 billion in sales in 2005!

Science and the media

FIGURE 4: Dolly, the first cloned mammal.

Dolly the sheep was a major biotechnology breakthrough and the media started to talk about miracle drugs and new ways to treat diseases such as cancer and even old age. On the other side some people began to worry about cloning humans and Frankenstein-designed monsters. Ten years later and little of this seems to have happened.

There is a problem in the way science is reported in the media. Sometimes complicated ideas are simplified to make exciting headlines for newspapers. These can mislead or even tell lies.

Biotechnology is a powerful science that will change the world. It should not be left to scientists to make all of the decisions. Ordinary citizens and governments should be involved. But do we know enough science to judge?

QUESTIONS

6 List the reasons why biotechnological developments should be reported by the media.

7 Do these reports do more harm than good? Give reasons for your answer.

QUESTIONS

4 When was the first cloned mammal produced?

5 Imagine you are writing an extension to the timeline in the year 2107. Add five more milestones with their dates and discoveries between 2007 and 2107.

Lo–tech biotech

You will find out:
- How bacteria are used to make yoghurt
- How a range of microorganisms create soy sauce

Mouldy food?

People have been using bacteria and fungi in foods such as yoghurt, cheese, tofu and beer for thousands of years. They are perhaps lo-tech biotech? We take them for granted but they made food taste better and last longer. And beer and wine have made celebrations go with a swing for thousands of years!

Making yoghurt

- Yoghurt is a useful way to make milk last longer. In the days before refrigeration fresh milk would last only a few days before it was spoilt. Yoghurt could preserve the milk for longer and cheese kept the valuable milk edible for months or even years.
- Yoghurt manufacture depends on bacterial activity. But not just any bacteria! The first job is to kill off any dangerous bacteria in the milk by boiling it and letting it cool.
- The particular bacteria needed to make yoghurt are then added. The easiest way to do this is to add a spoonful of live yoghurt. The milk is then covered and left in a warm place until it has set.
- The bacteria that make yoghurt are called *Lactobacillus bulgaricus*. They produce lactic acid which makes the milk curdle and give yoghurt its taste.

DID YOU KNOW?

Pasteurisation is used to make milk safe to drink. The milk is heated to 65 °C for a few moments to kill harmful bacteria. It is then cooled and bottled.

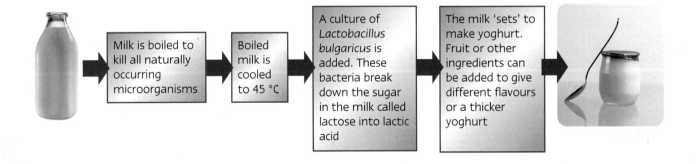

Milk is boiled to kill all naturally occurring microorganisms → Boiled milk is cooled to 45 °C → A culture of *Lactobacillus bulgaricus* is added. These bacteria break down the sugar in the milk called lactose into lactic acid → The milk 'sets' to make yoghurt. Fruit or other ingredients can be added to give different flavours or a thicker yoghurt →

FIGURE 1: How yoghurt is made.

QUESTIONS

1. What was yoghurt made from in the first place?
2. Why is milk boiled before the yoghurt is added?
3. What is the difference between pasteurising and boiling milk?
4. Why do refrigerated foods last longer?

...alcohol ...enzymes ...fermentation ...filter ...filtration

Fermentation

The process the bacteria use to make yoghurt is called **fermentation**. Fermentation is a kind of respiration that does not require oxygen. Many **microorganisms** carry out fermentation. Fermentation is much more varied than aerobic respiration and different microbes produce a wide range of waste products. The table shows the products of different fermentation reactions.

Microorganism	Fermentation product	Use by humans
yeast	ethanol	brewing alcoholic drinks
yeast	carbon dioxide	raising bread and other baked foods
Lactobacillus	lactic acid	converts milk to yoghurt and cheese
Acetobacter	ethanoic acid	converts wine to vinegar

Fermentation is only one part of the way microorganisms change the substrates they live on. They also secrete **enzymes** to break down complex chemicals to make them easier to absorb. They do this to get these chemicals into their cells so that they can be respired.

Soy sauce

Soya beans are an excellent source of protein – but difficult to digest and often a little tasteless. Tofu, or soya bean curd, is easier to digest but often even more lacking in flavour! Luckily, soya beans can be fermented to make a strongly flavoured sauce – soy sauce – used in many oriental dishes.

FIGURE 2: Homemade tofu for sale in a Chinese street market.

The soya beans are soaked, boiled and mashed to a paste. They are mixed with ground roasted wheat and spread on a large table. A culture called koji is added. Koji is a mixture of microbes but mainly *Aspergillus oryzae*.

The mixture is kept warm and aerated. After a few days, it is poured into large tanks and mixed with salt water. This liquid is left for up to six months to ferment into soy sauce.

During fermentation the mixture is kept warm and air is blown through it to increase the growth of the microbes. Fermentation breaks down starch and protein in the mixture to soluble chemicals.

At the end of the process the mix is **filtered** through layers of muslin. This **filtration** produces traditional soy sauce. This is filtered, pasteurised to kill any dangerous microbes, and then packed in sterile bottles.

Chinese rice wine

Chinese rice wine is made from a mixture of grains but mainly rice. A boiled mixture of grains is inoculated with rice infected with *Aspergillus oryzae* or a species of *Rhizopus*. These microbes break down the starch to a sugary liquor which contains **lactic acid**. The liquid is strained off and can be mixed with water to create the correct concentration.

Then yeast is added and fermentation of the sugar to **alcohol** begins. This can take several months, but some of the most expensive, and potent, wines may be left for decades. At the end the liquid is sold as yellow liquor. Sometimes this powerful liquid is distilled to produce a drink called white liquor or bai jiu. This can be up to 80% alcohol and is sometimes known as Chinese vodka.

FIGURE 3: Chinese rice wine – as strong as vodka but cheaper than a cup of coffee in Beijing!

QUESTIONS

5 What does the word 'culture' mean in the context of biotechnology?

6 What chemicals break complex molecules down into smaller ones so that the microorganisms can absorb them?

7 Which microbe helps to produce soy sauce?

QUESTIONS

8 What microorganism produces the alcohol in rice wine?

9 Why is rice wine distilled?

Foods from microbes

You will find out:

- About a range of microbial food products
- How these foods are produced
- How to make vegetarian cheddar cheese

Micro-factories

Microorganisms can make lot of things: medicines, many foods and a range of drinks, a range of important industrial chemicals and even enzymes for washing powders. One company has a bacterium that can digest crude oil! Will these creatures be the important micro-factories of the future?

Seaweed trifle, anyone?

The Irish call it carrageen. The Welsh call it laver bread. The Japanese have three or four names for it! Everyone else calls it seaweed. It comes in many different types and it produces some very useful stuff.

- Seaweed is rich in a range of minerals and very low in fat. It's a health food!
- The complex carbohydrate in the seaweed can be extracted to make a sort of organic glue. It is used to bind together everything from trifle to medicines and cosmetics. Therefore seaweed, or carragen, is known as a **gelling agent** because it firms liquid up into a gel.
- Agar jelly used to grow microoganisms in Petri dishes all comes from seaweed. The Chinese also use it to make a sort of cracker called an agar cake.

FIGURE 1: Agar cake for sale in a supermarket in Lhasa, Tibet. It's supposed to be good for the skin!

QUESTIONS

1 What is carrageen?
2 What characteristics make seaweed a healthy food?
3 What is a complex carbohydrate?
4 Give two uses of agar.

...amino acid   ...chymosin   ...citric acid

Other microbial products

DID YOU KNOW?

Enzymes are often used to make slow reactions go more quickly at low temperatures. This saves energy, so enzymes are helping to reduce global warming.

Vitamin C

Vitamin C manufacture is a multi-stage process. Some *Acetobacter* species can break down glucose some of the way using enzymes. Other bacteria can take it further but the final few steps to vitamin C involve strong acids and temperatures of about 100 °C. A research group in Scotland is looking at a way to bridge this final gap using genetically modified yeasts. This would make vitamin C production cheaper and more environmentally friendly.

Invertase

Invertase is an enzyme made by yeast and is used to convert sucrose into glucose and fructose. You will have enjoyed invertase in soft-centre chocolates. A solid paste in the middle is made with sucrose and a small amount of invertase. This is then covered with a thick layer of chocolate and left for a few weeks at 18 °C. The invertase converts the sugar to glucose and fructose making the centre semi-liquid and yummy!

FIGURE 2: The invertase makes this nice to eat!

Monosodium glutamate (MSG)

MSG makes food taste stronger. It is often added to Chinese food. The bacterium *Corynebacterium glutamicum* can produce **glutamic acid** which is then converted to MSG. Other bacteria can produce a range of **amino acids** which might be used in other foods or even protein drinks and supplements for bodybuilders.

FIGURE 3: Amino acid powders are used by bodybuilders.

Citric acid

Citric acid will turn up in many fruit squashes and fizzy drinks. It gives them a sharp taste and acts as a preservative. *Aspergillus niger* is a fungus used to produce citric acid from corn molasses at a temperature of about 27 °C. The world uses about 600 000 tonnes of citric acid every year!

FIGURE 4: Citric acid is found in drinks.

Vegetarian cheddar

Veggies eat a lot of cheese! But traditional cheeses use rennet extracted from a young cow's stomach to help the milk curdle. **Chymosin** is an alternative enzyme for this job – and no calves have to die. Chymosin is produced by the fungus *Mucor miehei* which is related to the pin mould you sometimes get on stale bread. Modern chymosin is actually made from genetically modified strains of the yeast *Kluyveromyces lactis* and two other bacteria.

FIGURE 5: How much of this cheese is vegetarian?

QUESTIONS

5 Which bacterium is used to produce vitamin C?

6 Draw a flow chart to show the production of soft-centre sweets.

7 What does MSG do to food?

8 What is the starting point for citric acid production by *Aspergillus niger*?

QUESTIONS

9 Why do vegetarians sometimes object to traditional cheeses?

10 Genetically modified bacteria are used to make many vegetarian cheddars. However, the manufacturer does not have to label the food as GM. Is this fair?

Healthy diets

You will find out:

- About foods that are supposed to promote health
- What a healthy diet contains
- About the dangers of the Western diet

Slow-motion suicide?

The major causes of death in the Western world are to do with the things we do to ourselves – voluntarily! We eat too much, we take too little exercise, we drink and smoke too much and … well, it is a bit like slow-motion suicide. Are we trying to kill ourselves?

Warning! Warning! Warning!

- Almost every week there is a new health scare about food, drink, exercise, lifestyle … almost everything nowadays seems to damage our health. In many ways this is good – it shows we understand the link between what we do and how healthy we are.
- But at the same time these constant warnings can be counter-productive. After a while we stop hearing them – 'It's just another scare and will pass!'

To be so fat that it affects your health is to be obese. Obesity now joins the main killers in the Western world. So what are the risks? The chart shows the result from a 24-year long study of nurses in the United States. The researchers followed the nurses for 24 years and counted how many died. The deaths could be due to any cause – cancer, heart disease or even a traffic accident.

FIGURE 1: Is this a bid to kill yourself?

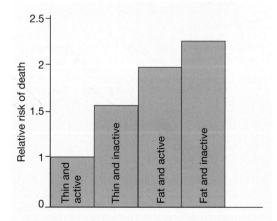

FIGURE 2: Obesity and inactivity increase the chances of dying early.

QUESTIONS

1. List **four** things that affect your health.
2. List **three** ways you could improve your own health.
3. In the American study which group was most likely to die?
4. How much more likely were the fat, inactive nurses to die compared with the thin, active ones?

WOW FACTOR!

Around 360 000 Americans die every year because of obesity. The health costs of treating obesity exceed $100 billion every year!

…cholesterol …esters

Balanced diets

A healthy diet and a good level of exercise have a very good effect on your life expectancy and general health. However, if you exercise regularly but are still overweight, your risk of an early death still rises.

So no vices allowed at all? Maybe healthy, vegetarian, non-drinkers and non-smokers don't live any longer. Is a healthy lifestyle boring?

In fact, the opposite is probably true. A healthy, balanced diet offers all sorts of benefits. One study showed that the chance of Alzheimer's disease was significantly reduced for people following a Mediterranean-style diet. So a healthy diet not only prolongs life but also helps you to avoid serious diseases such as Alzheimer's.

The study used a diet questionnaire with 2258 healthy men and women with no evidence of dementia. The results of the questionnaires were analysed and each person was put into one of ten groups, based on how close their typical diet was to the 'Mediterranean diet'. The group furthest from the Mediterranean diet was then taken as the baseline. Would a healthy diet protect the people in the other groups? The groups in the middle of the range were about 18% less likely to develop Alzheimer's, and in the groups with the best diets, the risk was reduced by up to 40%!

A Mediterranean diet includes fish, oils such as olive oil, pasta and a range of fresh, leafy vegetables. One study has even shown that a glass or two of red wine, not usually included in people's idea of diet, but typical of Mediterranean countries, also helps to prolong life.

FIGURE 3: A fruit and veg stall in Spain – healthier than a hospital in the UK?

> *A healthy diet not only prolongs life but also helps you to avoid serious diseases*

Functional foods?

Statins are chemicals found in certain types of plants. Research has shown that a diet high in these plant statins seems to lower cholesterol. High levels of **cholesterol** are linked to a range of heart problems. Manufacturers add statins to foods and market these as a way to lower your cholesterol. They work particularly well on cholesterol **esters** which are combinations of cholesterol and fatty acids.

Oligosaccharides are carbohydrates with a few sugar molecules linked together. They are not easily digested by the human gut and provide food for a range of bacteria. These are often called 'friendly bacteria' in advertising because they seem to help us to absorb calcium and magnesium and to break down other toxic compounds. Foods containing these chemicals are called **prebiotics**.

Both statins and oligosaccharides help to make so-called functional foods – they do something other than stop us being hungry!

▦ QUESTIONS ▦

8 What does statin do in the body?

9 Even though we cannot digest oligosaccharides easily they are useful. Why?

10 'There is no such thing as a healthy food – only a healthy diet'. Explain what this statement means.

▦ QUESTIONS ▦

5 List the kinds of things people are typically told to **avoid** to live a healthier life. List the kinds of foods that people are typically told to eat **more of** to live a healthier life.

6 Give **one** piece of evidence from the study quoted that shows a Mediterranean diet can prolong healthy life.

7 If olive oil is good for you then more olive oil will be better for you. What is the danger of a diet that includes excessive amounts of a single food?

Biotech promises

You will find out:
- What benefits biotechnology offers
- How biotechnology can help to feed the world
- About the potential problems of biotechnology

A new hope?

It's the great hope of scientists across the world – by using our understanding of science and technology we will be able to cure all diseases, feed everyone and provide for longer, healthier lives. Is it really true that we will eventually know enough to satisfy everyone?

Biotechnology everywhere

Biotechnology includes all technologies that have a biological basis. The word is normally used to include medical technologies, **genetic modification** and a range of agricultural developments. Some far-seeing scientists even talk about 'improvements' to the human body that include electronic and biological implants to give us more strength or better memories, or even a radio receiver that links directly to our brains!

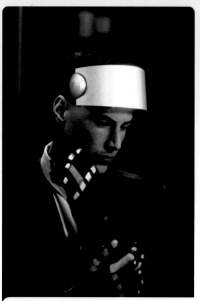

FIGURE 1: In this film about the future, Johnny Mnemonic (Keanu Reaves) has a biological memory chip in his head to allow him to carry valuable computer data through customs.

- Medical biotechnology includes development of new drugs to cure a range of diseases and even treatments that will allow us to eat whatever we want without getting fat.
- In the future doctors may be able to grow replacement organs such as kidneys and hearts in a laboratory to replace damaged ones in our bodies.
- Genetic engineers can already detect genetic problems – in the future they hope to be able to repair these before birth (or even in adults).
- Agricultural biotechnologists are looking at modifying plants or animals to produce more food with a wider range of useful chemicals. These could include drugs such as human blood proteins or complex chemicals that can be used to treat disease.

Biotechnology promises a lot – but just because we can do something, it does not mean that we should do it. Many of the decisions about biotechnology are about **ethics** rather than just being purely scientific.

■■ QUESTIONS ■■

1 What does the word biotechnology mean?
2 List **three** major areas of biotechnological research.
3 Design a poster for schools to show the potential benefits of biotechnology.

...biotechnology   ...ethics

The growth of biotech agriculture

Biotech agriculture is growing fast. This is driven by a number of factors, including the need to grow more food from the same area of ground.

It is difficult to argue against an increase in the food available to the world. Every year the global population rises and that means more mouths to feed. As countries such as China

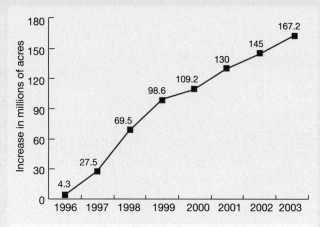

FIGURE 2: The increase in global area of biotechnology crops from 1996 to 2003.

and India become richer, their diets are changing to become more Western. These include more meat. This is much more expensive to produce in terms of land than their traditional plant-based diets. Is the rise of biotech agriculture both desirable and inevitable?

Increased yield?

The increases in yield produced by biotech agriculture comes from a number of sources – but rarely from an increase in the growth of the plants themselves. Yield is a complex variable and there is no single gene for increases in size. The days of the giant genetically modified apple or rice grain are still far away!

Most of the increase in yield comes from increases in:

- **resistance** to pests (this reduces wastage)
- tolerance of herbicides – this means that farmers can use more herbicides to protect against weeds
- drought tolerance – a lack of rain produces a much smaller drop in yield for GM plants than traditional varieties
- cold tolerance – dropping temperatures can have a serious effect on crop plants, but new GM varieties are better able to cope with these. This also means lands that were previously too cold to grow a crop can now be brought into productive use. This could increase food production dramatically.

FIGURE 3: Tibetan yaks are very hardy and can cope with the poor highland grass. But could genetically modified wheat grow here instead to produce much more food for the local people?

Problems?

The advantages of biotech crops are here and visible. The problems are often potential problems – they have not appeared yet although some research suggests that they are real. At the moment concerns about GM crops include:

- Unintended harm to other organisms – some butterflies appear to be harmed by pollen from some GM crops
- Pesticide effectiveness reduced – will the pests just evolve to cope with these higher levels of pesticide?
- Increased use of herbicides – farmers will use more knowing they will not harm the plants.
- Gene transfer to other species – will the modified genes spread to other species?

FIGURE 4: Have these butterflies been harmed by pollen from genetically modified crops?

QUESTIONS

4 List the factors that contribute to yield in a crop plant.

5 Why is there no single gene for yield in a plant?

6 Why might wheat plants that cope better with cold dry conditions be good news for Tibetan farmers?

QUESTIONS

7 List the potential problems with any biotechnological developments.

8 Suggest a way to reduce the dangers of **one** of the factors you listed in the answer to question **7**.

GM crops – better for whom?

SELF-CHECK ACTIVITY   CHALLENGE

CONTEXT

Some people have argued that the development of genetically modified (GM) crops would be a good thing. One of the advantages with GM crops is that they can be designed to be resistant to a weedkiller. This weedkiller can then be used to get rid of weeds where the crops are growing without affecting the crops themselves. However, one of the objections to this is that it may affect the presence of wild flowers, insects, birds and other organisms.

Government scientists carried out an investigation into trials in which GM crops were grown in similar conditions to, and near to, conventional (i.e. non-GM) versions of the same crop. Part of the report was about spring-grown oilseed rape. The report showed that:

- There were more weeds in conventional spring rape fields than in GM ones.
- There were more bees and butterflies in conventional spring rape fields than in GM ones.
- There were more springtails and one kind of beetle in the GM rape fields.
- In fields growing conventional crops, farmers tended to apply herbicides (to kill the weeds) before either the crops or the weeds had emerged, and sometimes again when the weeds were very small.
- With GM crops the herbicides were applied much later, when the weeds had grown quite large.
- Generally speaking, there was more animal and plant wildlife in conventional crop fields than in GM crop fields.
- Farmers tended to use broad spectrum weedkillers with GM crops and more specific herbicides with the conventional crops.

(Taken from *Managing GM Crops with herbicides: Effects on farmland wildlife*)

STEP 1

How did the GM and conventional crop fields compare in terms of wildlife to be found in the fields?

STEP 2

If the herbicides are applied to GM crops later in the growing period, what do you think will be true about the size of the weeds in those fields when they are killed?
Why do you think that the springtails might prefer that as an environment? The beetle is a carnivore. Why do you think it might be found there?

What is the advantage of being able to use a broad spectrum weedkiller? Why is a farmer likely to use a specific herbicide with a conventional crop?

Why do you think that, overall, there is likely to be more variety of wildlife in fields where conventional crops are growing?

Why do you think some people might favour conventional crops? Why might others favour GM crops?

Maximise your grade

These sentences show what you need to include in your work to achieve each grade. Use them to improve your work and be more successful.

Grade	Answer includes...
F	Identify one way in which the GM crop fields were different to the non-GM crop fields.
	Identify several ways in which the GM crop fields were different from the non-GM crop fields.
	Identify the advantages of one kind of herbicide.
	Compare broad spectrum and specific herbicides.
C	Explain why in this case conventional crops seem to be supporting a wider range of wildlife.
	Produce an overall comparison of conventional and GM crops.
A	Relate the concept of biodiversity to these tests.
	Relate the concept of biodiversity to these tests with effective handling of evidence.

Weeds and pests

You will find out:
- How much damage pests do to crops
- Why some people fear genetically modified organisms may harm the environment
- About genetically engineered T-shirts

What a waste!

Every year millions of tonnes of food are lost because of pests attacking crops, weeds choking fields and fungi making food rot before and after harvest. With so many people in the world starving, can we do something to save this 'lost food'?

Hired guns?

Weeds are a problem. They can reduce the yield of plants by anything from 35% to 100%. Yes, an infestation of weeds can destroy your whole harvest! What can be done? Well, **herbicides** are the hired guns of the farming world. These chemical assassins can clear a field of weeds with just one spraying. Unfortunately they can also damage the crops!

- A **selective** herbicide kills certain plants but leaves others untouched. In 1975 over 80% of the US soya bean crop was resistant to certain selective herbicides. This meant that you could spray a field of soya beans and weeds and only kill the weeds.
- Unfortunately, the weeds hit back. They evolved resistance to the herbicides and by 2006 there were over 290 resistant types of weed. Back to square one?
- Every year new herbicides are developed. It takes a while for weeds to develop resistance so these can be used for a while. But scientists and farmers are stuck in a constant race to beat the weeds. As soon as new herbicides are developed so resistance begins to appear.

FIGURE 1: Two months ago this allotment was cleared of all weeds by a mechanical digger. Just look at it now!

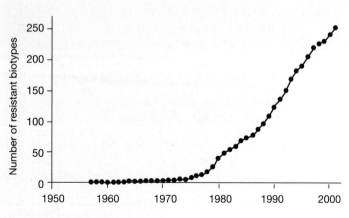

Source: Dr. Ian Heap www.weedscience.com

FIGURE 2: How resistance to herbicides has grown among weeds.

▥ QUESTIONS ▥

1. How much damage can be done by a weed in a field of wheat?
2. What can farmers do to reduce this damage?
3. What does the word 'herbicide' mean?
4. What does the graph show about herbicide resistance?

...genes ...herbicide resistance

Resistance is ... genetic

Some herbicides work well on weeds but also destroy the crops. Instead of looking for new selective herbicides, could we strengthen the crops to resist existing herbicides? Genetic engineers have found the **genes** that provide **herbicide resistance.** Can they get them into crop plants?

The bacterium *Agrobacterium tumefaciens* is a bacterium that causes galls in plants. Galls look like lumps of tissue growing on the surface of plants – in some ways you can think of them as 'plant cancers' or moles.

The bacterium causes these galls by injecting a length of DNA into the cells of the plant. Could we use the bacterium as a **vector** to carry the herbicide-resistant genes into a crop plant? In fact, this has been done.

But are herbicide-resistant plants a good idea? It means that farmers can use more herbicides and at a higher concentration. This kills more weeds but do the herbicides come through in our food? And if we multiply the number of organisms containing herbicide-resistant genes will it just make it more likely that these genes could jump species into the weeds we are trying to kill?

Frankencotton?

An alternative way forward might be to help the plants protect themselves against insect attack. *Bacillus thuringiensis* is a bacterium that produces a **toxin** that kills insects. Organic gardeners, who are normally against all genetic modification, have been using the bacterium as a biological control against insect pests for years. The bacteria are sprayed into greenhouses to kill insects that attack the plants.

FIGURE 3: The Just... shop in Leicester sells only fairly traded clothing. Does it need to also be organic and non-GM? Do we really care about organic cotton for clothes? And isn't the increase in yield for poor cotton farmers a good thing?

Genetic engineers have isolated the gene that produces the *B. thuringiensis* toxin, called Bt, and engineered it into cotton plants. These plants resist a range of insect pests 'naturally'. Is this a safer way forward? It is certainly popular. In a study in the United States, farmers using GM cotton applied half as much pesticide as farmers using the traditional varieties.

The table shows the area (in acres) of GM cotton in the United States as a proportion of total cotton area:

2001	2002	2003	2004
15 499 (69%)	14 151 (71%)	13 924 (73%)	13 947 (76%)

Cotton has one other advantage. We don't eat it. People are very worried about genetically modified (GM) food crops but seem much more relaxed about GM clothes. How could a GM T-shirt hurt us?

▤▤▤ QUESTIONS ▤▤▤

5   What is one of the biggest problems with herbicides?

6   How does *Agrobacterium tumefaciens* help to solve one of the biggest problems with herbicides?

7   Give **two** possible disadvantages of herbicide-resistant crops.

8   How does the approach taken with the toxin Bt differ from the approach adopted with *Agrobacterium tumefaciens*?

9   The area of cotton decreased in the United States from 2001 to 2004. Why might the total amount of cotton produced have increased?

10 What was the total area of cotton in 2004 in the United States?

11 Why is it less difficult to sell genetically modified cotton than genetically modified soya?

Stem cells

You will find out:

- How stem cell research could create new treatments
- Why some people have strong feelings about stem cell research

Superman?

Christopher Reeve was the actor who played Superman in the first modern movie of the story. He was the perfect American hero, a human rights activist and a keen sportsman. On 27 May 1995 he injured his spinal cord so badly he was paralysed from the neck down. Since nerve cells cannot regrow, he had to come to terms with living in a wheelchair for the rest of his life.

Nerves don't heal

Nerve cells are specialised cells that do not repair themselves when they have been damaged. This is why damage to the brain or spinal cord is so serious. Special cells called **stem cells** are able to develop into any sort of cell in the body. Could stem cells be used to grow new nerve cells?

Unfortunately, adult human bodies do not contain the right sort of stem cells. These cells have to be harvested from embryos. This kills the embryos. Doctors and researchers are faced with a difficult, ethical dilemma – is it right to use embryos to produce stem cells to try to cure other people?

It's not just brain and spinal cord injuries that might be cured by stem cell therapy. **Parkinson's disease** affects millions of people across the world. Cells in the brain die as a person with Parkinson's gets older. It shows itself as 'the shakes' at first but can lead to paralysis. A dose of stem cells might allow sufferers to regrow healthy brain cells and so cure the disease.

FIGURE 1: In films he could fly. In real life he could not even sit up unaided because of a tragic accident.

WOW FACTOR!

Research centres can buy human stem cells for $500 for a live sample.

QUESTIONS

1 Why are injuries to the spinal cord so serious?
2 What is special about stem cells?
3 What are the problems with using stem cells to treat disease?
4 How could stem cells help someone with Parkinson's disease?

...leukaemia   ...lymphoma

Stem cell research banned

Human stem cells were first isolated in 1998 by a team in the United States. This breakthrough is even more amazing because no government funding has been available for this area of research since 1995. It is an area that is starved of funding because President George W. Bush insists that it is unethical. Christopher Reeve himself appeared before the US Congress to try to overturn this ban but failed. When he died in 2004, stem cell research was well advanced – but not in his home country.

'Modern stem cell lines are developed from blood from the placenta of babies. No embryos are involved. Complaints from people who are anti-research are out of date and ill-informed.'

'Think how much money the US government spent on military research in the same time! How is that moral?'

'To treat human beings as 'cell factories' must be immoral. Life is something we are given not something you can buy in some sort of technological supermarket!'

'The ethics that interest me is why it is moral to deny people like me a cure. I have Parkinson's and I know I will get worse and worse as I get older. I need stem cell research – it's the only real hope I have.'

'The most valuable stem cells do still come from human embryos. But these embryos are produced by a cloning technique and the stem cells are removed before they are a week old. The cells can then be cultured to produce millions of cells in a laboratory.'

QUESTIONS

5 List reasons for supporting stem cell research.
6 List as many reasons as you can for not supporting stem cell research.
7 Would you support the research? Give a reason for your answer.
8 Who should decide which type of research is funded by the government? Give a reason for your answer.

Stem cells and medicine

People suffering from cancers such as **leukaemia** and **lymphoma** are often given strong drugs. These also kill the cells in the bone that make blood cells, so doctors remove so-called 'adult' stem cells from the bone before treatment begins and return them after it is complete. The cells in the bone marrow are a special type of stem cell called adult stem cells because they can produce cells that are very similar to them. Embryonic stem cells can produce any sort of cell in the whole body. Doctors hope to use embryonic cells to treat:

■ spinal cord injuries
■ muscle damage in the heart following heart attacks
■ blindness
■ baldness.

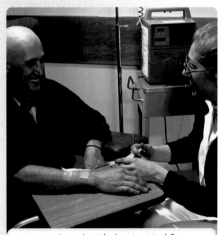

FIGURE 2: A patient being treated for leukaemia.

QUESTIONS

9 What is the difference between adult and embryonic stem cells?
10 List some of the illnesses that might be cured by stem cell therapy.

Doctor Gene

You will find out:

- About personalised medicine
- How gene testing can extend lives
- How human insulin is made

The drugs don't work?

Everyone reacts to drugs in slightly different ways. What works well for one person may fail on someone else – or produce serious side effects. At the moment doctors use trial and error to find the right one for you. Why can't we get medicine that is personalised for us in the same way as we can buy clothes 'made to measure'?

Genomics

The human **genome** includes all of the genes found in humans everywhere. **Genomics** is the study of the genes present in an individual. Genomics tries to predict how likely a person is to suffer from a particular disease or how they will react to a particular medicine. So, if my grandfather died of a heart attack, does that mean I will suffer from heart disease?

- Genes are important in disease. In fact, genes play a part in nine out of ten of the most common causes of death in the developed world.
- Your heart will be made using information from hundreds, possibly thousands, of genes. Some of these genes will probably be damaged. Most will be fully functional and your heart will be fine. However, if you smoke, eat the wrong foods and take little exercise the combination of gene damage and environmental damage could trigger heart disease.
- Gene testing could alert you to the presence of damaged genes. You can then take extra care to avoid disease.

FIGURE 1: Suits you, sir! Could all medicine be tailor-made in the future?

Genes play a part in nine out of ten causes of death in the developed world

---

⊞ QUESTIONS ⊞

1 What does the word genomics mean?
2 Why do people react differently to the same medicine?
3 If your father suffered from heart disease does that mean you will too?
4 If you have a family history of heart disease what should you avoid doing?

...blood sugar   ...genome

Insulin and blood sugar

Insulin is a relatively simple protein containing only 152 amino acids, joined together in a chain. It is a crucial hormone in the human body and controls the rate at which sugar is absorbed or released by cells.

Insulin is made by cells in the pancreas. They increase the rate of production when **blood sugar** rises. The insulin makes cells take sugar out of the blood and use it to make fat. When blood sugar level falls, the insulin production also drops. More sugar now passes from cells into the blood. In this way the level of blood sugar is kept roughly constant. In people with diabetes this control is broken because they cannot produce insulin.

In the past insulin could be extracted from the pancreas of pigs and purified and supplied to diabetics. By carefully monitoring their food intake and blood sugar level they knew when to inject a measured amount of insulin.

Manufacturing insulin

Insulin production used to be a very costly process. In the 1980s a biotechnological process using genetically modified bacteria was developed and purer, safer human insulin could be produced much more cheaply.

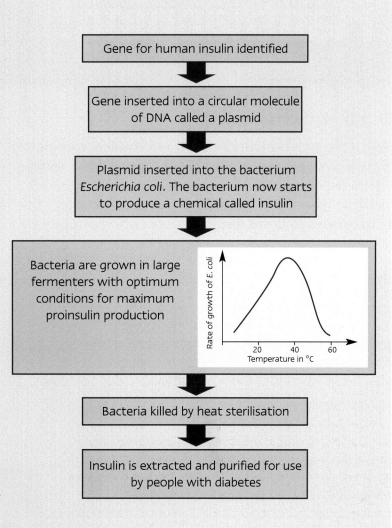

Gene for human insulin identified

Gene inserted into a circular molecule of DNA called a plasmid

Plasmid inserted into the bacterium *Escherichia coli*. The bacterium now starts to produce a chemical called insulin

Bacteria are grown in large fermenters with optimum conditions for maximum proinsulin production

Bacteria killed by heat sterilisation

Insulin is extracted and purified for use by people with diabetes

---

|||| QUESTIONS ||||

5   What type of chemical is insulin?

6   Where in the body is insulin made?

7   Give **two** advantages of genetically engineered insulin over traditional insulin from animals.

8   What is the optimum temperature for the growth of *E. coli*?

9   Does insulin supplied to diabetics contain any genetically modified components? Give a reason for your answer.

10 Some research is now looking at a way to inject the gene for insulin production directly into the pancreatic cells of diabetics. How might this help to cure the disease?

Plantnapping!

You will find out:

- About the ethical issues around use of living materials
- About patenting living materials

Raiders of the ark?

A plant growing in the Amazon jungle is a powerful but completely safe painkiller. It's worth a fortune – but who owns it? The tribe living in the area where it grows? The medicine man who knows about its painkilling properties? The biologist that collected it? Or the drug company that extracted the drug?

Plantnapping

Giant transnational drug companies are sending people into remote places all over the world to look for plants and animals that could be used to produce drugs. In many cases they ask local people to point out the plants that they use for medicines. The plants are taken back to laboratories and the **active ingredient** is isolated.

- Many of our earliest medicines came from plants. At first these were prepared as teas or eaten.
- Scientific research then isolated the active ingredient from the plant. The active ingredient is the chemical which acts as a medicine. A plant will contain many thousands of other chemicals that have no effect and may dilute the active ingredient.
- Once the active ingredient has been isolated, its concentration can be measured accurately. This will help to make sure that people get the correct dose of a chemical. For example, digitalin is a chemical made from foxgloves. At the correct concentration it is a useful medicine for treating some heart diseases. If the concentration is too high it acts as a poison and can kill you!
- Chemists might also try to synthesise the active ingredient in the laboratory. This is particularly useful if the plant that produced it is very rare or grows only in difficult to reach places.

FIGURE 1: Medicine man.

FIGURE 2: Foxgloves – a pretty garden flower that contains digitalin which can literally kill or cure you!

QUESTIONS

1 Where did the first drugs probably come from?
2 What does the phrase 'active ingredient' mean?
3 Give **two** advantages of isolating the active ingredient in a medicine from a plant.
4 Why is it important to get the dose of medicines correct?

...active ingredient   ...quinine

Plant pharmacy

Aspirin

The ancient Greek doctor Hippocrates (460–377 BC) used to prescribe a bitter tasting extract made from ground-up willow bark for pains and fevers. In 1828 the active ingredient was extracted and crystallised by a French chemist. He called it **salicin**. The powder was a good painkiller, but had unpleasant side effects. In 1897 a German chemist called Felix Hoffmann modified salicin to produce acetyl salicylic acid. This has been the formula for aspirin ever since.

FIGURE 3: Willow tree.

Taxol

Taxol is a powerful anticancer drug that comes from the bark of the Pacific yew tree. It took nearly 30 years from the discovery of the plant extract in 1963 to the sale of the purified drug in 1993, but in 2000 alone taxol earned $1.6 billion. But the Pacific yew tree is very slow growing and it takes six 100-year-old trees to produce enough taxol for a single patient! The breakthrough came when chemists learned how to manufacture taxol using extracts from some bacteria and a range of chemical processes.

FIGURE 4: Pacific yew tree.

Quinine

Malaria is a serious disease that kills up to 2.7 million people every year – mainly African children under the age of 11. **Quinine** was for many years the only way to treat malaria. It comes from the bark of the South American cinchona tree. Powdered tree bark was first used to treat malaria in Rome in 1631. At one point cinchona bark was almost as valuable as gold! In 1820 French researchers isolated the active ingredient from the bark and called it quinine. Even today nobody has found a better way to make quinine than to extract it from cinchona trees.

FIGURE 5: Cinchona tree.

Artemisinin

Artemisinin is a drug that can be used to treat malaria. It is also being studied as a possible cure for breast cancer. Artemisinin comes from *Artemesia annua*, a plant used in Chinese traditional medicine for over 1000 years. They call it qing hao, and the English name is Chinese wormwood. It was discovered when scientists tested 200 traditional treatments for malaria – only this one worked. Extraction of the chemical is easy but supplies of the plants are limited. Researchers have now used genetic engineering techniques to make a yeast produce a chemical that is easily converted to artemisinin.

FIGURE 6: Traditional Chinese medicine.

▦ QUESTIONS ▦

5   Where does aspirin come from?

6   What is the major disadvantage of the Pacfic yew tree as a source of taxol?

7   How have scientists solved this problem?

8   Give the names of **two** drugs used to treat malaria.

9   How was artemisinin discovered?

10 How would you go about testing a traditional herbal remedy to see if it could cure a disease?

Buy buy baby?

You will find out:

- How the choices we make affect the future
- That choices about technology are not always easy to make

It's about us!

Biotechnology is a very powerful technology that can frighten people. Why? It might be because it works on the cells and genes that make us human. If you clone yourself, is your clone really 'you' or someone else? If we change our genes to cure diseases will be become less 'ourselves'. What does it mean to be 'human'?

Boy or girl?

More boys are conceived than girls. More boys are born than girls. But women live longer. The number of males to females in a population is called the **gender ratio** and, conveniently, is always about equal. But could technology change all that?

In some societies boys are valued more than girls. Now that we can find out the sex of a baby very early on in the womb some parents are aborting females to make sure they have a son. Obviously this is not an easy decision to make.

In some countries the gender balance is being upset. Many more boys are being born than girls. In China the government has set up a campaign to encourage people to value daughters more highly to try to offset this problem.

In the future, biotechnology might make it possible to decide on the sex of a baby in advance. This is a much less stressful decision than considering an abortion. Will this mean the gender balance is upset even more?

FIGURE 1: Are we going to run out of women if people can choose the gender of their offspring?

The table shows the number of boys for every 100 girls in a range of countries.

		Boys
China	At birth	112
	Below 15	113
	15–64	106
	Over 65	91
India	At birth	105
	Below 15	106
	15–64	107
	Over 65	102
The Netherlands	At birth	105
	Below 15	105
	15–64	103
	Over 65	73
UK	At birth	105
	Below 15	105
	15–64	102
	Over 65	74

Source *CIA World Factbook* updated Aug 2005

QUESTIONS

1. How many girls are born for every 100 boys in the UK?
2. How many girls are born for every 100 boys in China?
3. Does it matter if the gender balance is not equal? Give a reason for your answer.
4. Why could biotechnological advances make this situation worse?

My brother's a spare part!

The biggest problem with transplant surgery is not the surgery – it's the rejection of the organ. If you can find someone with exactly the same genes as you their organs will survive in your body without any problems.

In the future, biotechnology might allow us to produce a clone of ourselves. Imagine someone catches an infection that destroys their kidneys. If the biotechnologists could produce a cloned younger brother or sister from their body cells the kidney could be transplanted safely. This type of cloning is called **reproductive cloning**.

Illegal and impossible

At the moment cloning for spare parts, or any reproductive cloning, is both impossible and illegal. However, biotechnology is progressing so rapidly that it might be possible in a few years. Indeed, one researcher has already claimed that he has cloned a human being. Most fellow scientists currently believe that he is lying. But the same scientists agree that in the future it might be possible.

Will it always be illegal? Most people think it should be and no funds are ever made available for this sort of research. However, a patient suffering from an incurable illness that a clone could save might feel very differently. What if the clone is not harmed and is given the same rights as everyone else? This is not a scientific decision, but an ethical and moral one. You don't have to be a research scientist to have an opinion about this.

The post-humans?

Biotechnology offers amazing possibilities: cures for diseases, drugs to make us more clever, perhaps the chance to live forever or to change our gender at will. Perhaps we could add electronic devices to our bodies: computers that fit inside our heads and communicate directly with nerve cells. A group called 'post-humans' are looking forward to this future. They believe that science will allow us to control our own evolution. Rael is only one of a number of post-human thinkers. Yet this vision of the future is exactly why some people want to cut back on research. The post-humans' heaven is their hell! What do you think?

FIGURE 2: A French ex-journalist who calls himself Rael and claims to be descended from extraterrestrials. His religious sect has funded cloning research and claims to have produced a human clone.

Life-saving donors

Charlie suffers from a disease that needs continual and painful treatment. It can be cured with a **stem cell** transplant from a suitable donor. His parents wanted a younger brother with exactly the right genes to make a good match – so they produced a number of embryos using *in vitro* fertilisation (IVF) and tested each one to see which had the best genetic combination. One was selected for implantation and Jamie was born in 2004. Both brothers are now happy, healthy and loved.

QUESTIONS

5 What is the biggest problem in transplant surgery?

6 How could this problem be solved?

7 Should reproductive cloning remain illegal? Think of at least **two** reasons on both sides of this argument.

8 Would you make reproductive cloning legal? Give a reason for your decision.

QUESTIONS

9 How do you think the parents felt throughout this?

10 How is this story different from reproductive cloning?

11 Do you think the parents did the right thing? Give a reason for your answer.

Unit summary

Concept map

Medical biotechnology looks at:
- development of new drugs
- matching drugs to patients through genomics
- genetic engineering to cure or prevent inherited defects.

Herbicide-resistant crops allow a wider range of herbicides to be used. Cotton containing genes from *Bacillus thuringiensis* are poisonous to some pests.

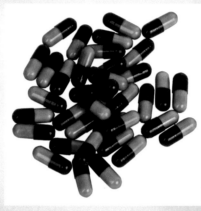

Stem cells are being investigated as a way to grow replacement human organs or repair damaged nerve tissues.
Traditional medicines are being investigated to isolate and improve any active ingredients.

Agricultural biotechnology looks at:
- producing new crops
- increasing the yield of existing crops
- modifying crops to produce new products.

Biotechnology has three main areas of study:
- medical
- industrial
- agricultural.
Many of these areas raise important ethical issues.

Industrial biotechnology looks at:
- engineering microbes to produce a range of useful products
- using enzymes to produce or modify products.

There are ethical issues about the morality of new developments. Currently there are concerns about genetic engineering, stem cell research and cloning.

Genetic engineers have produced microbes that can:
- digest crude oil to clean up spills
- produce vitamins, amino acids and a range of drugs (insulin, new antibiotics).

Unit quiz

1. What is special about stem cells and how can they help to cure Parkinson's disease?

2. Where was Dolly the first cloned sheep produced?

3. What is tofu made from?

4. What does milk mixed with *Lactobacillus* make if it is left in a warm place for a few days?

5. How do sweet manufacturers make chocolates with soft or liquid centres?

6. What does monosodium glutamate do to food?

7. What do statins do?

8. Give two problems of using herbicides.

9. How can the toxin from *Bacillus thuringiensis* help to protect cotton plants?

10. What is genomics?

11. How is human insulin made nowadays?

12. What is a plasmid?

13. Which important drug is made from willow tree bark?

14. Where does the anti-cancer drug taxol come from?

15. List four ways biotechnologists hope to increase the yield of crop plants.

16. Give two worries about the use of biotechnology in the future.

Literacy activity

Obesity

Obesity is a big killer in the West – why can't we take a pill to make us thin? This is the hope for a new medicine being developed from a plant called hoodia. The San tribe from southern Africa have known about hoodia for many thousands of years. They used it to stop themselves feeling hungry when they had to travel long distances without food. Researchers in South Africa, working with traditional medicine men, investigated the plant and found it did act as an appetite suppressant. They isolated an active ingredient and were granted a patent for an extract from the plant which they called P57. The size of the market for such a drug would be worth billions.

The researchers licensed P57 to a British drug company, which claimed that the San tribe had died out. This allowed them to license the drug to the giant transnational drug company Pfizer. But the San had simply been moved off their land by the apartheid government of South Africa. The tribe heard about the theft of their drug and took legal action. After much wrangling an agreement was reached and they will now receive a royalty for the drug when it becomes available.

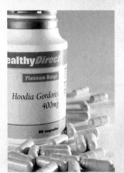

The story of hoodia is not unusual in that the traditional knowledge of tribes was taken but is unusual in that an agreement was reached to repay the native healers and their communities for their knowledge. It is to be hoped that this is a model for future developments.

QUESTIONS

1. How could an appetite suppressant help to treat obesity?

2. Prepare a statement for the drug company to be read out in court, explaining why they should not pay royalties.

3. Prepare a similar legal statement for the San tribe saying why they should receive royalties.

Exam practice

Exam practice questions

A Yoghurt production involves the fermentation of milk lactose. The yoghurt mixture is curdled milk and is often flavoured with fruit. It must be stored at 43–44 °C during production and two different bacteria are used in the process.

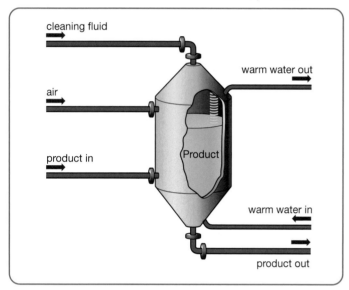

The diagram shows a modern yoghurt fermenting vessel.

i Milk solids are put into the vessel. What is the name of the milk sugar that undergoes fermentation?

.... [1]

ii After fermentation, what substance has this sugar been converted into?

.... [1]

iii Apart from fermentation, what is the name of the process that the bacteria *Streptococcus thermophilus* and *Lactobacillus bulgaricus* undertake in the production of yoghurt?

.... [1]

B The production of soy sauce also uses fermentation.

i What are the best conditions for the (aerobic) fermentation of the cooked soy beans (production of koji)?

....

....

.... [3]

ii What is the name of the mould that is used to ferment the koji?

.... [1]

iii What are the products of the fermented carbohydrates in the production of soy sauce?

.... [2]

(Total 9 marks)

2 The following statements are about the use of embryonic stem cells.

a The use of stem cells is unnatural and wrong, it should be banned.

b This treatment will be of use to many people.

c The treatment is too expensive to be used for all Parkinson's sufferers.

d In the long term this could reduce the cost of treating Parkinson's.

Which statement is most likely to have been made by:

i Someone with religious beliefs.

.... [1]

ii Someone in favour of stem cell research

.... [1]

B Describe the main processes in producing and using stem cells for Parkinson's research.

....

....

....

.... [3]

(Total 5 marks)

Worked example

1 In many countries, genetically modified crops are being grown. There is controversy surrounding the growth of genetically modified foods and plants used for other purposes such as cotton.

   a Briefly explain what genetic modification is.   [2]

   b Explain how the bacterium *Agrobacterium tumefaciens* is used to genetically modify plants.   [3]

   c It is hoped that plants that are resistant to herbicides can help developing countries. Discuss this statement.   [4]

A correct answer that clearly states two points about genetic modification of plant species.

a Genetic modification of a plant would involve adding the genes of another plant, or sometimes insect, to a plant species so that the original species takes on the trait that the gene codes for.

This is a very weak answer. The examiners will be looking for much more detail than simply repeating the information given in the question. There are several things to talk about here including how the bacterium is capable of mixing its own genes with those of the plant and how it is easy for scientists to modify the bacterium's own DNA so that it can be used as a **vector,** much like a virus.

b Agrobacterium tumefaciens is a bacterium that is used to genetically modify plants it infects the plant and that is how the modification of the plant's genes happens.

A good answer overall but you need to be aware of the 'waffle factor'. You should try to make your answer more concise.

c Plants that are resistant to herbicides are much stronger than their unmodified cousins. This means that, when they are grown, more herbicides can be used to stop weeds and unwanted plants growing. Weeds steal nutrients from the soil and this stops the crops from growing properly. If herbicides are used then the crops will grow. The more crops that grow means that this can help the developing world as they will have more food to eat and more things like cotton to sell.

Overall Grade: B

How to get an A

This is the extension paper and examiners will be looking for the ability to demonstrate what you know and to be able to apply your knowledge to different situations. Take note of how much you are going to write on you paper and ensure that your answers are kept brief and to the point. Do not run out of time writing things that will get you no marks.

BEHAVIOUR IN HUMANS AND OTHER ANIMALS

The kitten's eyes are focused intently on the ball as it waits for the exact second to strike with its paw.

Cats have retractable claws which they can pull into their paws. This keeps the claws sharp, making them all the better for gripping and killing their prey.

The kitten has a camouflaged coat, enabling it to get close to its prey before it pounces.

Instinctive behaviour

You will find out:

- That animals inherit instinctive behaviour from their parents
- That inherited behaviour is part of natural selection

The diving reflex

Surely someone should rescue this drowning baby! Actually babies can swim really well. Like whales, seals and other mammals that live in water, human babies have a **diving reflex**. This ensures that they manage very well in water. This diving reflex disappears when babies reach the age of about 12 months. Many biologists think that the diving reflex is left over from a period in human **evolution** when we lived a semi-aquatic lifestyle.

FIGURE 1: This baby's ability to swim is instinctive.

Reflex actions

The baby in the photograph did not have to be taught how to survive underwater. He has inherited the ability from his parents. It is called **instinctive** or innate **behaviour** and is a **reflex** action. The stimulus for the reflex seems to be submerging the face in cold water. The response is to reduce the amount of energy used by the body. The heart beats more slowly and blood is diverted from the arms and legs to the essential organs such as the brain, heart and lungs. A small flap of tissue, called the epiglottis, closes off the trachea, keeping water out of the lungs. Obviously the baby needs to come to the surface to breathe air but the diving reflex helps him to survive much longer underwater.

There are many species of dung beetle found around the world. The beetles roll a ball of dung and lay an egg in it. They then bury the dung ball. The egg hatches and the larva feeds on the dung, before becoming an adult. The dung beetle never meets its parents so it does not learn about making dung balls from them. It is instinctive behaviour.

WANT TO KNOW MORE?

Find out about our semi-aquatic ancestors at
http://www.seashepherd.org/ocean_realm/ocean_realm_spr01.html

FIGURE 2: Dung beetles' behaviour is instinctive.

QUESTIONS

1. What do you think a 'semi-aquatic lifestyle' means?
   Can you think of some examples of semi-aquatic mammals?
2. Explain how the diving reflex helps a baby survive under water.
3. How can we be sure that behaviour in dung beetles is instinctive, rather than learned?

Human babies have a diving reflex and manage really well in water

...behaviour   ...diving reflex   ...evolution   ...inherited

Inherited behaviour

You will remember from the topic 'Environment' that animals have evolved by **natural selection**. Some individual animals have a particular characteristic that helps them to survive longer and to be healthier than other individuals. These individuals have more chance of passing on the gene for the characteristic.

Behaviour is also **inherited** from an individual's parents. Imagine a characteristic that increases an individual animal's chance of survival. A gene that causes white fur would be helpful to bears living in the Arctic. White bears will probably live longer, be healthier and have more offspring. The white fur gene is likely to become widespread in the bear population.

Now imagine a behaviour that increases an individual's chance of survival. Stroke a new-born baby on the cheek and the baby will turn his or her mouth to your finger. This is called the 'rooting' reflex. It enables the baby to find the mother's nipple to start feeding.

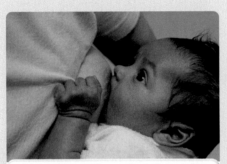

FIGURE 3: The rooting reflex helps a baby to feed successfully and increases his or her chances of survival.

The rooting reflex increases the baby's chance of survival so it seems that this could be an example of inherited behaviour. But how can this be? In the topic 'Inside living cells' you learnt that genes are made of DNA and that DNA carries the code for making proteins. Surely it is not possible for a single protein to be responsible for the way a baby behaves? But remember that enzymes are proteins and are responsible for making almost all of the different substances in the body, including those in the hormonal and nervous systems. Maybe it is a combination of many different substances, the production of which is controlled by a number of different genes, that lead to a particular behaviour.

WANT TO KNOW MORE?

Read *The Selfish Gene* by Richard Dawkins.

QUESTIONS

4   Why does white fur increase a bear's chances of survival in the Arctic?

5   How does the rooting response help a baby's chance of survival?

6   Explain how the production of proteins is controlled by genes.

7   Why is it likely that the rooting reflex is instinctive?

Lagerspetz's experiment

A scientist called Lagerspetz carried out an experiment with mice. He noticed that some mice were more aggressive than others. He measured aggressiveness by the time it took one mouse to attack another when they were put together in a cage. The most aggressive mice were bred together, as were the least aggressive mice. Over a few generations two separate groups of mice developed, one much more aggressive than the other. It is clear that this behaviour had been inherited but it is not clear how. It is also worth noting that the two different groups of mice in Lagerspetz's experiment also showed differences in other aspects of behaviour. For example, the more aggressive mice were more likely to explore when placed in a new environment.

FIGURE 4: Experiments with mice show that some behaviour is inherited.

QUESTIONS

8   How did Lagerspetz identify the most and least aggressive mice?

9   Suggest how patterns of behaviour could be passed on in DNA.

Learning

You will find out:

- That an animal's behaviour is affected by its early experiences
- That habituation and conditioning are ways in which animals learn
- That humans can make use of conditioning when training animals

Bird brain!

The scarecrow in the photograph isn't doing a very good job. There's a bird on its head! When the scarecrow was first put in the garden it kept birds away. The birds had learnt that humans might harm them. After a while the birds got used to the scarecrow and learnt that it was harmless.

The study of animal behaviour is called ethology. To ethologists, **learning** is a change in behaviour as a result of **experience**.

FIGURE 1: This bird has learnt that the scarecrow is harmless.

Familiarity breeds contempt

Birds can be a problem at airports because they can damage aircraft, for example by being sucked into their engines. Airport authorities are always on the lookout for ways of scaring birds away. Ideas that have been tried include putting models of hawks and owls around the airport and playing recordings of the distress calls of birds. At first these methods keep birds away from the airport. After a while, however, the birds learn that there is no danger from a model hawk or that a distress call does not mean there is a predator about. They start to come back to the airport where they pose a danger to aircraft once more.

This form of learning is called **habituation**. The birds get used to a stimulus, see no danger and no longer respond to the stimulus.

Another example of habituation is seen in the tropical fish called guppies. If a shadow passes over the aquarium the guppies respond by swimming under plants and rocks, where they are protected from predators. If, however, a shadow passes over the aquarium every two minutes the guppies become *habituated* to it and ignore it. If there is no shadow for about 24 hours, however, then when a shadow passes over the aquarium again it seems as if the guppies have forgotten about the lack of danger and respond by diving for cover again.

DID YOU KNOW?

In 2004 a US air force plane hit a flock of geese, jamming its engines. The plane crashed, killing 24 people.

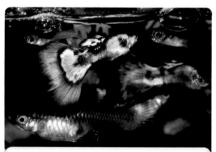

FIGURE 2: Guppies quickly learn that a shadow over their tank poses no threat.

QUESTIONS

1 Why do models of hawks initially scare other birds away from airports?
2 What is meant by habituation?
3 Why does a shadow passing over an aquarium cause a response in guppies?
4 How do guppies respond to a shadow passing over their aquarium?

Habituation

Young animals learn by habituation. It prevents them from wasting energy by responding to stimuli that are probably harmless. Habituation is a bit of a gamble – how do the advantages of responding to signs of danger compare with the disadvantages of wasting time and energy responding to stimuli that are probably harmless?

Imprinting

Much of an animal's learning takes place as a result of its early experience of life. Ducklings and goslings (young geese) are ready to leave the nest a few hours after hatching. They follow the first moving thing that they see (usually their mother). This is called **imprinting**.

Once young birds have become imprinted, they will continue to follow the first moving object the saw after they hatched – this is usually their mother. In some cases, however, chicks can be persuaded to follow something else. The photograph shows the ethologist Konrad Lorenz being followed by a group of ducks. Lorenz made sure that he was the first thing the ducklings saw when they hatched and they responded to him as if he was their mother! It doesn't even have to be a living creature. Experiments have shown that ducklings will follow a model duck or even a cardboard box, especially if it is the same colour as a female duck.

FIGURE 3: Konrad Lorenz and his family of ducks.

The takahe is a very rare bird found in New Zealand. To save it from extinction, some young takahes are raised in captivity. To make sure the takahe chicks do not imprint on the people caring for them, they are raised in a box beside a model of a female takahe and fed using a glove that looks like a takahe's head!

DID YOU KNOW?

Konrad Lorenz invented the word 'ethology', meaning the study of animal behaviour.

Sexual imprinting

Experiments have shown that there is a period after birds hatch when imprinting is most likely to occur. This is called the sensitive period. If young birds do not imprint within this period, they may not imprint at all. Imprinting is important as it ensures that animals know what species they belong to. Adult birds show sexual behaviour towards the object of imprinting. Brightly coloured birds of species such as ducks, pigeons, domestic fowl and finches have been raised by adults of other breeds with different coloured feathers. When the chicks become adults they will mate with birds that have the same colours as their foster parents' breed, rather than their own.

FIGURE 4: A black rooster raised by a brown hen will prefer to mate with brown females.

QUESTIONS

5 What is meant by imprinting?

6 Why is it important that young takahes do not imprint on the people feeding them?

7 Can you think of any other precautions that the carers must take to avoid the takahes imprinting on them?

QUESTIONS

8 What is meant by the sensitive period?

9 Why is imprinting important?

10 Apart from actually mating, what do you think is meant by sexual behaviour?

Conditioning

You will find out:

- How animals can learn through conditioning
- How humans can make use of conditioning when training animals

Good dog!

What a well-trained dog! Dogs do lots of different jobs and they need to be properly trained to do them. Even dogs that are kept as pets need to be trained. You wouldn't want to live with a dog that wasn't housetrained!

Training a dog needs patience and relies on something called **conditioning**. All animals, including humans, learn through conditioning. It is the most important way in which animals learn.

FIGURE 1: Sit!

Pavlov and his dogs

Ivan Pavlov is most famous for his experiments on conditioning and learning in dogs, but that was not what he set out to investigate. Initially he was trying to find out the effect of different foods on the amount of saliva produced by dogs. A small hole was cut in the dog's cheek so that saliva ran out down a tube. The saliva was collected and Pavlov could then measure the amount made.

Pavlov soon made an interesting observation. The dogs began to salivate as soon as they heard him approaching and long before they could see or smell the food.

Pavlov decided to investigate further. Each time he gave a dog some food he also rang a bell or flashed a light. After doing this a few times he noticed that the dog would salivate just at the sound of the bell or the flash of the light, even if no food was given to the dog. The dog had learnt to associate the sound of the bell with food. Pavlov called this a conditioned reflex.

FIGURE 2: Ivan Pavlov, with the beard, was awarded the Nobel Prize for medicine and physiology in 1904. He is seen here demonstrating his most famous experiment.

◾ QUESTIONS ◾

1. Write down some jobs that dogs are trained to do.
2. Why is it important that pet dogs are well trained?
3. Do you think Pavlov's experiment was cruel? Should he have been allowed to do it?
4. Can you think of any conditioned reflexes that occur in you?

...conditioned reflex ...conditioning ...negative

The Skinner box

B.F. Skinner invented a useful tool for the study of animal behaviour, the 'Skinner box'. This is a cage that has a lever that an animal can press. When the animal presses the lever, it gets a reward, usually food. When the animal is first put in the box, it does not press the lever. Eventually, however, it will press it by accident as it is moving about. Once it has done this a few times it will learn that it can get food any time it wants, just by pressing the lever. A Skinner box can be used to measure the ability of animals to learn.

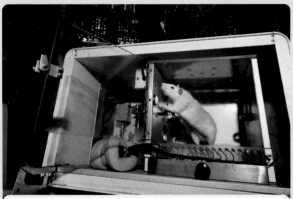

FIGURE 3: The rat in this Skinner box has learnt to press a lever to get a drink of water.

Animals in Skinner boxes can also learn to avoid something unpleasant. In one experiment, rats soon learnt that the lever could be used to turn off a very bright light.

Of course, the Skinner box is an artificial means of observing learning. Can animals learn in similar ways in their natural environment?

- Imagine a bird accidentally turns over a leaf and sees an insect it can eat. After doing this a few times it will learn that insects are more likely to be found hiding on the underside of leaves.
- Imagine a young animal eats a wasp and gets stung. It learns that yellow and black striped things are not good to eat and avoids them in future. Bees and wasps are yellow and black to help avoid being eaten. Every time one bee or wasp gets eaten it saves many others because the animal that eats it learns not to do it again!

DID YOU KNOW?

B.F. Skinner invented an 'air-crib', a glass fronted, air-conditioned cot in which his daughter slept until she was two.

QUESTIONS

5 How could the Skinner box be used to measure the learning ability of two species of animal?

6 Hoverflies are harmless insects yet they have a yellow and black striped body like a wasp. Why?

Animal training

Conditioning is used to train animals. The trainer has a task that the animal has to learn. If the animal completes the task correctly it gets a reward or **positive reinforcement**. This could be food, but it doesn't have to be. Dogs are rewarded by being patted and praised by the trainer. The dog learns to do the task because it associates the task with the reward.

Punishments or **negative reinforcement** can also be used to train animals. Most people do not want their dog to climb on the furniture. Each time it does it gets a telling-off and is put back on the floor. The dog becomes conditioned to link climbing on furniture with being told off.

FIGURE 4: Animal trainers use conditioning.

QUESTIONS

7 Do parents and teachers use conditioning to 'train' their children? Can you think of some examples?

8 What do you think is more important – reward or punishment?

Communication

You will find out:

- That animals communicate by a combination of sounds, chemicals, body language and facial expressions
- That facial expressions are species specific
- That human communication is much more complex than that of animals

Talk to the animals

Any wolf will easily recognise the message that this wolf is making – 'Go away'. The wolf in the photograph is eating and is making it quite clear to any other wolf that he is not going to share his food. Most other wolves will quickly back away rather than get in a fight and risk being injured.

Animals **communicate** in a number of ways, including facial expressions, body posture, sounds and chemicals.

FIGURE 1: It's obvious what this wolf is telling us!

Facial expressions

Only mammals have sufficient control over their facial muscles to be able to change their **facial expression**. Primates (apes and humans) have most control and can communicate most clearly using facial expressions. Chimpanzees live in large groups and it is important that they get along most of the time. Facial expressions communicate to other chimps how they are feeling, when they want to be left alone, when they want to play or when it would be a good idea to get out of the way! Scientists observing chimps have been able to work out what some facial expressions mean.

FIGURE 2: Happiness

FIGURE 3: Aggression.

FIGURE 4: Fear.

FIGURE 5: Submissive behaviour – communication in action.

Body language

Mammals also communicate by body language or **posture**. The photograph shows a wolf submitting to another wolf. The submissive wolf has rolled onto its back and is exposing its throat. The dominant wolf could easily kill it, but by showing this **gesture** of submission, the weaker wolf is safe from further harm. This demonstrates the importance of communication, especially among animals that live in groups.

QUESTIONS

1. Name some ways in which animals communicate.
2. All of the chimpanzees are showing their teeth. Describe the ways in which their facial expressions differ.
3. Explain why submissive behaviour is important.

...communicate   ...emotions   ...facial expression   ...gesture

Chemical communication

Many animals use chemicals for communication. The photograph shows a dog marking its territory. Dog urine contains a type of chemical called a **pheromone**. Other dogs smelling it will recognise that they are in an area that another dog claims as its own.

Many other animals use pheromones:

- Some ants lay down a trail of pheromones when they carry food back to their nest. This allows other ants to find the food source.
- Some bees release a pheromone when they are attacked by a predator. This warns other bees of the danger.
- Many female animals release pheromones to **signal** that they are available for breeding. Some butterflies and moths can detect pheromones from 10 km away!

FIGURE 6: This dog is using chemical communication to mark out its territory.

Some butterflies and moths can detect pheromones from 10 km away!

Sounds

The animal vocal communication with which we are most familiar is probably birdsong. In most species of birds it is the male that sings, often to warn other males away from its territory and also to attract a female. This is partly connected with territorial singing: a large territory will provide plenty of food to feed chicks. In some species, however, males and females take it in turn to sing. This duetting behaviour helps to strengthen the male–female bond.

Birds are not alone, however, in using **sounds** communicate:

- Many species of monkey communicate by sound as it is particularly useful in their forest habitat.
- Frogs often attract mates with their characteristic calls.
- Whales make sounds called 'whale song', which is used for complex levels of communication.

FIGURE 7: Robins sing to help mark out their territory.

WOW FACTOR!

Whales can detect the songs of other whales from over 2000 miles away!

WOW FACTOR!

Some insect pests are trapped by attracting them with artificial pheromones.

QUESTIONS

4 The pheromone used by ants to mark their food trail disappears quite quickly. Explain how this stops ants from wasting time when the food has gone.

5 What is meant by duetting in birds?

6 Why is vocal communication important for monkeys?

Human communication

Humans have the most complex systems of communication of all animals. Language makes it possible to transmit knowledge of past events, **emotions** and complex ideas to other humans. Language means that humans can exchange ideas and discuss and refine them.

As well as speech, humans also use written language to convey ideas. And the really clever thing about written language is that it is permanent. People can refer back to things written in the past. People can take time to consider the written word. Written ideas are less likely to be forgotten. Having learned how to use language, humans can use language for further learning. That leads to more and more ways of communicating to more and more people over greater distances.

FIGURE 8: Was this cave painting made to teach people how to hunt or as a reminder of a successful day?

QUESTIONS

7 Make a list of the ways in which humans communicate.

8 Do other animals have language?

...pheromone ...posture ...signal ...sound

Herbivore feeding

You will find out:
- That feeding behaviour depends on the type of food being eaten
- That herbivores need to spend a lot of time feeding
- That herbivores often feed in large groups
- That herbivores have to avoid being eaten by predators

On the move

The continual search for food takes a vast herd of wildebeest on a permanent migration through part of Africa. Over 1.4 million wildebeest and 200 000 zebras and gazelles follow the rain on an annual trek of 1800 miles through Tanzania and Kenya to find fresh grass. Their journey has no beginning or end as the animals are constantly on the move, risking being eaten by crocodiles as they cross rivers and by lions as they cross the plains.

Wildebeest

The wildebeest or gnu is the largest of the antelopes. Like zebras and gazelles, they are **herbivores**, animals that eat plants. Grass is not a food that is rich in nutrients and it is especially lacking in amino acids needed to make protein. In order to get all of the nutrients they need, herbivores need to eat a lot of food. They have to spend a lot of time eating. In many parts of Africa, rain is seasonal. This means that the grass is brown and lacking in nutrients for much of the year. Especially in dry countries, large herbivores often have to migrate to follow the rain so they can eat fresh, nutritious grass. Wildebeest are constantly on the move with the herd. A wildebeest calf is able to walk and run with the herd within minutes of being born.

So if food is hard to find, why do the wildebeest stay together in a huge herd? Wouldn't it be easier to find food if they all lived in separate small groups? The big advantage of living in a herd is that being part of a group can reduce the chances of being eaten by a predator. It offers more **protection**.

FIGURE 1: Wildebeest and zebra risk being eaten by crocodiles as they cross a river on their migration.

FIGURE 2: A wildebeest calf can run with the herd within minutes of being born.

QUESTIONS

1. What is meant by the word 'herbivore'?
2. Why do herbivores need to spend such a lot of their time eating?
3. Why do large herbivores in Africa have to migrate?
4. Why do wildebeest calves need to be able to run soon after being born?

...altruistic behaviour ...herbivores

Following the herd

How does being in a herd protect individual **vertebrates** from being eaten by predators?

- *Dilution.* The more animals in a herd, the less chance there is of any one animal being the one that gets eaten.
- *Confusion.* When lions attack a herd of hundreds of wildebeest it is very difficult for them to decide which one they are actually trying to catch. One feature of a successful hunt is that the lions manage to separate one individual wildebeest from the herd and concentrate on catching it alone. Shoals of fish move around in rapidly changing directions, confusing predators.
- *Vigilance.* The group of animals as a whole benefits from having many pairs of eyes and ears on the lookout all at the same time. A single wildebeest with its head down, eating grass is not going to have much chance of spotting a lion. In a herd, there will always be some animals watching, so others can concentrate a larger amount of time on feeding.

  Meerkats are mammals that live in small groups in Africa. When feeding, they have been observed to take turns to climb a tree or stand on a high point and watch for predators. If one appears the watching meerkat calls a warning to the others to take cover. Later other meerkats take their turn on sentry duty. This sort of social behaviour is called **altruistic behaviour**.

FIGURE 3: Meerkat on sentry duty.

- *Group defence.* Many herd animals can use their superior numbers to defend themselves against predators when a single animal could not. Musk oxen are found in Arctic Canada. When being attacked by wolves, they form defensive circles around their young with their horns facing out.

FIGURE 4: Would a wolf fancy its chances of getting past that row of musk ox horns?

Selfish herd

Do all of the animals in a herd decide that they will all help each other out and work in a cooperative manner? Probably not. A herd is simply made up of lots of individual animals that group together to avoid being eaten, in which each animal looks after itself. The individuals in a selfish herd coincidentally produce behaviour that protects the majority.

Adelie penguins live in the Antarctic. Leopard seals eat Adelie penguins. They wait in the water for the penguins to take to the sea. Which penguin will dive in first? Eventually hundreds of penguins are standing at the edge of the ice and a few are pushed in by the ones behind. As the leopard seals eat these penguins, the rest take advantage to get past them and out to the open sea – the selfish herd at work.

FIGURE 5: A leopard seal waits for Adelie penguins to take to the sea. Who fancies jumping in first?

QUESTIONS

5 What is a vertebrate?

6 How does a herd's increased vigilance help individual animals?

7 What is meant by altruistic behaviour?

8 Do groups of animals show any similar behaviour to teenagers in gangs?

QUESTIONS

9 What is meant by a selfish herd?

Mammals on the move

CONTEXT

Ashley was watching a wildlife programme on TV. It was about the Serengeti National Park in Africa and featured animals called wildebeests. He was fascinated by the odd appearance of these animals, with their large heads, curved horns, big shoulders and spindly rear legs; then the programme explained that their journey is the biggest mammal migration in the world. One reason for the migration is the need for fresh grazing areas – short grass is their preferred diet. They cannot go without water for more than a day or so. They have several predators, including hyena and lions. An adult will live for up to 20 years.

The females calve in May, giving birth to a single calf; they don't seek shelter but give birth surrounded by the herd. Most of the females in the herd give birth within two or three weeks of each other. The calf can stand and run within minutes of being born and, within a few days, can run fast enough to keep up with the herd. The herd starts to migrate north soon after that and travels at a relentless pace through day and night; many are lost, injured or even killed. In November the return journey south commences.

Ashley was intrigued by the programme and couldn't understand why the wildebeests lived the way that they did. The young seemed to have a really rough time; they had to be up and on the move in a very short time and sometimes perished before reaching adulthood. Surely they would stand a better chance of survival if they weren't all born at about the same time, or if the herd stayed in the same area for several months until the calves were older and stronger?

It made a really good programme but he was so glad that humans didn't raise their young like that.

STEP 1

Why do wildebeest have to repeatedly move on?

STEP 2

If the wildebeest lived in smaller herds all the year round (instead of just during the breeding season), thought Ashley, perhaps they would be able to settle in one area. Why do you think they don't do that?

Why do you think the females give birth in the middle of the grassy plain, surrounded by the herd instead of finding a sheltered place? Why is it that most of the females giving birth at around the same time gives an advantage in terms of survival?

Ashley found the mass migration a stunning sight, with a great number of animals relentlessly pressing on. They didn't stop, even if some members of the herd got injured or left behind. Surely they would stand a better chance of survival if they cared more for each other? What do you think?

Use some of the ideas you have gathered to explain how the need for survival has influenced the adaptation of the wildebeest.

Maximise your grade

These sentences show what you need to include in your work to achieve each grade. Use them to improve your work and be more successful.

Grade	Answer includes...
F	State one reason why the wildebeest keep moving on.
	State several reasons why the wildebeest keep moving on.
	Suggest one reason why large group size aids survival.
	Suggest several reasons why large group size aids survival.
C	Explain how being out in the open aids survival.
	Explain why many females giving birth at around the same time aids survival.
A	Explain with reference to one feature of the wildebeest's behaviour how survival has influenced them.
	Explain with reference to several features of the wildebeest's behaviour how survival has influenced them.

Carnivore feeding

You will find out:

- That feeding behaviour depends on the type of food being eaten
- That meat is rich in protein so carnivores need to spend less time eating
- That some carnivores hunt in packs while others hunt alone

Hunting for meat

We get our food nicely prepared and served up on a plate. It's all quite easy. For many carnivores, however, it's a lot trickier than that. Most carnivores first have to catch their prey and the prey does not want to be eaten! Carnivores have evolved behaviour that helps them to hunt successfully; some alone and others in packs.

FIGURE 1: A group of lionesses feeding on a wildebeest.

Predators

Animals that eat meat are called **carnivores**. Animals that catch animals of other species and eat them are called predators. The animals they eat are their **prey**. Hunting and catching prey is called **predation**.

Meat is a very nutritious food, containing high levels of nutrients, especially protein. Herbivores have to spend a lot of time eating, just to get enough nutrients from the food they eat. Carnivores don't need to spend nearly as much time actually eating. Hunting, however, takes a lot of effort and many chases are unsuccessful. Predators spend a lot of time hunting and resting between hunts. Even carnivores that are not predators, such as vultures, often have to spend a lot of time searching for food.

Predators may hunt alone or in groups. There are many different names for groups of animals, such as a pride of lions, but a group of animals hunting together is called a **pack**. What are the advantages of being part of a pack?

- Pack hunting is much more successful than individual hunting. A pack of animals is twice as likely to make a kill as an individual but, of course, food caught by a pack of animals has to be shared.
- A pack can bring down much larger prey than an individual.
- Once prey has been caught, it is easier for a pack of animals to defend it against scavengers.

DID YOU KNOW?

Hunting alone is not easy. It is estimated that tigers catch their prey only once out of every ten attempts.

FIGURE 2: Not all carnivores are predators – black vultures feed on 'road kill'.

QUESTIONS

1. What is meant by the word 'carnivore'?
2. Give some examples of carnivores that are not predators.
3. What is meant by a 'pack'?
4. Draw a table summarising the advantages and disadvantages of hunting in a pack.

Pack hunting

Lions are fast and can reach a top speed of about 55 km/h but they lack the stamina to keep this up for very long. Females are faster than males and, in prides that live in open country, it is the lionesses that do most of the hunting. In prides that live in wooded areas the males hunt more, often using their greater strength to capture larger prey.

Lions need to get close to their prey to avoid a long chase. Hunting in a pack makes it easier to get close to the prey. When a group of lions hunt together, they work as a team. At first some of the lions stalk the prey, keeping low and using camouflage to get close. Then some members will start running towards the prey, causing panic, in an attempt to separate an individual from the herd, then chasing it into an ambush of other well-hidden lions.

The lions strike at the prey and attempt to pull it down to the ground. They then use their powerful jaws to suffocate the prey by biting down on its windpipe. Once the prey has been caught, the pride will eat it. Even if the prey was caught by the females it will be the dominant males who feed first, followed by the lionesses, and then the younger lions and cubs.

FIGURE 3: One advantage of hunting in a pack is that larger prey can be killed.

Solo hunting

Tigers and most cats other than lions as well as most bears usually hunt alone. As individuals they cannot use cooperation and teamwork to get close to their prey. Instead they rely on stealth and camouflage to get close enough to ambush their prey and so avoid being involved in a long chase.

DID YOU KNOW?

Hunting in a pack is easier. It is estimated that a wolf pack is successful in one attempt out of every three.

QUESTIONS

5 Draw a flow chart or a comic strip to summarise the stages in a hunt by a group of lions.

6 Why do lions and tigers need to get close to their prey to make a kill?

7 Describe the importance of camouflage in hunting behaviour.

In pursuit

There are two main types of pursuit:

- Guided pursuit in which the predator constantly checks what the prey is doing and keeps on altering its own direction. This is observed in predators such as the cheetah, which, once it has caught up with its prey, will follow it closely as it zigzags to try to escape.

FIGURE 4: The cheetah will match each twist and turn as this impala tries to escape.

- Ballistic attack is much simpler in that the predator guesses which way the prey is likely to go, then launches itself in that direction. Even if the prey changes direction, the predator will continue on its original path. This sort of pursuit is commonly seen in several species of fish and in octopus.

FIGURE 5: The octopus makes a ballistic attack on its prey.

WOW FACTOR!

A cheetah can run at 70 mph – the speed limit on a motorway – but only for about 400 metres.

QUESTIONS

8 Explain the difference between guided pursuit and ballistic attack.

9 What factors do you think could influence whether an animal makes a guided pursuit or a ballistic attack?

Reproductive behaviour

You will find out:

- That sexual reproduction requires the finding and selection of a suitable mate and that this may involve courtship behaviour
- That some animals mate for life, while others may have several mates during the mating season

Passing on the genes

Animals have evolved many different forms of reproductive behaviour but they all have one thing in common – to ensure that an animal's genes are passed on as often as possible. To achieve a high level of reproductive success, an animal needs to make sure it has as many *surviving* offspring as possible.

Many male animals have evolved complex courtship behaviour, aimed at attracting females to mate with them.

How many mates?

Sexual reproduction involves mating and the mixing of genes. The number of mates that an animal has depends on the social organisation of each species. Some species are monogamous, which means they mate with only one partner. Monogamy is most common among birds. Many other species are polygamous, which means they mate with more than one partner. Polygamy usually means one male mates with several females, but in a few species one female may mate with several males.

Male animals make millions of sperm but, in most species, females make far fewer eggs. This means that males can ensure that their genes are widely spread by mating with as many females as possible. For a female it is more important that the male she mates with is healthy and is therefore likely to carry genes for healthy offspring.

In some species males fight to establish who has the right to mate with the females. The winner benefits by passing on his genes through as many females as possible (although, obviously, most males don't get to mate at all). The females benefit because they mate with the males with the 'best' genes. Male elephant seals battle with each other to establish who controls a 'harem' of up to 50 females. The female does not get much choice about who she mates with, as she is less than half the size of the male. Genes for large males have a greater chance of being passed on as large males are more likely to get the chance to mate.

FIGURE 1: The more 'eyes' in a peacock's tail, the more attractive he is to the peahen.

WOW FACTOR!

A peacock's tail weighs 3 kg when wet.

FIGURE 2: Male elephant seals are more than twice as heavy as females.

▪▪ QUESTIONS ▪▪

1 Why is reproductive success measured in number of *surviving* offspring?
2 What is meant by monogamy and polygamy?
3 Do you think genes for small female elephant seals are more likely to be passed on than genes for large females?

...courting   ...hybrids

Courtship

Courtship is usually carried out by males. A male animal uses it to persuade females that he is the best choice of mate. Courtship has several functions:

- It is a type of *advertisement* designed to attract females and warn away other males. In many species the male is much more brightly coloured than the female. In species living in dense woodland, for example, it is not easy to see a display, and vocalisation plays a more important role in courtship.

- It allows the female to *assess* the male and decide if he will make a suitable partner. In many **courting** rituals the male offers food to the female. This gives the female some idea about the male's ability to find food and his suitability as a parent. Other courtship behaviour can include nest building, as is seen in sticklebacks, where the male shows off the nest he has built and tries to entice the female to lay her eggs in *his* nest. Female sticklebacks are not just interested in the quality of the nest, however. As the male carries out his display he will shake his body. Males who are good body shakers are attractive to females because the male uses body shaking to send water with oxygen over the eggs.

FIGURE 3: The peahen lacks the peacock's bright colours.

FIGURE 4: Having persuaded the female to lay her eggs in his nest, the male stickleback will follow her and deposit his sperm. Then he will care for the eggs.

- It helps to ensure that the partner is of the *same species*. Closely related species can produce offspring which are **hybrids**. These are sterile, so the parents' genes pass no further. Species that look alike will have different courtship rituals.
- It can determine whether the female is *fertile*. There is no point a male wasting his sperm mating with a female who does not have any eggs ready.

QUESTIONS

4 Summarise the reasons for courtship behaviour.

5 When is vocalisation more useful than a visual courtship display?

6 What is a hybrid?

7 What similarities are there between animal and human courtship?

Why the big tail?

Peahens are attracted to peacocks with long tails, yet the tail does not help the male to survive. A lot of nutrients are used up growing it and it slows him down when he is chased by a fox. What's the attraction? Four suggestions have been made:

- Carrying around such a large handicap proves the male *must* be fit.
- A healthy tail proves that he is not carrying parasites.
- Long-tailed males are more likely to have long-tailed sons, increasing the chances of passing on the female's genes.
- A long tail is the result of females favouring genes for long-tailed males. At the same time, genes for choosing long tails in males will also be passed on. The result is the runaway **selection** of an otherwise useless characteristic by sexual selection.

QUESTIONS

8 What is the purpose of all reproductive behaviour?

9 Will peacock tails keep on getting longer forever?

10 What do you think is meant by 'sexual selection'?

Bringing up baby

You will find out:

- That birds and mammals have special behaviours that contribute to parental care
- That parental care involves extra risk to parents but increases the chances of survival of their genes

Good old dad!

The jawfish is unusual. Its mouth is full of eggs but it is not eating them. It is protecting its eggs by carrying them in its mouth. After the eggs hatch, the babies return to the mouth for safety. This fish is very unusual because it is the male that cares for the eggs. Paternal care is unusual in animals. Males that care for their offspring usually do it jointly with the mother.

FIGURE 1: The male jawfish cares for its eggs in its mouth!

Parental care

Parental care can range from the very basic to the very complex. Many species just lay their eggs and leave them. Some animals show a bit more care. The female digger wasp makes a hole in the ground. Before laying an egg she catches and paralyses an insect. She puts this in the hole, ready to feed the wasp larva when it hatches. Then she flies away and never sees her own offspring.

Many fish, amphibians and reptiles simply lay their eggs and leave them to hatch. Some species, however, look after their eggs until they hatch and may care for the young afterwards.

In **birds** and **mammals**, **parental behaviour** is highly evolved. Most birds build nests and have to incubate their eggs, keeping them at the correct temperature until they hatch. Once the chicks have hatched they need to be fed. This takes so much parental time and effort that it is common for male birds to help. Males and females often share tasks such as incubating the eggs and bringing food for the chicks.

FIGURE 2: Alligators are unusual reptiles as they care for their young.

Parental behaviour is triggered by the behaviour in the young. Baby birds in the nest open their mouths wide and make 'begging' sounds. Parents respond by favouring the noisiest chick. The bigger chicks get more food than the smaller ones. From the parents' point of view this is good as it produces some fit offspring who are more likely to pass on their genes. The weaker chicks may die or be pushed from the nest by the others.

FIGURE 3: The noisiest chick will get the most food.

▪▪ QUESTIONS ▪▪

1. What is meant by paternal care?
2. What does incubate mean?
3. How do adult birds benefit when a smaller chick dies?
4. Do humans respond differently to their noisiest children?

...birds ...mammals

Mammals

Mammals are different from other animals. Females have evolved mammary glands which produce milk to feed babies. This part of parental care can *only* be carried out by the mother. Monogamy is rare in mammals and males care for the young in few species. Exceptions are some primates, wolves and naked mole rats. Even after young mammals have been **weaned**, many stay with their mother. As well as protection, young mammals benefit by learning things like hunting skills from their mothers.

FIGURE 4: All mammals make milk but seals have the creamiest of all, with 45% fat.

WOW FACTOR!

Naked mole rats are strange mammals. Their social behaviour is like that of insects, with a queen looked after by workers.

There are several reasons why mothers, rather than fathers, do most of the parenting in mammals:

- Females have mammary glands.
- Females invest a lot of time, energy and nutrients in their babies in pregnancy, and need to ensure that they survive to pass on her genes.
- Males can never be certain that they are the real father of 'their' babies, so why risk wasting time caring for babies that may not carry their genes? Females, having given birth, can be certain that they are caring for their own genes.

Selfish genes

Having babies is all about passing on genes. Many biologists argue that animals are simply 'machines' that guarantee the survival and passing on of genes.

Prides of lions consist of several females and their offspring, and one or two males. The males are sometimes replaced in the pride by other males. The first thing the new male does is kill the younger cubs fathered by the old males. The females then become fertile and the new male mates with them. It sounds cruel but why would a male want to waste his energy protecting the genes of another male?

WANT TO KNOW MORE?

Find out about naked mole rats at http://nationalzoo.si.edu/publications/zoogoer/2002/3/nakedmolerats.cfm

QUESTIONS

5 What does 'weaned' mean?

6 Can females always be certain that they are the mothers of their offspring? In which species can they be more certain and in which can they be less certain? Is there a connection with the amount of care they give their offspring?

Parental investment

Animals exist to pass on their genes. Parental care reduces opportunities for mating and takes up a lot of resources:

- *Time* spent caring for babies or incubating an egg could otherwise be used to get more food or to mate more often.
- *Energy* that could be used to find more mates is used making milk for babies.
- *Nutrients* that could be used to grow stronger and more attractive to the opposite sex are used making milk.
- *Risk* is increased when caring for babies because they slow parents down and make them more vulnerable.

So why invest all of those resources in caring for babies? Parental care has evolved as a means of ensuring that genes are passed on. Reproductive success is measured in terms of number of *surviving* offspring.

FIGURE 5: This chick hatched from an egg incubated on the feet of a male emperor penguin which stood in the Antarctic winter for two months without food.

QUESTIONS

7 How do animals that do not show parental behaviour increase their reproductive success?

8 Why do emperor penguins incubate eggs on their feet?

Humans as apes

You will find out:
- That humans are one of the great apes
- That human and animal behaviours should not be compared directly although they may have factors in common

Great ape fact files

Meet the **great apes**, our closest relatives. Yes, we are great apes too!

Name: Chimpanzee

Size:
male 45 kg, 1.4 m tall
female 40 kg, 1.2 m tall

Habitat: forest and open savannah, West and Central Africa

Community: in mixed groups of about 50 headed by an 'alpha' male

Diet: fruit, plants, eggs, insects, meat

Name: Gorilla

Size:
male 190 kg, 1.8 m tall
female 90 kg, 1.5 m tall

Habitat: tropical rainforest, Central Africa

Community: in troops of up to 30, one male, several females and their children

Diet: plants and some insects

Name: Orang-utan

Size:
male 90 kg, 1.4 m tall
female 50 kg, 1.1 m tall

Habitat: tropical rainforest, Borneo

Community: mostly live alone except for mothers and their children

Diet: mostly fruit

Name: Bonobo or pygmy chimpanzee

Size:
male 35 kg, 1.0 m tall
female 30 kg, 1.0 m tall

Habitat: rainforest, Central Africa

Community: in mixed groups of about 30 headed by dominant females

Diet: fruit, plants, and some meat

The Bonobo is our closest related species

Name: Human

Size:
male 90 kg, 1.8 m tall
female 70 kg, 1.6 m tall

Habitat: thrives worldwide, can survive in all habitats

Community: in societies, increasingly based around cities, populated by millions

Diet: fruit, plants, grain, eggs, meat, fish, burgers, pizzas, curries, pasta, oriental take-away, tapas, fried chicken, etc.

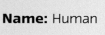

❚❚ QUESTIONS ❚❚

1. Which is the only great ape that does not live in Africa?
2. Which great ape has a diet closest to that of humans?
3. Which great apes are the biggest?
4. Which great apes are the smallest?

...anthropomorphism   ...conscious

Animal builders

Bonobos are the animals most closely related to us. They live in rainforests in central Africa. At night they make nests in trees so that they can sleep in relative safety well above ground level. The next night they will make a nest elsewhere, so bonobo nests are temporary structures.

Many species of birds, however, build nests to which they return year after year. Termites build huge air-conditioned mounds, like cities, housing millions of termites. Humans are 'more advanced' than other animals including the great apes, but how? Humans build cities that can be seen from space. Humans have changed the environment permanently; almost all traces of the 'natural' environment have disappeared.

FIGURE 1: Humans build huge cities.

Animal tool makers

Humans make a huge range of tools from a simple lever to a printing press and the computer on which this book was written. Do animals make tools? The Galapagos woodpecker finch uses a cactus spine to pick insects from tree bark but it doesn't actually *make* a tool, it just uses something handily lying around.

Chimpanzees use twigs to get termites from inside their mounds. They actually *make* tools as they strip off the leaves from twigs and snap them to make sure they are the right length. Chimpanzees use a piece of wood as an anvil and a stone as a hammer to crack open nuts. They also use leaves as a 'sponge' in order to collect drinking water.

When humans make a tool, they keep it so that they can use it again in the future. Animals do not keep tools but we cannot be sure whether this shows a lack of foresight or simply reflects the ease of making simple tools.

FIGURE 2: A chimpanzee uses a 'tool' to get termites from their nest.

QUESTIONS

5   Explain the difference between using and making a tool.

6   List the examples of animal tools mentioned on this page. Use the internet to find out about some more.

7   How does the way in which humans use tools differ from other animals?

Anthropomorphism

It would be foolish to say that human behaviour is totally different from animal behaviour, as there are many parallels. However, people often make the mistake of interpreting animal behaviour in terms of human behaviour. This is called **anthropomorphism**. Many species of insect mimic the yellow and black stripes of wasps to avoid being eaten. An anthropomorphic interpretation might imply that the insect is deliberately disguising itself in the same way that a soldier might use camouflage. In reality the insect does not know that it is 'disguised'. It just follows a set pattern of behaviour as it flies around in full view of potential predators.

While it is true that humans are animals, we are quite exceptional animals who are **conscious** of the outcomes of our actions. Humans have the ability to learn, use complex language to express emotions, tell lies, understand humour and show **self-awareness**.

QUESTIONS

8   Do you think that animals tell lies?

9   What do you think is meant by 'self-awareness'?

10 Write down as many things as possible that show that humans are different from other animals.

11 Write down as many things as possible that show that humans are animals.

Humans and other animals

You will find out:

- About the numerous different ways that humans use animals
- That there are ethical considerations on the 'rights' of animals

Hunting with animals

It is illegal in the UK to hunt with dogs although humans have been doing so for a very long time. Dogs and horses were **domesticated** many thousands of years ago, probably originally to help in hunting for food. Of course, there's a difference – we don't eat foxes!

Hunter-gatherers

Early humans were hunter-gatherers, gathering plant food such as berries, roots and leaves as well as hunting for animals. Dogs were domesticated at least 10 000 years ago, as humans used their sharp senses and speed to help catch food.

Early humans were often **nomadic**, which means they moved around, often following herds of animals which they used for food and other resources. Eventually these herds of animals were domesticated and were generally kept in one place.

Sheep, cattle, goats and pigs provide humans with a constant and dependable supply of food. All can be used for meat, while cows, goats and sheep provide milk, although the Maasai people of East Africa use a mixture of blood and milk as their main source of protein. They cut into a vein and collect blood, then use mud to stop further bleeding. Some human societies still follow herds of animals. The Lapps of northern Scandinavia, for example, depend on the herds of reindeer they follow.

FIGURE 1: Fox hunting uses two different domesticated animals.

Animal materials

In addition to food, humans use animals as a source of a great many materials including:

- wool
- feathers for making pillows and quilts
- skins including fur coats, leather and suede
- glue – traditionally made from cows' hooves and horns
- fat for making candles
- pig bristles for making brushes
- intestines for making tennis racquets and violin strings
- dyes, some of which are made from snail shells and insects.

WOW FACTOR!

In China seabirds called cormorants were used to catch fish for humans.

QUESTIONS

1. Why is it illegal to use dogs to hunt foxes?
2. Make a list of all of the animals that humans commonly eat.
3. Try to think of further products obtained from animals. Sort them into those that are obtained by killing the animal and those that keep it alive.

The Maasai people of East Africa use blood as a source of protein

...domesticated

Working animals

In the UK the working animals we see most are dogs and horses. Working dogs have many uses:

- *Guard* dogs and *police* dogs use their speed and strength to catch and restrain criminals.
- 'Sniffer' dogs use their sense of smell to find substances such as drugs and explosives. *Tracker* dogs and *rescue* dogs use their sense of smell to find people who are missing, who have escaped or who are trapped in natural disasters.
- *Assistance* dogs help people who are blind or deaf to carry out everyday tasks.
- *Herding* dogs help to control flocks of sheep and herds of cattle.

- *Sledge* dogs have an important job moving people and equipment around in Arctic regions.
- *Performing* dogs are trained to do tricks in circuses or to 'act' in films and television. Greyhounds and whippets are regularly raced, with people betting on the winner.
- *Hunting* dogs are used in a wide variety of ways including cross-country chases and retrieving shot birds.

Horses are used for work much less than in the past. In the UK they are still used by the police and for sport but are seldom used for other purposes.

Other working animals used worldwide include elephants, llamas, oxen, camels and even birds such as pigeons.

In addition people keep pets for companionship and for the interest of watching animals. Many of us also visit wildlife parks and zoos as a form of entertainment and education.

WOW FACTOR!

In France, specially trained pigs are used to sniff out truffles, a very expensive fungus found underground.

QUESTIONS

4 Draw a table showing some of the ways in which dogs are used for work. Explain what special features of the dogs are being used in each job.

5 Write down a list of the ways in which horses have worked in the past.

6 Do zoos and wildlife parks have any functions other than those mentioned above?

Medical uses

Many animals are used in medical research and to produce medicinal products. Some people are opposed to any form of medical research using animals, and believe that animals have the same rights as humans. Other people believe that the use of animals in medical research is essential if scientists are to develop new dugs and medical techniques.

Animals used in medical research include:

- *Dogs* were used in the research that showed that diabetes was caused by a lack of insulin. Prior to this, people with diabetes suffered a slow death. Research using dogs enabled ways to be found of preventing tissue rejection following organ transplants.
- *Pigs* were used for many years to produce insulin for treating diabetics. Pig heart valves are used to replace faulty human heart valves.
- *Horses* have been used for making many medical products such as tetanus antitoxin.

QUESTIONS

7 Ignoring your personal beliefs, write down **three** reasons to support using animals in medical research and **three** reasons for opposing it.

8 It is illegal in the UK to use great apes for medical research. Do you agree with this? Explain your answer.

Unit summary

Animals inherit certain patterns of behaviour from their parents, known as instinctive behaviour.

An animal's early experiences in life have a big impact on the way in which it behaves as an adult.

Animals learn through habituation and conditioning.

Humans can use conditioning to train animals.

All animals communicate by means of chemical, visual and auditory signals of varying levels of complexity.

Humans use animals as a source of entertainment (hunting, racing, circuses, wildlife parks) and companionship.

There are ethical considerations that should be taken into account when using animals.

Humans exploit animals in a number of ways including as food, as a source of materials and for testing drugs.

Carnivores and herbivores behave differently because of the nature of their food and the precautions needed for successfully and safely obtaining food.

Some animals show parental care and feed their young.

Some animals use tools to help them to obtain food.

Animals have special behaviour that helps them to select a mate.

Some animals mate for life and share parental care.

Unit quiz

1 What is meant by the 'rooting reflex' in a baby?

2 Give an example of 'habituation'.

3 What is meant by 'imprinting'?

4 Give an account of Pavlov's experiment into conditioned reflexes.

5 How could you train a dog to perform a trick?

6 What is meant by a 'submissive' body posture?

7 What is a 'pheromone'?

8 Why do wildebeest in East Africa have to continually migrate?

9 Give three advantages for herbivores of living in a herd.

10 Give three advantages for carnivores of hunting in a pack.

11 Give one disadvantage for carnivores of hunting in a pack.

12 What is meant by 'altruistic' behaviour?

13 What is meant by 'monogamy'?

14 Give three reasons why animals might carry out courtship displays.

15 What is meant by sexual selection?

16 What are the advantages to an animal of caring for its young?

17 What are the disadvantages to an animal of caring for its young?

18 Name the great apes.

19 Give three examples of animal tool use.

20 List six materials we use that are obtained from animals.

Literacy activity

Animal research

More mice are used in medical research than any other vertebrate animals. The use of mice in medical research is likely to increase now that the mouse genome has been mapped in the same way as in the Human Genome Project. About 99% of human genes are present in mice so human genetic diseases can be studied in detail. One way of finding out the function of a human gene is to insert it into mouse DNA and observe what happens. Alternatively the mouse version of a human gene can be removed from the mouse DNA and the results observed. About 97% of all genetically modified animals used in research are mice.

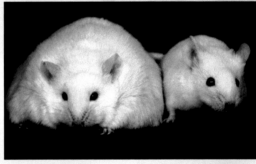

The mouse in the photograph has a mutation on a gene that controls body fat, with the result that the mouse becomes obese even when fed a low-energy diet. This variety of mice is specially bred to carry out research into obesity, the results of which may be relevant to obesity in humans.

QUESTIONS

1 Why are mice increasingly used in medical research?

2 What is meant by 'ethical'?

3 What are the benefits to humans of using mice to study obesity?

4 What are the benefits to mice of studying obesity in mice?

5 Is it ethical for scientists to breed 'unhealthy' strains of mice and other animals in order to carry out research for the benefit of humans?

Exam practice

1   In 1904, Ivan Pavlov was awarded the Nobel prize for physiology or medicine. His work was to do with responses in dogs. Pavlov noticed that his laboratory dogs were drooling at apparently random times. He eventually worked out that his dogs were drooling at lab coats, because the dogs were fed by people wearing lab coats.

Following this, Pavlov realised that if he rang a bell before the dogs were fed, the dogs became conditioned by the sound of the bell.

A   What patterns of behaviour do animals learn from their parents?

.... [1]

B   What would you have observed the dogs doing in Pavlov's experiment when the bell was rung?

.... [1]

C   The process of conditioning can be used when training animals to give certain responses. Explain in your own words how this would be achieved. You may choose to write about any animal.

....

....

....

.... [4]

(Total 6 marks)

2   **A**   Why do buffalo feed in a herd?

.... [1]

B   Does this method of evading predators protect every member of the herd?

.... [1]

C   Which members of the herd are more vulnerable?

....

.... [2]

D   The buffalo is an herbivore. It is also a large mammal. Why would the buffalo need to eat more food than a carnivore?

....

....

.... [3]

E   Buffalo may fall victim to a lion. How is a lion adapted to catch its prey?

....

....

.... [3]

(Total 10 marks)

1 a Give an example of an animal that mates for life. [1]

b A female lion will often have sexual intercourse with many males whilst on heat. Each cub in the litter she produces for that year may have a different father. Explain why this is a good evolutionary strategy. [2]

c Many birds and mammals have developed strategies for caring for their young. Using an example of your choice, explain how this benefits the young. [4]

Any answer would be appropriate here, as long as the organism in question does actually mate for life. You will need to be careful, as though some species are listed as being monogamous, they are actually not. For example, the grey wolf is usually monogamous but will mate with other females if food is plentiful.

a Geese

b This is a good evolutionary strategy because it means that the young that are produced have different sets of genes. This will ensure that diversity amongst the pride remains high.

The lion is an organism that cares for its young. When the babies are born they stay with the mother for a long period of time. This is so that the mother can care for and feed the young. In the time that the young will stay with the mother it will learn many things and this will ensure its survival.

This is an excellent answer. The student has talked about the reasons why female lions have intercourse with many males and the result of this action. The clue for this question is evolution. You must think about what would happen to the diversity of the gene pool over a long period of time if this were not to happen.

This answer could be extended to describe what things the young lion will learn from the mother. For example, how to hunt, what predators are in the area, and how to avoid these predators. When the cubs are born they will need to stay with the mother because they are suckling, they require their mother's milk as it is rich in fat, which is needed for the cubs to grow, and contains antibodies the cubs will need to protect them from disease.

Overall Grade: B

How to get an A

A good set of answers here. Remember that this is part of the extension unit and is composed of exam-style questions and not multiple choice. If you wish to gain a high grade you will need to know and be able to apply your knowledge to different situations.

CHEMICAL DETECTION

What do forensic scientist do? Their job is to analyse various crime scenes and collect evidence that can then be used in court. How do they do this?

Why do we need to analyse substances in our lives? What would happen if no analysis took place with food, for example? Would this be a good thing?

The labels on food show what ingredients are supposed to be present. How do we know? Is it possible to include unreliable or wrong information?

The ability to be able to detect the presence of chemicals is very important if you are a forensic scientist. Analytical chemists also detect chemicals using some special techniques, and they can also measure how much there is.

Why is water so important in our lives? We may need it to live, but why are there so many concerns about the water that we drink? Will these concerns grow in the future?

How do we detect drugs that may be present at the scene of a crime? How do we measure how much there is, in someone's blood, for example? Is it possible to identify drugs when even minute quantities are present?

Chemical formulae

You will find out:
- Why chemical formulae are so useful to the chemist
- That some compounds have very similar chemical formulae, but often have very different chemical properties
- How to write balanced chemical equations

John Dalton

John Dalton was the first chemist who thought deeply about what matter is made of. He was the first to realise that atoms combined with other atoms to form compounds. In compounds a fixed number of atoms join together. Water was known to be made of one part oxygen and two parts hydrogen, so the formula of water was H_2O.

John Dalton suffered from colour blindness and thought that the liquid in his eye was blue – this was the cause of his problem, so he thought. He instructed a surgeon after his death to cut open his eye to see if this was the case. It was found that this was not true.

FIGURE 1: The eye of John Dalton.

What's important about chemical formulae?

All chemical compounds and elements have a **chemical formula**. It is a type of code or shorthand and if we understand it, it can be very helpful.

Chemical formulae tell us:

- the elements present in a compound
- the number of each type of atom present in the compound.

The formula of sulphuric(VI) acid is H_2SO_4 – this means that there are two atoms of hydrogen, one atom of sulphur and four atoms of oxygen in one molecule of sulphuric acid.

FIGURE 2: The formula of sulphuric(VI) acid is H_2SO_4.

Watch Out A chemical formula doesn't just tell us which elements are present, it also tells us how many atoms there are of each type.

■ QUESTIONS ■

1 The chemical formula for carbon dioxide is CO_2. What does this formula tell us about a molecule of carbon dioxide?

2 The formula for ethanol is C_2H_5OH. Which elements are present in ethanol, and how many atoms of each type are present in an ethanol molecule?

3 Find out the chemical formulae for methane, magnesium chloride and hydrogen peroxide.

DID YOU KNOW?

Oxygen gets its name from 'acid maker' or 'oxy', meaning 'acid' and 'gene' meaning maker. It was once thought that all acids contained oxygen.

Dual personality?

Iron is a metallic element with the symbol Fe. In many ways, it reacts like a typical metal, for example in its reaction with chlorine gas.

However, the reaction of iron with chlorine is not as simple as it seems – two possible reactions may take place:

Iron + chlorine gas → iron(II) chloride

$Fe(s) + Cl_2(g) → FeCl_2(s)$

Iron + chlorine gas → iron(III) chloride

$2Fe(s) + 3Cl_2(g) → 2FeCl_3(s)$

FIGURE 3: The reaction of iron with chorine.

So, iron reacts with chlorine to produce two different compounds – both are chlorides of iron, but they have different chemical formulae. Iron(II) chloride consists of two chlorine particles for every one iron particle, whereas iron(III) chloride consists of three chlorine particles for every one iron particle.

Describing the change

Chemical equations describe a chemical change. In a chemical equation:

- the formulae of the **reactants** are written on the left of the arrow
- the formulae of the **products** are written on the right of the arrow
- the equation is then balanced so that the numbers of each type of atom are the same on both sides.

The reaction below is between aluminium and iodine:

- The word equation for the reaction is:

  Aluminium + iodine → aluminium iodide

- The unbalanced symbol equation for this is:

  $Al + I_2 → AlI_3$

- **Balancing** gives:

  $2Al + 3I_2 → 2AlI_3$

- Adding state symbols ((s) for solid, (l) for liquid, (g) for gas and (aq) for a substance dissolved in water) gives:

  $2Al(s) + 3I_2(s) → 2AlI_3(s)$

FIGURE 4: The reaction between aluminium and iodine.

QUESTIONS

4   What are the chemical formulae for iron(II) chloride and iron(III) chloride? What is the difference between these two formulae?

5   Balance the equation: $H_2O_2 → H_2O + O_2$

6   Write a balanced equation for the reaction between magnesium and dilute hydrochloric acid, including state symbols.

$Mg^{2+} + 2HCl → MgCl_2 + H_2$

REMEMBER

We must balance equations so that the numbers of particles on each side of the equation are equal, otherwise mass is not conserved.

How many types of sulphuric acid are there?

We all know that sulphuric acid is H_2SO_4, but did you know that there were three types of sulphuric acid?

- Sulphuric(IV) acid – H_2SO_3

This weak acid is formed when sulphur dioxide gas dissolves in water. It is one of the main acids responsible for acid rain.

- Sulphuric(VI) acid – H_2SO_4

This acid is used in many experiments. It is also one of the most important chemicals made by the chemical industry.

- Peroxymonosulphuric acid – H_2SO_5

This is like sulphuric(VI) acid with an extra oxygen added – it is therefore a strong and highly oxidising agent as well as an acid. It is otherwise known as Caro's acid and is made by reacting sulphur trioxide with concentrated hydrogen peroxide.

$SO_3 + H_2O_2 → H_2SO_5$

Watch Out   Many students think that some elements, such as chlorine, always go round in twos. This is only true as an element, not as a compound!

QUESTIONS

7   What is the chemical formula for peroxomonosulphuric acid?

8   Write a balanced chemical equation to show how peroxomonosulphuric acid is made from sulphric (VI) acid.

9   What is meant by an oxidising agent?

$H_2SO_4 + O_2 → H_2SO_5$

- loses electrons
- addition of oxygen

Chemical analysis

You will find out:

- What is meant by the term 'chemical analysis'
- How some substances containing ions may be tested
- How reactions can sometimes form coloured precipitates, which can be useful when identifying ions

What's in our food?

We all need food every day, since it provides us with energy and necessary nutrients. However, many people are concerned about the quality of the food that they eat. Chemical additives are added to make the food look nicer and to make it last longer, but sometimes it is difficult to know exactly what is in the food – we do not always believe the label!

We therefore must have a way in which substances can be analysed so that we can determine what is in them.

FIGURE 1: We use chemical tests to tell us what is in certain foods like these tomatoes.

What is chemical analysis?

Chemicals occur everywhere. They make up everything, for example: you and me, mountains, seas, the moon, trees and the sun. Without chemicals, nothing would exist. Many chemicals have also been used to make our lives more comfortable and of a better quality. Pharmaceutical drugs, detergents, paints, polymers (plastics) and glues are just a few of the substances that are made by humans that have been very important in making our lives more comfortable.

Chemicals that are used in our lives have been rigorously tested and should all be safe. However, this is not always the case.

It is therefore important to be able to devise chemical tests that enable scientists to detect the presence of some chemicals (a **qualitative** test), and also to measure how much of the chemicals may be present (a **quantitative** test). This is called chemical analysis.

FIGURE 2: Using chemical analysis to detect the presence of substances.

> **REMEMBER**
>
> A chemical test must be unambiguous. In other words, a positive test must be linked to the substance being tested, and no other.

> **REMEMBER**
>
> An ion is a charged atom, or molecule. Most ions have a full outer shell of electrons.

■ QUESTIONS ■

1. Explain why food must be chemically analysed before it is eaten.
2. What is the difference between a *qualitative* and a *quantitative* test?

...*electrons* ...*ionic substances* ...*ions*

Testing for ions

Many substances are made up of **ions**.

- Most ions are formed when metal atoms react with non-metal atoms.
- **Electrons** move from the metal atom to the non-metal atom.
- The metal atom forms a positively charged ion, and the non-metal atom forms a negatively charged ion.

FIGURE 3: Salt crystals are made up of ions.

Figure 3 is a photograph taken by a scanning electron tunnelling microscope of sodium chloride (table salt). If these crystals were magnified called even further, particles called ions would be seen. The sodium ions are positively charged. The chlorine ions are negatively charged.

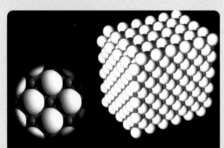

FIGURE 4: Sodium and chloride ions in a sodium chloride crystal.

When we are devising a test to measure the presence of certain ions, we make sure that the test for each ion is unique. This means that the test only shows the presence of a certain ion and not other ions.

Ionic substances are identified by detecting the positive and negative ions in different tests. The results of each test are then collated to determine the actual compound being analysed.

Many ions react with other chemicals to form **precipitates** (insoluble solids), many of which have characteristic colours. The colours of the precipitates can sometimes be used to tell us which metal ions are present.

FIGURE 5: A bright yellow precipitate of lead(II) iodide forming in a reaction between two solutions.

DID YOU KNOW?

A forensic scientist detects the presence of substance present at the scene of a crime. The results of these tests may be used to accuse someone of murder.

REMEMBER

When testing for ions, many coloured precipitates may form that can then be used to identify the original metal ion present.

QUESTIONS

3 Describe what is meant by an ion, and explain how ions are normally formed.

4 Why must chemical tests be carried out more than once?

5 What is a precipitate?

Making precipitates

Precipitation occurs when one solution reacts with another to form a compound that is insoluble in water.

Lead(II) iodide is a bright yellow precipitate and can be formed by the reaction between lead(II) nitrate solution and sodium iodide solution:

Lead(II) nitrate solution + sodium iodide solution → lead(II) iodide precipitate + sodium nitrate solution

$Pb(NO_3)_2(aq) + 2NaI(aq) \rightarrow PbI_2(s) + 2NaNO_3(aq)$

Copper(II) hydroxide is a light blue precipitate and forms when copper(II) ions and hydroxide ions combine. The formation of this precipitate can be described by the **ionic equation**:

$Cu^{2+}(aq) + 2OH^-(aq) \rightarrow Cu(OH)_2(s)$

Copper(II) ions + hydroxide ions → copper(II) hydroxide

FIGURE 6: Blue copper(II) hydroxide precipitate forming in a solution.

QUESTIONS

6 What is the chemical formula for lead(II) iodide? What is its colour?

7 Explain how a pure, dry sample of lead(II) iodide would be made in the laboratory.

8 Give an ionic equation showing the formation of a precipitate of lead(II) iodide.

Testing for positive ions

You will find out:

- How chemists test for the presence of acids
- How some metal ions give coloured flames, which can be used to identify the metal ion present
- How some metals ions form coloured precipitates with sodium hydroxide solution, and these colours can be helpful for identification

Testing for acids

Everybody is familiar with acids. There are many types of acid – and they are found everywhere. Sometimes, we like to be able to measure how much acid is present in a solution, and for this we use an acid–base **indicator**.

Indicators change colour depending on how much acid is present – all of the colours of the rainbow can be seen using a full range Universal incidator: red, orange, yellow, green, blue, indigo and violet.

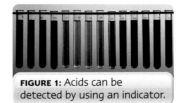

FIGURE 1: Acids can be detected by using an indicator.

Indicators

In Key Stage 3, you may have taken a red cabbage and used its juice to detect the presence of **acids** and **alkalis**. This works because red cabbage juice contains an acid–base indicator. The indicator changes colour depending on the pH of the solution being tested.

- When an acid–base indicator is added to an acid or an alkali, the colour seen depends on the pH of the solution.
- All acids contain hydrogen ions, H^+. The more of these there are in a certain volume, the greater the concentration of them, the more acidic the solution and the lower the pH.
- With alkalis, the ions present are hydroxide ions, OH^-. The more concentrated the hydroxide ions in solution, the more alkaline the solution and higher the pH.
- Acid–base indicators give a measure of the pH of a solution by displaying different colours.

REMEMBER

All acids contain hydrogen ions – they have the chemical formula: H^+.

DID YOU KNOW?

Some acids are very, very strong. Some can even dissolve glass. I wonder what you would keep them in?

QUESTIONS

1. How does universal indicator tell us how acidic a substance is?
2. Which ion is common to all **a** acids and **b** alkalis?

...acids   ...alkalis   ...flame test

Flame tests

When some metal ions are placed into a blue Bunsen flame, the flame may change colour. The colour seen depends on the metal ion present.

Metal ion being tested	Formula of ion	Colour of flame
Sodium	Na^+	Orange-yellow
Potassium	K^+	Lilac
Calcium	Ca^{2+}	Brick-red
Copper	Cu^{2+}	Green

The photograph shows a **flame test** being carried out.

FIGURE 2: Which metal is being tested here?

Tests with sodium hydroxide solution

When sodium hydroxide solution, NaOH(aq), is added to some metal ions, **precipitates** are formed. The colours of these precipitates may be used to identify the presence of certain metal ions.

Here is a summary of what is observed when sodium hydroxide solution is added to various metal ions.

FIGURE 3: A light blue precipitate of copper(II) hydroxide.

Metal ion being tested	Formula of ion	Colour of precipitate	Formula of precipitate
Aluminium	Al^{3+}	White but dissolves in excess NaOH(aq)	$Al(OH)_3(s)$
Calcium	Ca^{2+}	White suspension	$Ca(OH)_2(s)$
Copper(II)	Cu^{2+}	Light blue precipitate	$Cu(OH)_2(s)$
Iron(II)	Fe^{2+}	Dark green precipitate	$Fe(OH)_2(s)$
Iron(III)	Fe^{3+}	Brown precipitate	$Fe(OH)_3(s)$

The picture shows what happens when sodium hydroxide solution is added to separate solutions containing iron(II) and iron(III) ions:

FIGURE 4: Hydroxides of different colours form when sodium hydroxide solution is added to iron (II) and iron (III) ions.

QUESTIONS

3 A substance produces a lilac flame when placed into a Bunsen flame. What metal is present in the compound?

4 A substance produces a white suspension when sodium hydroxide solution is added. If more of the substance is added, the suspension disappears. When hydrochloric acid is added to the solution, carbon dioxide gas is produced. What is the white suspension?

Watch Out Ammonia gas is NH_3 – a chemical compound. NH_4^+ represents the ammonium ion – this is only *part* of a compound, like ammonium nitrate.

Testing for ammonium ions

Ammonium ions have the formula NH_4^+. They occur in compounds, often made from ammonia, NH_3, for example ammonium chloride, ammonium nitrate, ammonium sulphate.

Name of compound	Formula of compound
Ammonium chloride	NH_4Cl
Ammonium sulphate	$(NH_4)_2SO_4$
Ammonium nitrate	NH_4NO_3

The presence of ammonium ions in a compound is detected as follows.

- Place the compound under test into a test tube.
- Add a few drops of sodium hydroxide solution and warm the test tube gently.
- Place a piece of moist red **litmus** paper at the mouth of the test tube.
- If the litmus paper goes blue, ammonium ions must have been present.

The gas formed that turns litmus blue is ammonia and is formed because the hydroxide ion removes a hydrogen ion from the ammonium ion leaving ammonia gas.

QUESTIONS

5 What is the formula for **a** ammonia and **b** the ammonium ion?

6 A pale green solid, X, is dissolved in water and sodium hydroxide solution is added. A dark green precipitate is formed. It is also observed that a gas is formed that turns moist red litmus blue. Give the formula of two ions that are present in X.

...indicator   ...litmus   ...precipitate

Testing for negative ions

You will find out:

- How the formation of carbon dioxide in some chemical tests can be useful in identifying some substances
- How sulphate and sulphite ions may be detected
- How halide ions may be detected using silver(I) nitrate solution

Fizzy drinks

Fizzy drinks are often called carbonated drinks. This is because carbon dioxide gas is added to a drink under pressure. It then gives the drink a fizzy sensation, which many people like.

Carbon dioxide is also produced in some chemical tests, and this can be very useful when working out which substances may be present.

FIGURE 1: Carbon dioxide gas makes this drink fizzy.

Testing for carbonates

Carbonates are very common chemicals and they all contain the negatively charged carbonate ion, CO_3^{2-}. This ion may be detected in the following way:

- Place a sample of the suspected carbonate in a test tube. Carefully add a small quantity of dilute hydrochloric acid.
- Bubbling will take place if a carbonate is present because of the formation of carbon dioxide gas.
- This gas may either be poured into **limewater** in another test tube, or a delivery tube can be fixed to the test tube to enable bubbling of the gas through limewater. In both cases, the limewater should turn milky.

In the reaction above, magnesium carbonate is added to dilute hydrochloric acid. The following equations show what is happening in the reaction:

Magnesium carbonate + hydrochloric acid → magnesium chloride + water + carbon dioxide

$$MgCO_3(s) + 2HCl(aq) \rightarrow MgCl_2(aq) + CO_2(g) + H_2O(l)$$

FIGURE 2: This is what happens when acid is added to a carbonate.

■■ QUESTIONS ■■

1   What is the formula for the carbonate ion?
2   How may the presence of carbonate ions in limestone be confirmed?

DID YOU KNOW?

Sulphite ions, in the form of sodium sulphite, are sometimes added to wine. These ions react with hydrogen ions in the wine to make sulphur dioxide, and this preserves the wine.

...carbonates   ...dichromate   ...halide   ...limewater

Sulphates, sulphites and halides

There are many negative ions that need to be detected apart from carbonate ions. Each of these chemical tests results in specific reactions that only the ions being tested undergo – this makes each test unambiguous.

Sulphates and sulphites

Sulphates contain the negative ion SO_4^{2-}, and **sulphites** contain the ion SO_3^{2-}. Although these ions sound similar and even have similar chemical formulae, they are chemically very different, and are tested in different ways.

■ Sulphates or sulphates(VI). When *barium chloride* solution, $BaCl_2(aq)$, is added to a solution of a suspected sulphate, a *white* **precipitate** of barium sulphate is formed.

■ Sulphites or sulphate(IV). When dilute *hydrochloric acid* is added to a solution containing a sulphite, *sulphur dioxide* gas is formed. This gas may be detected by lowering into the test tube a strip of paper soaked in potassium **dichromate**(VI). The paper turns from orange to green if sulphur dioxide is present.

FIGURE 3: This is what is observed when barium chloride solution is added to a solution of a sulphate.

Halides

Halide ions include the chloride, Cl^-, bromide, Br^- and iodide, I^-. These ions may be detected by adding *silver(I) nitrate* solution. Precipitates of different colours are formed.

Halide ion	Formula of halide ion	Colour of precipitate formed	Formula and name of precipitate
Chloride	Cl^-	White	AgCl(s) silver(I) chloride
Bromide	Br^-	Cream	AgBr(s) silver(I) bromide
Iodide	I^-	Yellow	AgI(s) silver(I) iodide

FIGURE 4: Which halide ion do these test tubes contain?

REMEMBER

Silver(I) nitrate solution can be used to distinguish chloride, bromide and iodide ions by forming precipitates of differing colours.

QUESTIONS

3 A compound forms a cream precipitate with silver(I) nitrate solution. What are the name and formula of the ion present in the solution?

4 Indicate how silver(I) nitrate solution may be used to distinguish between solid sodium iodide and sodium chloride.

Watch Out When we write ionic equations, we remove the spectator ions. What is left is the chemical 'business' that is actually taking place in the reaction.

Equations involving Ions

Reactions involving ions may be written to show the actual chemistry taking place. Many ions are not involved in the reaction and are called **spectator ions** – these are removed from the equation.

The formation of a barium sulphate precipitate, $BaSO_4(s)$, involves the simple combination of barium ions and sulphate(VI) ions:

$$Ba^{2+}(aq) + SO_4^{2-}(aq) \rightarrow BaSO_4(s)$$

The formation of silver(I) halide precipitates may be written as:

$$Ag^+(aq) + Cl^-(aq) \rightarrow AgCl(s)$$

Equations of this type are called ionic equations, and only involve those ions that are involved in the chemical change.

Watch Out A halide ion is not the same as a halogen. A halogen is a chemical element; a halide is a halogen present in a compound.

QUESTIONS

5 What is the chemical formula for **a** barium sulphate and **b** silver(I) chloride?

6 Aluminium hydroxide is a white solid of formula $Al(OH)_3$. Write an ionic equation to show aluminium hydroxide precipitate forming from its constituent ions.

Amount of substance

You will find out:

- What is meant by the term 'the mole'
- That mass can be measured and it can then be used to tell us the number of atoms present
- How many particles there are in one mole of a substance

How heavy is our Galaxy?

Our Galaxy is called the Milky Way. It is very large, about 10 000 light years across. This means that it would take 10 000 years for light to travel from one side to the other!

The picture shows an image of the Milky Way's **mass** being measured. It would have a mass of about 10^{42} kg – that is 1 with 42 zeros after it. This mass is about 2000 billion times the mass of our own Sun.

FIGURE 1: How massive is the Milky Way?

Mass of substances

This picture shows several ingots of gold. Each one has a mass of one kilogram.

How many atoms would there be in one ingot of gold of mass one kilogram? Who cares? It is very important to know the answers to questions such as this, since all matter is made of atoms.

In chemistry, we are often interested in atoms too, and how many atoms there may be in a certain mass of substance. However, atoms are very small. So even in a small mass, say one gram of a substance, there will be millions and millions of atoms.

In chemical reactions, we like to know how many atoms are involved in the reaction, but we are not going to count them – it takes too long. We record a substance's mass instead.

We count by weighing!

FIGURE 2: All matter, even these gold bullion bars, are made of atoms that are very, very small.

■ QUESTIONS ■

1. What is the approximate mass of the Milky Way?
2. What is the mass of half the mass of the Milky Way?
3. An atom has an approximate diameter of 10^{-10} metre. How many atoms would be required to form a queue of length 1 mm?

Watch Out When we measure a substance's mass, we are measuring the amount of substance that it contains.

...amount   ...Avogadro constant

Comparing masses

Atoms of different elements have different masses, so it makes sense to use one atom as the standard with which all other are compared. Its name is carbon.

Carbon has a mass number of 12 and an atomic number of 6. It is often found in the periodic table as:

^{12} – the mass number

C

6 – the atomic number

The number of atoms in exactly 12 g of carbon is used as the standard. It has a fixed number of atoms in it, and this number is very large:

600 000 000 000 000 000 000 000 atoms, or 6×10^{23}

This number is called the **Avogadro constant**.

Figure 3 shows what 12 g of carbon looks like – not much, considering how many atoms are in it.

The mass of substance that contains as many atoms as there are in 12 g of carbon is called one **mole**.

The substances in Figure 4 all contain one mole of particles, but they have different masses.

The **amount** of substance is measured in moles.

FIGURE 3: How many atoms are there in the 12 g sample of carbon being weighed here?

FIGURE 4: Each of these chemicals contains the same number of particles, but consists of different numbers of what?

How to work out the amount of substance

- Find the mass number for the element. This is the same as the mass of one mole of that element.
- Work out the mass of the substance you have, in grams, divided by the mass of one mole.
- The answer to this simple sum is the number of moles that are present.

For example, calculate the amount of substance in 4.0 g of magnesium.

Amount of substance = 4.0/24 (the RAM of magnesium)   = 0.017 moles

Another example: I would like 3.0 moles of iodine atoms. What mass would this be?

Mass of iodine (in grams) = 3.0 × 127 (the RAM of iodine)   = 381 g

REMEMBER

Even though the masses of substances may be different, they can contain equal numbers of particles, because atoms of different elements have different masses.

QUESTIONS

4   What is the amount of substance present in the following?
   a) 12.0 g of carbon   **b)** 240 g of magnesium   **c)** 38 g of sulphur
   (RAM data: C = 12, Mg = 24, S = 32)
5   What is meant by the Avogadro constant?

REMEMBER

The number of particles (atoms, molecules or ions) in 1 mole of any substance is the same.

A mug of tea!

It is important that we are able to make estimations, since sometimes these give us a good idea of the huge numbers involved.

Let us consider how many water molecules there would be in a typical mug of tea.

What volume of water is in a typical mug of tea? Answer: 200 cm³

What mass of water is this? The density of water is 1.0 g/cm³. Answer: 200 g

What amount of water is this (in moles)?

Amount of water = mass/mass of 1 mole
                = 200/(16 + 1 + 1)
                = 11.1 moles

How many water molecules is this?

Answer:

In 1 mole of water molecules, there are 6×10^{23} molecules, so 11.1 moles will contain $11.1 \times 6 \times 10^{23}$ molecules, that is 6.6×10^{24}.

But since this is only an estimate, the number of molecules is about 7×10^{24}.

DID YOU KNOW?

If I owned 1 mole's-worth of pound coins and shared it out with everybody in the world, I would still have enough left to make a tower of coins that would stretch from the Earth to the Sun, and back!

QUESTIONS

6   Why is the numerical value of the mass of water in the mug and its volume the same, that is, 200?
7   How many molecules of water present in 18 g of water?
8   Estimate the number of water molecules in a thimble of water.

What's the white powder?

CONTEXT

Tim liked doing Chemistry topics in Science. He loved using a bunsen burner and seeing what happened when chemicals were mixed and heated.

One day, Tim's teacher produced a jar of white powder. She told the class that they were going to learn some ways of identifying chemicals, and use this one to practise on.

'First of all you need to add some acid,' she said, and told them how. 'I want you to look carefully (goggles in place) and discuss what you see happening.'

The acid was a dilute one, hydrochloric, that the class had used before. When it was added to the powder it fizzed. Sarah said she thought it was a gas that was being given off, but she didn't know what.

They then repeated the reaction in a test tube with a delivery tube so that the gas was guided into a second tube. In the second tube they put a special clear solution and the gas bubbled through it, turning it a milky colour.

Then they went back to the white powder they started with and used a nickel-chromium wire loop with a wooden handle. Out came the Bunsen burners at this point, and the class dipped the wire loops in the white powder and then into the flame. This produced a sudden change in the colour of the flame; above the wire loop it showed an intense yellow, only briefly but very clearly. Sarah and Tim then took the wire loop back to the teacher for cleaning (this had to be done with concentrated acid, which is pretty unpleasant stuff) so that they could try another one.

The second chemical they investigated was a pale green powder and it also reacted with dilute hydrochloric acid to release a gas that turned the 'special solution' milky. However, the flame test produced an emerald green colour.

STEP 1

What was the 'special solution' that turned milky?
What was the gas that turned it milky?

STEP 2

Look at the colour from the flame test on the first white powder. What element was present?

What was present in the white powder that Sarah and Tim started with?

What was the name of the chemical that they started with? (Hint: put the name of the metal first, and shorten the name of the gas.)

Look at what they found out about the second chemical, and work out what that was.

When they were doing the flame test, why was it important that the wire was nickel-chromium and not, for example, steel?

Maximise your grade

These sentences show what you need to include in your work to achieve each grade. Use them to improve your work and be more successful.

Grade	Answer includes...
F	Recall gas being tested.
	Recall test for gas being released.
	Use flame test colours in the identifying of an element.
	Having identified two substances present in a powder, make a reasonable attempt at the chemical name of the powder.
C	Having identified two substances present in one powder and being told the chemical name of the powder, can identify two substances present in the other powder and work out its name.
	Having identified two substances present in powder, can work out its name.
A	Suggest why certain kinds of metal are unsuitable for the metal loop used for flame testing.
	Complete steps with particular accuracy and clarity.

Masses and equations

You will find out:

- How an understanding of the mole can be very helpful
- How masses of reactants and products in a reaction can be calculated

Making important chemicals

The ability to make new chemicals is very important to us. Pharmaceutical drugs, paints, polymers, fabrics are often made in laboratories

It is important to a chemist to know how much chemical substance may be made in a process. This can be calculated so that they know how much to expect.

FIGURE 1: What do you think they are making in this laboratory?

A firework display

The Thermite reaction is an amazing reaction, and you may have seen it in your laboratory at school.

The reaction taking place is as follows:

Iron(III) oxide + aluminium → aluminium oxide + iron

$$Fe_2O_3(s) + 2Al(s) \rightarrow Al_2O_3(s) + 2Fe(s)$$

If we start with 5.40 g of aluminium, what mass of iron could form?

(Relative atomic mass data: Al = 27, Fe = 56)

Follow these steps to solve this problem:

- Step 1: Convert into an amount (in moles) any masses that are given.

    Amount of aluminium = 5.40/27 (RAM of Al) = 0.20 moles

- Step 2: Using the equation, write down the amount of the substance that you are trying to find out.

    Ratio of aluminium to iron is 2:2, or 1:1, so amount of iron = 0.20 also.

- Step 3: Convert the amount from step 2 into a mass.

    Mass of iron = 0.20 × 56 (RAM of Fe) = **11.2 g**

FIGURE 2: Which chemicals are reacting in this show of chemical magic?

DID YOU KNOW?

The temperature in the Thermite reaction may reach over 1500 °C!

REMEMBER

Remember the three steps in these calculations: moles, equation, mass.

REMEMBER

Remember that the amount of substance is given by:

$$Amount~(in~mol) = \frac{mass~(in~g)}{molar~mass~(in~g)}$$

❚❚ QUESTIONS ❚❚

1 How many moles of aluminium are present in 2.70 g?
2 What mass of iron forms if 2.70 g of aluminium are used in the Thermite reaction?

...combustion   ...moles

Burning petrol in a combustion engine

Petrol is a mixture of alkanes varying in size from 5 carbon atoms up to 12 carbon atoms. Let us assume that the average size of a molecule consists of 8 carbon atoms, and let's called it octane.

Octane burns in lots of oxygen to form carbon dioxide gas and water vapour.

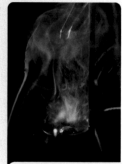

FIGURE 3: Where does the heat energy come from in this combustion reaction?

The chemical equation for this **combustion** process is:

Octane + oxygen gas → carbon dioxide + water

$$2C_8H_{18}(l) + 25O_2(g) \rightarrow 16CO_2(g) + 18H_2O(l)$$

What mass of carbon dioxide gas will form when 1.00 kg of octane burns?

(Relative atomic mass data: C = 12, H = 1, O = 16)

- Step 1: Convert into an amount (in moles) any masses that are given.

  Amount of octane = 1000 g/[8 × 12 + (18 × 1)] = 1000/114 = 8.77 moles

- Step 2: Using the equation, write down the amount of the substance that you are trying to find out.

  Ratio of octane to carbon dioxide is 2:16, or 1:8, so amount of carbon dioxide formed is 8 × 8.77 = 70.2 moles

- Step 3: Convert the amount from step 2 into a mass.

  Mass of carbon dioxide = 70.2 × [12 + (16 × 2)] = 70.2 × 44 = **3090 g**, or **3.09 kg**

The mass calculated of **product** will represent the theoretical mass obtained, but this mass in practice will rarely be obtained:

- Side reactions take place. In other words, reactions happen other than the one being considered.
- Some product is lost as some escapes from the reaction vessel.
- The reaction may be a reversible one, so some product formed may re-form the **reactants**.

We measure the amount of product formed as a proportion of the maximum mass; the lower this value, the lower the **purity**.

■■■■ QUESTIONS ■■■■

3   Give the names of two products formed when petrol burns in excess oxygen.
4   What is the mass of one mole of pentane, C_5H_{12}?
5   Give an environmental problem associated with one of the products from the reaction above.

Working backwards

Sometimes, we may want to know the mass of reactants required to form a certain mass of product. The calculation for this is almost identical to the previous examples.

The reaction below is between potassium and water:

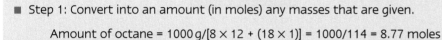

FIGURE 4: How do you know that the reacting metal is potassium?

Potassium + water → potassium hydroxide + hydrogen

$$2K(s) + 2H_2O(l) \rightarrow 2KOH(aq) + H_2(g)$$

If we want to make 5.00 g of hydrogen gas, what mass of potassium is required?

(Relative atomic mass data: H = 1, K = 39)

- Step 1: Convert into an amount (in moles) any masses that are given.

  Amount of hydrogen = 5.00/(2 × 1) (RAM of H_2) = 2.50 moles

- Step 2: Using the equation, write down the amount of the substance that you are trying to find out.

  Ratio of potassium to hydrogen is 2:2, or 1:1, so the amount of potassium needed is also 2.50 moles.

- Step 3: Convert the amount from step 2 into a mass.

  Mass of potassium = 2.50 × 39 (RAM of K) = **97.5 g**

■■■■ QUESTIONS ■■■■

6   How many moles of hydrogen molecules are present in 10 g of hydrogen?
7   Give **two** safety precautions that you would take if using potassium in the above experiment.

Gases and the mole

You will find out:

- Many reactions involve gases as products or reactants
- A Bunsen burner works by burning methane in oxygen from the air
- How to use Avogadro's law in calculations involving gases

What is a flame?

When reactions take place, energy is often produced. This energy may be in the form of heat or light, and sometimes we see this as a flame.

The photograph shows a flame produced by burning lots of waste gas from an oil platform. This gas is mainly methane, which has the chemical formula CH_4.

FIGURE 1: What is burning in this reaction?

The Bunsen burner

The photograph shows a lit **Bunsen burner** burning with a blue flame.

The colour of the flame indicates how much oxygen is being mixed with the fuel. A blue flame indicates a high oxygen content, while a low oxygen content would result in a yellow flame. The reaction taking place in lots of oxygen is:

Methane gas + oxygen gas → carbon dioxide gas + water **vapour**

$$CH_4(g) + 2O_2(g) \rightarrow CO_2(g) + 2H_2O(l)$$

The flow of oxygen is controlled by the valve at the base of the Bunsen burner. The valve is ring-shaped and contains holes through which a varying supply of air is provided. The Bunsen burner is named after the German chemist Robert Bunsen (1811–1899), who popularised its use.

FIGURE 2: A chemical reaction involving gases.

> ### REMEMBER
> The numbers used to balance the chemical equation are the same as the ratios of the gases in their simplest ratios.

QUESTIONS

1. What is the name and formula of the waste gas formed on oil rigs?
2. What are the chemical formulae of the products formed when a Bunsen burner is lit?
3. Who invented the Bunsen burner?

A chemist called Avogadro

Amedeo Carlo Avogadro (1776–1856) was an Italian physicist and chemist. He was very interested in reactions involving gases.

Avogadro stated that equal volumes of all gases, under the same conditions of temperature and pressure, contain the same number of particles.

This hypothesis, **Avogadro's law**, was not widely accepted until after his death.

Let us see what his law means.

Figure 4 shows the reaction between magnesium ribbon and hydrochloric acid. Hydrogen gas is formed.

If we burn the gas formed in oxygen, the following reaction takes place:

FIGURE 3: Why is this chemist famous?

Hydrogen gas + oxygen gas → water

$$2H_2(g) \quad + \quad 1O_2(g) \rightarrow 2H_2O(g)$$

The equation tells us that:

2 moles of hydrogen react with **1** mole of oxygen to form **2** moles of water vapour

Using Avogadro's law, we can also say:

2 volumes of hydrogen react with **1** volume of oxygen to form **2** volumes of water vapour

So, $200\,cm^3$ of hydrogen react with $100\,cm^3$ of oxygen to form $200\,cm^3$ of water vapour

The volume ratio of $H_2 : O_2 : H_2O$ is always **2 : 1 : 2**

FIGURE 4: What happens if we place a lighted splint above this beaker?

WOW FACTOR!

The distance between gas molecules at room temperature and pressure is about 15 times the diameter of the molecules themselves.

Making carbon dioxide gas

When dilute hydrochloric acid is added to marble chips, carbon dioxide gas is formed:

$$CaCO_3(s) + 2HCl(aq) \rightarrow CaCl_2(aq) + H_2O(l) + CO_2(g)$$

What volume of gas is formed at room temperature when 10.0 g of marble chips are added to excess dilute hydrochloric acid?

RAM data: Ca = 40; C = 12; O = 16

1 mole of gas at room temperature occupies $24\,000\,cm^3$. This is the **molar volume**.

Molar mass of $CaCO_3$ = 40 + 12 + (3 × 16)
= 100 g

Amount of calcium carbonate = 10.0/100
= 0.100 mol

Amount of carbon dioxide formed is also 0.100 mol (from equation)

So volume of gas = 0.100 × 24 000
= **2400 cm^3**

WOW FACTOR!

Molecules of hydrogen at room temperature and pressure move at about 750 miles per hour. That's fast!

Watch Out! The volume of a gas depends on the number of moles (the amount) of gas present.

QUESTIONS

4 What is Avogadro's law?

5 What is the ratio of gas volumes in the following reaction?
$$2NO_2(g) \rightarrow N_2O_4(g)$$

6 What volume of $N_2O_4(g)$ forms from $500\,cm^3$ of NO_2 in the reaction in question **5**?

QUESTIONS

7 What volume of carbon dioxide forms if 40.0 g of calcium carbonate is added to excess dilute hydrochloric acid?

8 1 mole of carbon dioxide gas occupies $24\,000\,cm^3$ at room temperature. What is the density of carbon dioxide at these conditions in g/cm^3?

The mole and solutions

You will find out:

- What is meant by a solution and its concentration
- How the concentration of a solution is measured by chemists
- How to carry out calculations involving reactions

Intravenous drips

An intravenous drip bag is used to give various chemicals to a patient, usually through a vein in the forearm.

The solution used may contain saline, which is used to replace body fluids in dehydrated patients. Drips may also be used to give blood or plasma, to maintain body fluids in patients who are unable to eat or drink, or to give certain drugs. It is important that the doctors know how much of the active chemical is dissolved in the solution – this can often make the difference between life and death!

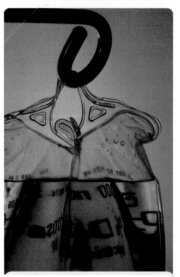

FIGURE 1: An intravenous drip bag.

What is a solution?

A solution is formed when a substance, the **solute**, is dissolved in a liquid, the **solvent**, to form a solution.

The amount of solute dissolved in a certain volume of solution is called its **concentration**.

For example, the picture shows a person testing their blood **glucose** concentration. This is carried out by using a special testing strip that changes colour depending on the concentration of glucose in the blood.

The concentration of the glucose in this case was given as 240 mg/100 ml of blood, and this is a high reading expected of someone who may have diabetes. This person's blood therefore had 240 mg, or 0.240 g, of glucose dissolved in 100 ml, or 100 cm^3, of blood.

FIGURE 2: How do you think these strips may work?

QUESTIONS

1. Complete the following: A solution is formed when a .... dissolves in a ....
2. How many grams in 750 mg?
3. A student asks, 'What is meant by the **ml** symbol on a measuring cylinder?' What do you say?

Watch Out A solvent can be any liquid that can dissolve another substance. It does not have to be water.

What about the mole?

Concentration, in a chemistry laboratory, may be measured in several different ways. It may have units of:

$$g/dm^3 \text{ or } mol/dm^3$$

The dm^3 (the decimetre cube) is a unit of volume. It is the same as $1000\,cm^3$, or 1 litre.

The amount of solute dissolved in a certain volume of water is given by the following:

FIGURE 3: Do you know what this measuring device is called?

$$\text{Number of moles} = \frac{\text{volume of solution (in cm}^3)}{1000} \times \text{concentration (in mol/dm}^3)$$

Example 1

A solution is made by dissolving $5.85\,g$ of sodium chloride in $100\,cm^3$ of water. What is the concentration of the solution in g/dm^3 and mol/dm^3?

(RAM data: Na = 23; Cl = 35.5)

Molar mass of NaCl = 23 + 35.5 = 58.5 g

Amount of NaCl used = 5.85/58.5 = 0.10 moles

We therefore have 0.10 moles dissolved in $100\,cm^3$ of solution. This is the same concentration as **1.0 mol/dm³**, or:

$$\text{Number of moles} = \frac{\text{volume of solution (in cm}^3)}{1000} \times \text{concentration (in mol/dm}^3)$$

so $0.10 = \frac{100}{1000} \times$ concentration (in mol/dm³)

concentration (in mol/dm³) = $0.10 \times \frac{1000}{100}$ = **1.0 mol/dm³**

Example 2

$50.0\,cm^3$ of a solution of hydrochloric acid of concentration $2.00\,mol/dm^3$ is placed into a conical flask. What amount, in moles, of hydrochloric acid is present in the conical flask?

$$\text{Number of moles} = \frac{\text{volume of solution (in cm}^3)}{1000} \times \text{concentration (in mol/dm}^3)$$

$$= \frac{50.0}{1000} \times 2.00 = \textbf{0.10 mol of HCl}$$

REMEMBER

Remember, and know how to use:

Number of moles = volume of solution (in cm³)/1000 × concentration (in mol/dm³)

Watch Out Calculations involving solutions can sometimes appear tricky, so make sure that you practise lots of them.

QUESTIONS

4   Give **two** units that chemists use to measure the concentration of a solution.

5   What formula is used to calculate the amount of solute in a solution?

6   How many moles are present in $50.0\,cm^3$ of a $2.00\,mol/dm^3$ solution?

REMEMBER

Remember!
$1\,dm^3$ is the same as $1000\,cm^3$.

Reactions and solutions

When a reaction takes place, we may be required to calculate something that involves a solution.

Example 3

Consider the following reaction:

magnesium + dilute sulphuric acid → magnesium sulphate + hydrogen gas

$$Mg(s) + H_2SO_4(aq) \rightarrow MgSO_4(aq) + H_2(g)$$

What volume of dilute sulphuric acid of concentration $0.400\,mol/dm^3$ reacts exactly with $2.00\,g$ of magnesium?

Amount of magnesium used
= 2.00/24
= 0.083 moles

The answer is in moles since the molar ratio between magnesium and sulphuric acid is 1:1.

Using:

$$\text{Number of moles} = \frac{\text{volume of solution (in cm}^3)}{1000} \times \text{concentration (in mol/dm}^3)$$

We can say for the sulphuric acid:

$$0.083 = \frac{\text{volume in cm}^3}{1000} \times 0.40\,mol/dm^3$$

so volume (in cm³) = 0.083 × 1000/0.40 = **207.5 cm³** or **208 cm³** (to 3 significant figures)

QUESTIONS

7   Why is the molar ratio of magnesium to sulphuric acid 1:1?

8   Why cannot the answer to the calculation be quoted to more than 3 significant figures?

Titrations

You will find out:

- What is meant by the important analytic process known as a titration
- How to carry out a titration
- How to choose an indicator

Analysing chemicals

Chemists often have to detect the presence of substances. They also have to measure the amounts, or concentrations, of chemicals that may be present in, say, a solution.

Chemists carry out a procedure called a **titration** to measure the amounts or concentrations of substances dissolved in a solution.

FIGURE 1: Do you recognise any of the apparatus in this photograph?

How to do a titration

When we are carrying out a titration, we normally have a solution of known concentration, and this is used to determine the concentration of another substance in solution.

- A burette is filled with the solution of known concentration. This is carried out using a funnel, and the burette tap is rotated so that the burette jet is also filled up with the solution.
- A pipette and filler are then used to transfer a known volume of the other solution to a conical flask.
- A few drops of **indicator** are added to the solution in the conical flask, and the flask placed on a white tile.
- The solution from the burette is then slowly added to the solution in the conical flask until one drop permanently changes the colour of the indicator.
- The volume of the solution from the burette is then noted.
- The experiment is repeated until the values are consistent.

Remember that a titration can be used to determine the exact amount of a soluble substance dissolved in a solution.

Watch Out A titration is an experiment that is fiddly because it involves lots of glassware. It needs to be done accurately. Therefore, make sure you have a go at doing one.

FIGURE 2: What is the name of the apparatus seen here?

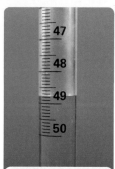

FIGURE 3: This is a close-up of which piece of apparatus?

QUESTIONS

1. What is a burette used for in a titration?
2. Why are experiments often repeated more than once?
3. What is the reading on the burette in the photograph above?

REMEMBER

Burettes and pipettes are accurate pieces of apparatus that need to be used with care.

...acid ...base ...indicator

Calculations involving titrations

Consider the following titration experiment. 25.0 cm^3 of dilute hydrochloric acid is added to a conical flask by a pipette. A burette is then filled with sodium hydroxide of concentration 0.750 mol/dm^3. It was found that 22.3 cm^3 of the sodium hydroxide was required for a complete neutralisation.

Calculate the concentration of the dilute hydrochloric acid.

■ Step 1: Write a balanced equation for the process:

$$NaOH(aq) + HCl(aq) \rightarrow NaCl(aq) + H_2O(l)$$

■ Step 2: Determine the amount of substance from the burette.

$$Concentration = \frac{mass\ of\ substance}{volume}$$

Mass of substance = volume × concentration

$$Amount\ dissolved\ (mass\ in\ moles) = \frac{volume\ (cm^3)}{1000} \times concentration\ (mol/dm^3)$$

So amount of NaOH = $\frac{22.3}{1000} \times 0.750 = 0.0167$ moles

■ Step 3: Using the chemical equation, deduce the amount of hydrochloric acid.

The ratio of HCl(aq) to NaOH(aq) is 1:1, so the amount of HCl(aq) used is also 0.0167 moles

■ Step 4: Determine the concentration of the hydrochloric acid solution.

$$Amount\ dissolved\ (in\ moles) = \frac{volume\ (cm^3)}{1000} \times concentration\ (in\ mol/dm^3)$$

So, 0.0167 moles = $\frac{25.0}{1000} \times$ concentration (in mol/dm^3)

So, concentration = $0.0167 \times \frac{1000}{25.0}$ = **0.668 mol/dm^3**.

Choice of indicator

There are many different acid–base indicators that are available for use in titrations. The indicator that is used depends on the strength of the **acid** and **base** used in a titration.

Strength of acid	Strength of base	Example	Indicator used
Strong	Strong	HCl(aq) and NaOH(aq) – hydrochloric acid and sodium hydroxide	**Phenolphthalein**
Strong	Weak	HCl(aq) and NH$_3$ (aq) – hydrochloric acid and ammonia solution	**Methyl orange**
Weak	Strong	CH$_3$COOH(aq) and NaOH(aq) – ethanoic acid and sodium hydroxide	**Phenolphthalein**
Weak	Weak	CH$_3$COOH(aq) and NH$_3$ (aq) – ethanoic acid and ammonia solution	No indicator possible

QUESTIONS

4   What mass of sodium hydroxide is dissolved in 50.0 cm^3 of a 3.00 mol/dm^3 solution?
(RAM data: Na = 23, O = 16, O = 1)

WOW FACTOR!

There are hundreds of different acid–base indicators. Universal indicator is just one indicator of many.

REMEMBER

The liquid in a burette can be measured to ±0.1 cm^3, so your readings must also be quoted to this level of precision.

Determining a concentration of a pollutant

Sulphuric(VI) acid has been found as a contaminant in a river supply. A sample of volume 500 cm^3 was removed for analysis.

25.0 cm^3 of the solution was removed and titrated against sodium hydroxide solution of concentration 0.0500 mol/dm^3. It was found that 10.5 cm^3 of the sodium hydroxide solution was required for neutralisation.

Determine the concentration of the sulphuric(VI) acid in the river water in moles/dm^3.

$$H_2SO_4(aq) + 2NaOH(aq)$$
$$\rightarrow Na_2SO_4(aq) + 2H_2O(l)$$

Amount of NaOH(aq) used
$$= \frac{10.5}{1000} \times 0.0500$$
$$= 5.25 \times 10^{-4}\ moles$$

Amount of sulphuric(VI) acid therefore is $5.25 \times 10^{-4}/2$ (using the equation), that is, 2.625×10^{-4} dm^3 moles.

So, 2.625×10^{-4} moles of sulphuric(VI) acid is present in 25.0 cm^3, so the concentration is $\frac{1000}{25.0} \times 2.625 \times 10^{-4}$

$$= \textbf{0.0105 mol/dm}^3$$

QUESTIONS

5   Why would an indictor be needed in the experiment above?

6   Why is the amount of sulphuric(VI) acid multiplied by 1000/25 in the final stage of the calculation above?

It's a watery world

You will find out:

- Where all of the water comes from on our planet
- Why water is a precious resource
- Some reasons why water is so special as a chemical substance

It all came from volcanoes!

We all know that a lot of our planet is covered with water. Nearly 75% of the planet is covered with water. It is able to **evaporate** into the air and contribute to our weather as rain, snow or sleet.

When the Earth first formed, there was no water at all, other than the steam that was produced from volcanoes. That steam then cooled to make the oceans that we see today.

FIGURE 1: Where does all this water come from?

FIGURE 2: What is added to water to kill diseases such as cholera?

A precious resource

You would have thought that with so much of the planet covered with water, that we would never be in short supply of water. Everybody must have lots of water to drink and this then keeps them alive. This is very far from the truth.

Many millions of people in the world do not have clean water to drink. Much of the water is contaminated with diseases such as malaria, cholera and typhoid, making it impossible to drink. If you do, you may die.

Many parts of the world are very dry because rain is rare. In these countries, water is obviously going to be difficult to find.

FIGURE 3: Are floods like this going to be more common in future?

Scientists believe that global warming will give rise to extreme weather patterns, and countries that are now hot and dry may be cold and wet, and the opposite may also be true. This means that the supply of water may be unpredictable.

Global warming may give rise to severe flooding. If this happens, sewage systems may burst and this may contaminate clean water supplies.

We are now beginning to realise that clean drinking water will be one of the most sought-after resources in the future.

REMEMBER

Water is a precious resource. We need to protect our fresh water supplies.

DID YOU KNOW?

Life, as we know it, originated from water on our planet. This may be because water can maintain a constant temperature and therefore preserve life.

QUESTIONS

1 Where does the water come from on our planet?
2 Why is there so little fresh water fit to drink even though nearly three-quarters of our planet is covered with water?

...condense ...covalent bonds

Water on the move

Water is always moving from one place to another. Its presence in our seas and in the air makes our weather relatively calm and predictable (but not always!). How does water move from one place to another?

Liquid water is constantly being heated by the Sun. When this happens, evaporation takes place and water vapour is formed. It is then possible for the water vapour to **condense** to form water droplets, and it may then rain. Snow and other forms of precipitation all occur in a similar fashion. The various ways in which water moves throughout the natural world are summarised by the water cycle.

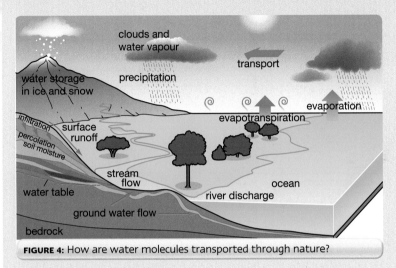

FIGURE 4: How are water molecules transported through nature?

Water is special!

It may not be obvious, but water is considered to be special. There are many reasons for this.

- Water molecules are weakly attracted to each other by an intermolecular force called the hydrogen bond. This means that water molecules are more difficult to pull apart from each other than other molecules. This gives water higher boiling and melting points than expected. Water is a liquid at room temperature and pressures without hydrogen bonding it would be a gas!
- Water expands when it freezes. It is the only substance to do this. When water freezes, the molecules move slightly further apart from each other. This makes the ice less dense, and so it floats and forms icebergs.
- Water has a **surface tension**. This means that there is a 'pull' on those molecules at the surface of the liquid, causing them to behave in an odd way. The water acts as if it has a skin.

FIGURE 5: Why does ice float on water?

▦ QUESTIONS ▦

3 Give **three** special properties of water.

4 What is the name of the process by which water forms a vapour?

5 Explain why energy is required for the process in question **4** to take place.

What is a hydrogen bond?

The hydrogen and oxygen atoms in a water molecule are bonded together by **covalent bonds**. In this type of bond, there are electrons being shared between the atoms, and we normally assume that the share is a 50:50 one, that is, a fair share!

However, the oxygen atom has a bigger pull on the bonded pair of electrons than the hydrogen atom. This gives rise to a slight negative charge on the oxygen atom and a slight positive charge on the hydrogen atom.

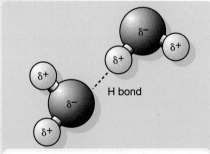

FIGURE 6: Hydrogen bonding between water molecules.

A water molecule therefore has a slightly charged nature, and the negative end of one molecule may attract the positive end on another molecule. This gives rise to a special intermolecular force called a hydrogen bond.

▦ QUESTIONS ▦

6 What is the name of the type of bond that **a** holds hydrogen and oxygen atoms together in a water molecule and **b** exists between molecules of water?

7 Neon has a relative atomic mass of 18, and water has the same mass too. Explain why water is a liquid, but neon is a gas at room temperature and pressure.

Unit summary

Concept map

These compounds are normally soluble in water and have high melting points.

Chemical tests can be devised that can detect whether a positive or negative ions is present in the compound.

Some metal ions can be identified by carrying out a flame test. In this test, a colour is produced in the flame that can be used to identify the metal present.

Compounds often appear in two parts – a positive ion and a negative ion. Compounds of this type are called ionic compounds, and have giant ionic structures.

Qualitative chemical tests

Elements react together to form compounds. If a metal is present, ions may be present.

Ammonium ions, NH_4^+
If sodium hydroxide solution is added to an ammonium compound, ammonia gas is formed. This gas turns moist red litmus blue.

Some metal ions can also be identified by the formation of coloured precipitates when sodium hydroxide is added.

Sulphite ions, SO_3^{2-}
When dilute acid is added, sulphur dioxide is formed, and this gas has a characteristic odour.

Carbonate ions, CO_3^{2-}
When dilute acid is added, carbon dioxide is formed that then turns limewater milky.

Negative ions are also detected using chemical tests. These ions include: carbonate, sulphite, sulphate and halide ions.

Sulphate ions, SO_4^{2-}
Barium chloride solution is added to a solution of the sulphate, and a white precipitate of barium sulphate is formed.

Chloride, Cl^-, bromide, Br^-, iodide, I^-
A solution is made of the halide in water, and a few drops of silver(I) nitrate are added.

The masses of atoms may be compared on a scale called the relative atomic mass scale. Atoms have different masses because of the differing numbers of neutrons and protons in the nucleus.

The atom to which all other atoms are compared on the RAM scale is carbon-12, or ^{12}C.

In chemical reactions, we often like to know the numbers of atoms involved in a reaction.

Quantitative chemical tests

The amount of substance is equal to the mass of substance (in g)/the molar mass of the substance.

The mole is the SI unit of amount of substance.

The mole is a mass of substance that has as many atoms as there are in 12 g of ^{12}C. One mole of an element is simply its relative atomic mass, expressed in units of grams. This is also called the molar mass.

One mole of a gas has a fixed volume at a certain temperature and pressure. At room temperature, this volume is $24\,000\,cm^3$.

A titration involves the use of a burette to measure exactly an unknown concentration of a solution.

The amount of substance dissolved = volume (in cm^3)/1000 × concentration (in mol/dm^3).

Solutions are formed when a solute dissolves in a solvent. Solutions have a concentration that is either measured in g/dm^3 or mol/dm^3.

Unit quiz

1. What are the formulae for the following compounds?
   a) sodium chloride   **c)** potassium sulphate
   b) sulphuric(VI) acid   **d)** aluminium oxide

2. Write a balanced chemical equation for magnesium reacting with sulphuric(VI) acid.

3. What is a cation?

4. Describe how you would test for these ions:
   a) Fe^{2+} **b)** NH_4^+ **c)** K^+ **d)** SO_4^{2-} **e)** Ca^{2+} **f)** CO_3^{2-}

Questions **5–7** involve the following information.

X is a white solid that dissolves in water to form a colourless solution. When acidified silver(I) nitrate is added to a solution of X, a white precipitate A is formed. When sodium hydroxide solution is added drop-wise to solid X, a gas B is formed that turns moist red litmus blue.

5. Name and give chemical formulae for substances A and B and identify substance X by name and by formula.

6. What does the result with moist litmus indicate about the acid-base nature of gas B?

7. A solution of substance X does not give a white precipitate with barium chloride solution. What does this tell us about X?

RAM data for questions **8–11**: Al = 27, O = 16; assume that 1 mole of gas occupies 24 000 cm³ under the conditions at which the reaction takes place.

8. Balance the chemical equation:
   $$..........Al(s) + ...O_2(g) \rightarrow .... Al_2O_3(s)$$

9. How many moles of oxygen molecules react with 2 moles of aluminium in this reaction?

10. 2.7 g of aluminium is heated in excess oxygen. What mass of oxygen is actually required?

11. What volume of oxygen gas is required to react with the same mass of aluminium as in question **10**?

12. What mass of aluminium oxide will form when 50.0 g of aluminium is heated in excess oxygen?

Questions **13–15** are about the following experiment.

25.0 cm³ of dilute hydrochloric acid of unknown concentration is added to a conical flask. A burette is filled with sodium hydroxide solution of concentration 0.100 mol/dm³ and titrated into the hydrochloric acid solution. It was found that 22.1 cm³ of the sodium hydroxide solution were required for complete neutralisation.

13. What is the name given to this type of experiment?

14. Calculate the amount of sodium hydroxide solution used in the experiment.

15. Write a balanced equation for the reaction and hence determine the concentration of the hydrochloric acid solution.

Literacy activity

Analytical chemistry is the science of obtaining, processing and communicating information about the composition and structure of matter. It is the art and science of determining what matter is and how much of it exists.

Analytical chemists perform **qualitative** and **quantitative** analyses; use the science of sampling, defining, isolating, concentrating and preserving samples; validate and verify results through calibration and standardisation; perform separations based on differential chemical properties; create new ways to make measurements; interpret data in proper context; and communicate results.

They use their knowledge of chemistry, instrumentation, computers and statistics to solve problems in almost all areas of chemistry. For example, their measurements are used to ensure compliance with environmental and other regulations; to ensure the safety and quality of food, pharmaceuticals and water; to support the legal process; to help physicians diagnose disease; and to provide chemical measurements essential to trade and commerce.

Analytical chemistry is a challenging profession that makes significant contributions to many fields of science.

Analytical methods using robots and instrumentation specifically designed to prepare and analyse samples have been automated. Increasingly powerful computers are enabling the development and use of increasingly sophisticated techniques and methods of interpreting instrumental data.

Adapted from: http://www.chemistry.org/portal/a/c/s/1/acsdisplay.html?DOC=vc2%5C3wk%5Cwk3_analytical.html

QUESTIONS
1. What is the meaning of '**qualitative** and **quantitative**'.
2. Why do analytical chemists need to be able to communicate their results and findings effectively?

Exam practice questions

1 A Complete this table to show the tests for some ions in solution.

Formula of ion	Reagent added	Result
	Sodium hydroxide solution then warmed	No precipitate but ammonia detected
Fe^{3+}	Sodium hydroxide solution	
	Dilute hydrochloric acid	Sulphur dioxide detected

[3]

B i How would you test for the presence of a halide ion?

....

.... [2]

ii What result would you expect if an iodide ion was present? [1]

C A flame test was carried out on substance A and a yellow colour was observed. Some dilute hydrochloric acid was then added, followed by some barium chloride solution. A white precipitate was observed.

i Which metal ion is present in A?

.... [1]

ii Which negative ion was present in A?

.... [1]

iii Give the formula of A.

.... [1]

(Total 9 marks)

2 Sodium hydroxide solution was added to five unlabelled samples of solution. The solutions contained Al^{3+}, Ca^{2+}, Cu^{2+}, Fe^{2+} and Fe^{3+}.

A Use the results below to work out which is which and complete the table.

Few drops of NaOH(aq) added change	NaOH(aq) added until no further	Ion present
Pale blue precipitate forms	Precipitate remains	
Dull green precipitate forms	Precipitate remains	
White precipitate forms	Precipitate re-dissolves	
White precipitate forms	Precipitate remains	
Brown precipitate forms	Precipitate remains	

[5]

B i Describe how to carry out a flame test on a sample containing K^+. What colour would the flame be?

....

.... [4]

(Total 9 marks)

3 Describe how to find the mass of salts dissolved in a $1\,dm^3$ of seawater.

....

....

.... [4]

(Total 4 marks)

4 The label on a bottle of potassium chloride (KCl) says that it contains $0.5\,mol/dm^3$. What mass of potassium chloride would be dissolved in $1\,dm^3$?

.... [2]

(Total 2 marks)

5 A chemist is asked to produce $4.00\,kg$ of magnesium oxide by the thermal decomposition of magnesium carbonate. The equation for this reaction is:

$$MgCO_3(s) \rightarrow MgO(s) + CO_2(g)$$

A Calculate the mass of magnesium carbonate the chemist must start with (assuming that the carbonate decomposes completely).

....

....

.... [3]

B If 1 mole of gas occupies $24\,dm^3$ at room temperature and pressure, what volume of carbon dioxide would be produced in this process?

....

.... [2]

(Total 5 marks)

Judith has been asked to find the molar mass of lithium by two different methods.

Firstly she has been told to weigh a small piece of lithium then react it with water and collect the gas formed and use its volume to calculate a value of the A_r of lithium.

The equation for this reaction is: $2Li(s) + 2H_2O(l) \rightarrow 2LiOH(aq) + H_2(g)$

Her results are Mass of lithium = 0.14 g   Volume of hydrogen = 240 cm^3

a   i   Calculate the number of moles of gas formed. [1]
   ii   Calculate the number of moles of lithium that must have reacted. [1]
  iii   Calculate the A_r of lithium. [1]

Secondly she is told to titrate the LiOH solution formed, with some 1.0 mol/dm^3 hydrochloric acid which reacts according to the equation:

$$HCl + LiOH \rightarrow LiCl + H_2O$$

A phenolphthalein indicator was made available.

b   Describe in detail how she should carry out the titration. Include in your answer the apparatus that is used and the colour change at the end point. [7]
c   From the titration, 20.0 cm^3 of 1.0 mol/dm^3 HCl was needed to react completely with all the LiOH in the flask.
   i   Calculate the number of moles of HCl used. [1]
  ii   Calculate the number of moles of LiOH present. [1]
  iii   Use the first equation to calculate the number of moles of lithium present. [1]
  iv   Calculate the A_r of lithium. [1]

Excellent. The calculation has been set out really well and the correct answer arrived at.

a   i   *1 mole of gas = 24 000 cm^3. So moles gas = $\dfrac{240}{24\,000}$ mol = 0.010 mol*

   ii   *From the equation 1 mol of gas is formed from 2 mol Li so 0.020 mol Li*

  iii   *moles lithium = mass/A_r. Rearranging this gives A_r = mass/moles = 0.14/0.02 = **7***

Some points missed here. The flask should be swirled all the time to mix the acid and alkali. Acid should be added slowly near the end point. The colour change at the end point has not been given. Phenolphthalein is pink in alkali and will turn colourless at the end point.

b   *A few drops of phenolphthalein is added to the lithium hydroxide solution in the flask.*
The volume of HCl in the burette is noted.
HCl is added from a burette.
When it has neutralised the alkali LiOH, stop adding acid.
Make a note of the burette volume and calculate the volume of acid added.

c   *From the titration, it was found that 20.0 cm^3 of 1.0 mol/dm^3 HCl was needed to react completely with all of the LiOH in the flask.*
   i   *Moles of HCl = $c \times v$ = 1.0 × 20.0 = 20 moles*
  ii   *The HCl and LiOH react in a 1 : 1 ratio so there must be 20 moles of LiOH present as well.*
  iii   *For every mole of LiOH there is 1 mole of Li so there must be 20 moles of lithium*

The student is right. The answer is 1000 times smaller than the answer achieved in **a**. This should have given the hint. In **i**, the number of moles should be $\dfrac{1.0 \times 20}{1000}$ mol = 0.020 mol.

  iv   *Moles = mass/A_r, so A_r = mass/moles = 0.14/20 = 0.007. I know this is a silly answer but I can't see why.*

Overall Grade: B

How to get an A

When trying to describe a practical procedure you should always imagine yourself back in the laboratory carrying it out. That way you will not miss steps out so easily. You must always remember that when using $n = cv$ to calculate moles in solution, the value of v must be in dm^3. This means that you must divide the volume in cm^3 by 1000.

CHEMISTRY WORKING FOR US

These are granules of biological washing powder under an electron microscope.

Inside each granule are strands of enzymes. These are biological substances. They break down and 'digest' biological stains, such as food and blood, that are difficult to wash out with normal detergents.

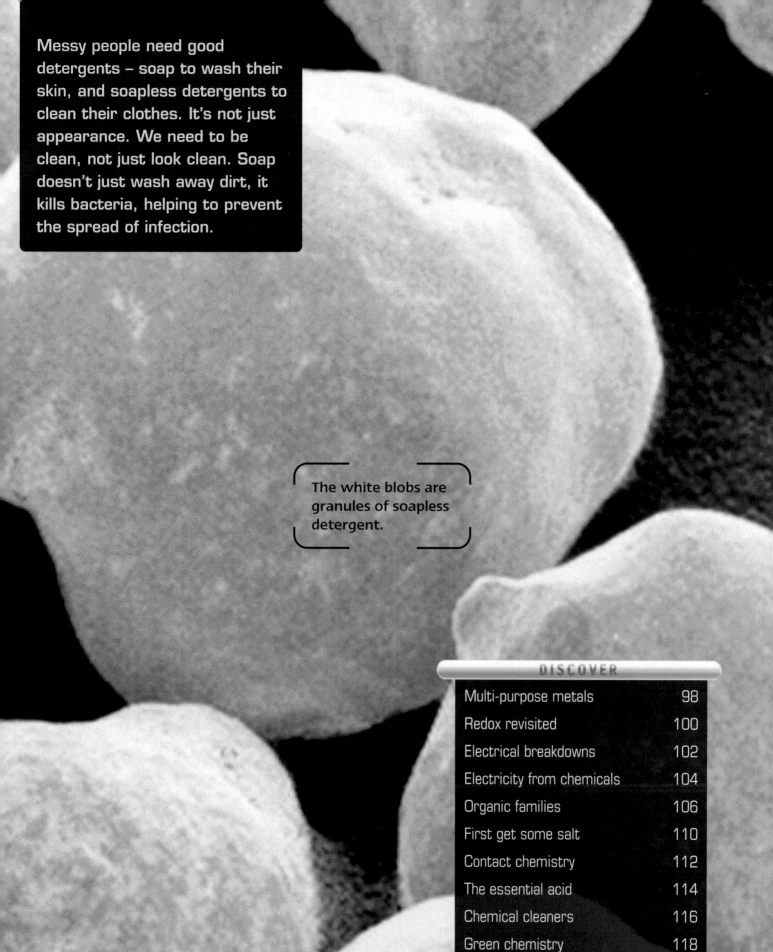

Messy people need good detergents – soap to wash their skin, and soapless detergents to clean their clothes. It's not just appearance. We need to be clean, not just look clean. Soap doesn't just wash away dirt, it kills bacteria, helping to prevent the spread of infection.

The white blobs are granules of soapless detergent.

Multi-purpose metals

You will find out:

- Why so many objects are made from metals
- Which properties make transition metals so useful
- Some important uses of transition metals and their compounds

Red, white and blue blood

We call royalty blue-blooded, but they're not really. Like all humans, their blood is red. Red blood cells contain haemoglobin – a red **pigment** containing iron. It combines with oxygen, and carries it around the body. Snails, slugs, crabs and octopuses really do have blue blood. The oxygen-carrying blue pigment is haemocyanin, which contains copper instead of iron. White blood cells don't carry oxygen, and have *no* pigment.

FIGURE 1: Collecting a horseshoe crab's blue blood for research. Like human blood donors, the crab is unharmed.

More obvious uses of metals

If asked to give some uses of iron or copper, you would probably think of making steel or copper wires, rather than blood. But which is more important? Cavemen managed without steel or wires, but couldn't have lived without iron in their blood. Usually, however, it's the metals themselves we think of, rather than metal compounds.

Iron, mainly as steel, is the most widely used. Its everyday uses include:

- girders in buildings and bridges
- pressed sheets for vehicle bodies, domestic 'white goods' (cookers, fridges, washing machines, etc.) and cans
- cables for cranes, lifts and suspension bridges
- machines and tools – for both home and industrial uses
- stainless steel – e.g. kitchen equipment and cutlery.

Copper and its **alloys**, brass and bronze, have more specialised uses:

- electrical wires, cables, motors and other parts
- plumbing – water pipes, boilers and hot water tanks
- heat exchangers, to save energy in industrial processes
- coins – bronze, cupro-nickel and brass. (Modern 1p/2p coins are copper-coated steel.)

FIGURE 2: Copper stills at a whisky distillery. Why is copper used?

WOW FACTOR!

Cereals that are 'fortified with iron' actually contain tiny iron filings. You can extract them from crushed cereals with a magnet.

EXAM HINTS AND TIPS

Transition metals have high density and melting point, and are good conductors of heat and electricity.

> **QUESTIONS**
>
> 1 **a** What is an alloy?
>   **b** Name **five** alloys mentioned in the passage above
> 2 Which metal is used more than any other?
> 3 Modern 1p and 2p coins look like copper, but are magnetic. Explain why.

...alloys ...catalysts ...electrical conduction ...enzymes

Typical transition metals

Most metals used for making things are **transition metals** – those in the middle block in the periodic table. They include iron, copper, nickel, titanium, silver and gold. (*Note:* Zinc is not strictly a transition metal.)

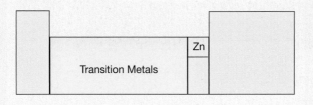

FIGURE 3: The periodic table.

[Zn]

Transition Metals

Transition metals have typical metallic properties:

- High **melting point** – can be heated to high temperatures without melting, which is useful for cooking equipment, boilers and furnaces.
- Good heat conduction – heat passes through easily – essential for cooking equipment, boilers and furnaces, radiators and heat exchangers.
- Good **electrical conduction** – can carry an electric current – essential for all electrical equipment.
- High density (usually over 6000 kg m^{-3}) – solid objects are heavy for their size – a disadvantage when they must move, since movement needs more energy.
- Not brittle – can be bent into shape and pulled into wires without breaking.

Matching properties with uses

We don't make wires out of wool or saucepans from cement. They wouldn't work. We must use materials with the right properties. The physical and chemical properties of transition metals make them suitable for many different uses.

The table shows some uses of transition metals.

Use	Properties needed	Suitable metal
electrical wiring	good electrical conduction can be drawn out into thin wires bends round corners	copper (one of the best conductors)
saucepans	good heat conduction high melting point not corroded by salt water or acidic fruit juices	stainless steel or copper
hammer	high density (small but heavy) rigid, hard and strong	steel (density 7700 kg m^{-3})
bicycle frame	low density (light weight) rigid and strong	titanium (density 4500 kg m^{-3})
light bulb filament	conducts electricity glows white hot without melting	tungsten (the highest melting point metal)

QUESTIONS

4   Which properties are needed for the heating element in a toaster?

5   Why do we use stainless steel rather than ordinary steel for saucepans?

6   What is the scientific word for 'can be hammered (or pressed) into shape'?

7   What is the scientific word for 'can be drawn out into a thin wire'?

Colourful compounds

Transition metal compounds are coloured. Insoluble ones are often used as pigments, such as copper acetate and chrome yellow. Others include Prussian blue (an iron compound) and the blood pigments haemoglobin and haemocyanin.

Catalysis

Transition metals and their compounds are important **catalysts**:

- Vanadium(V) oxide: Contact process – oxidising sulphur dioxide to sulphur trioxide in sulphuric acid manufacture.
- Iron: Haber process – converting nitrogen and hydrogen into ammonia.
- Nickel oxide: making hydrogen for the Haber process from methane and steam.
- Nickel: hydrogenating vegetable oils to make margarine.
- Platinum/rhodium: catalytic converters in car exhausts.

FIGURE 4: Platinum gauze, worth several thousand pounds, used in the manufacture of nitric acid. In daylight it is silvery-grey, not red.

Many **enzymes** (biological catalysts) contain ions of copper, cobalt, manganese or other transition metals.

QUESTIONS

8   The colour of a salt often shows which transition metal it contains. Give some examples.

9   Why are small amounts of transition metals essential in our diets?

...melting point   ...pigment   ...transition metals

Redox revisited

You will find out:

- How electrons are involved in oxidation and reduction reactions
- That oxidation and reduction can occur without oxygen
- Why transition metals and their compounds are good catalysts

The value of aluminium

What would you think if your dinner was served on an aluminium plate, while everyone else had silver? Not long ago it meant you were an honoured VIP. There's more aluminium in the Earth's crust than any other metal. Yet it was discovered less than 200 years ago, and at first was more valuable than silver. Even now, aluminium costs nearly ten times as much as iron. Have you ever wondered why?

Reducing aluminium oxide

Extracting a metal from its oxide using carbon is called **reduction**. Two important changes take place:

- The metal oxide loses oxygen, leaving the metal itself.
- Positively charged metal **ions** (e.g. Fe^{2+} or Pb^{2+}) in the compound become metal atoms.

Both changes happen when we extract aluminium from bauxite ore (impure aluminium oxide). However, this cannot be done by just heating bauxite with carbon. Aluminium is too reactive. It won't let go of the oxygen.

- Electricity is needed. Electricity is a flow of electrons. During reduction, each aluminium ion, Al^{3+}, picks up three electrons. This reduces their charge from 3+ to zero. The ions become atoms.
- Extracting 1 tonne of aluminium uses 15 000 units (kW h) of electricity. That's enough to run 15 000 electric fires for an hour. It's why aluminium is so much more expensive than iron.

This process is called **electrolysis**. It works only with liquids, so the aluminium oxide must be melted before the electric current can flow through it.

FIGURE 1: A boat-load of bauxite, aluminium ore.

FIGURE 2: Rows of electrolysis cells extracting aluminium. The white powder everywhere is aluminium oxide.

Watch Out Oxidation and reduction reactions need not involve oxygen. It is only necessary for electrons to pass from one chemical to another.

QUESTIONS

1. Which **two** things get less when we reduce a metal oxide?
2. What is bauxite?
3. Why does it need three electrons to reduce an aluminium ion to an aluminium atom?

WANT TO KNOW MORE?

Page 102 describes how electrolysis works.

...catalyst   ...electrolysis

A different view of redox

Almost any metal reacts with oxygen, forming the metal oxide. This contains positive metal ions and negative oxide ions. For example, magnesium burns, forming magnesium oxide, containing Mg^{2+} and O^{2-} ions.

As you should already know, converting a metal into its oxide is oxidation. But you can't have oxidation without reduction. In the above example, oxygen must be reduced, since it is the only other reactant.

This gives another view of redox reactions. Instead of passing oxygen between substances, we can think of redox as passing electrons.

■ Oxidation involves losing electrons, e.g. $Mg - 2e^- \rightarrow Mg^{2+}$
■ Reduction involves gaining electrons, e.g. $O + 2e^- \rightarrow O^{2-}$

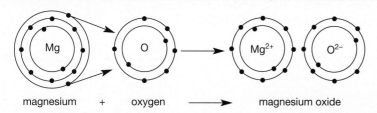

magnesium + oxygen ⟶ magnesium oxide

FIGURE 3: When magnesium reacts with oxygen, electrons transfer between the atoms.

■ When we reduce a metal oxide with carbon, it's the metal ions that are reduced. They gain electrons, e.g. $Fe^{2+} + 2e^- \rightarrow Fe$ or $Al^{3+} + 3e^- \rightarrow Al$
■ It is oxide ions, O^{2-}, that are oxidised. They lose electrons by sharing them in covalent bonds with carbon. They no longer have the electrons to themselves.

Redox without oxygen

When oxidation and reduction involve passing electrons, the reactions don't necessarily involve oxygen.

■ Metals reacting with acids are oxidised to their ions. Hydrogen ions in the acid are reduced to hydrogen gas;.

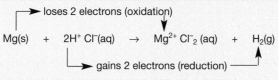

loses 2 electrons (oxidation)

$$Mg(s) + 2H^+ Cl^-(aq) \rightarrow Mg^{2+} Cl^-_2 (aq) + H_2(g)$$

gains 2 electrons (reduction)

■ In displacement reactions, the more reactive metal is oxidised to ions. Ions of the less reactive metals are reduced to the metal; e.g.

$$Zn(s) + Cu^{2+}(aq) + SO_4^{2-}(aq) \rightarrow Zn^{2+}(aq) + SO_4^{2-}(aq) + Cu(s)$$

■ The same rules apply to non-metals. Chorine oxidises bromide ions to bromine, and is itself reduced to chloride ions.

$$Cl_2(aq) + 2K^+(aq) + Br^-(aq) \rightarrow 2K^+(aq) + Cl^-(aq) + Br_2(aq)$$

FIGURE 4: Zinc displacing copper from copper sulphate solution.

■■■■ **QUESTIONS** ■■■■

4 Why can't you have oxidation without reduction?
5 When a metal loses electrons to form ions, where do the electrons go to?
6 When zinc displaces copper from copper sulphate solution, is the zinc oxidised or reduced?

Redox and catalysis

Transition metals each have two or more types of ion; for instance, Fe^{2+} and Fe^{3+}, or Cu^+ and Cu^{2+} ions. They can easily change from one to the other and back again. This is why they make good **catalysts** for redox reactions.

■ Suppose substance X reduces Y slowly, but reduces Fe^{3+} ions more quickly.

$$X + Fe^{3+} \rightarrow X^+ + Fe^{2+}$$

■ The Fe^{2+} ions produced then reduce Y.

$$Fe^{2+} + Y \rightarrow Fe^{3+} + Y^-$$

■ The overall result is that Y is reduced to Y^-, and X oxidised to X^+, even though they have not reacted with each other.
■ The original Fe^{3+} ions have been regenerated. They speeded up the reaction, but weren't used up. They acted as a catalyst.

FIGURE 5: Not coal, but a catalyst – vanadium(V) oxide used in sulphuric acid manufacture.

EXAM HINTS AND TIPS

Remember OIL RIG:
Oxidation Is Loss (of electrons)
Reduction Is Gain.

■■■■ **QUESTIONS** ■■■■

7 Suggest what happens if Fe^{2+} ions, instead of Fe^{3+}, are added to the X/Y mixture.
8 Why do transition metal ions catalyse redox reactions, rather than other types of reaction?

...ion ...oxidation ...reduction

Electrical breakdowns

You will find out:

- How to purify copper
- Why electricity causes some chemicals to decompose
- How we make use of electrolysis

Perfectly pure

Click. 'Let there be light!' – or heat, sound or movement. We rely on electricity working at the flick of a switch. Electrical wiring is usually copper because it's the best conductor apart from silver. However, even slight impurities increase its resistance, so it must be super-pure. Smelting ores gives 99% pure copper – but that's not good enough. We need 99.99%. Fortunately, purifying copper isn't difficult – but this too relies on electricity.

FIGURE 1: Copper cable for wiring mains sockets in a house.

Recipe for super-pure copper

- Hang a large plate of impure copper in some copper sulphate solution.
- Hang a small plate of very pure copper alongside it.
- Connect them to a direct current (DC) electricity supply; impure plate to the positive (+), pure to the negative (–).

Copper passes from the positive plate to the negative, forming a slab of super-pure copper. In industry they use large tanks with many **electrodes**, not just two.

How does it work?

A solution conducts electricity only if it contains **ions**. Copper sulphate contains copper ions, Cu^{2+}, and sulphate ions, SO_4^{2-}. An electric current flowing through the solution causes chemical changes. The process is called **electrolysis**.

At the negative plate, or **cathode**:

- Copper ions, Cu^{2+}, in the solution gain electrons and become Cu atoms.
- The atoms stick to the plate, building up a super-pure copper cathode.

The opposite happens at the positive plate, or **anode**:

- Copper atoms, Cu, in the impure plate lose electrons to become Cu^{2+} ions.
- These ions go into solution, so the impure anode dissolves away.
- Impurities fall off and sink to the bottom.

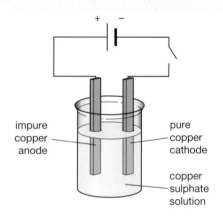

FIGURE 2: Simple circuit for purifying copper.

99% pure copper isn't good enough. We need 99.99%

QUESTIONS

1 What is the maximum amount of impurity in electrical grade copper wire?
2 Does a copper ion have more electrons than a copper atom, or fewer?
3 Why does the impure copper anode get smaller?
4 Where do the electrons come from to convert copper ions into atoms?

Watch Out Metal and carbon anodes give different results. Metal anodes dissolve away. Carbon anodes release a gas from the anions.

...anion ...anode ...cathode ...cation ...electrode

Breaking down ionic compounds

The scientific word for decomposition (breaking down into simpler substances) is 'lysis'. Electrolysis means decomposing a chemical electrically. It works with any ionic solution or molten compound, not just copper sulphate. Electrolysis needs:

■ an **electrolyte** – a liquid containing ions, so it conducts electricity. This can be a metal compound or an acid
■ two electrodes – pieces of metal (or sometimes graphite) that dip into the electrolyte to conduct the electricity in and out
■ a DC electricity source – battery or rectified mains supply.

The anode is the electrode connected to the positive (+) electricity supply. The cathode is negative (–). When the current is switched on, reactions decompose the electrolyte.

■ At the cathode, **reduction** occurs. (Remember OIL RIG.) Positive ions in the electrolyte gain electrons and become atoms. The metal atoms form a layer on the cathode. It gets electroplated; e.g.

$$Ag^+(aq) + e^- \rightarrow Ag(s)$$

■ If the electrolyte is an acid, hydrogen gas is evolved.

$$2H^+(aq) + 2e^- \rightarrow H_2(g)$$

■ **Oxidation** occurs at the anode. If it is metal, its atoms lose electrons and form ions. They dissolve in the electrolyte, replacing those removed at the cathode.

$$Ag(s) \rightarrow Ag^+(aq) + e^-$$

■ If the anode is graphite (carbon), the negative ions in the electrolyte lose electrons to form atoms, then gas molecules; e.g.

$$2Cl^-(aq) \rightarrow Cl_2(g) + 2e^-$$

FIGURE 3: Rows of brine electrolysis cells. for making chlorine.

Some applications of electrolysis

Electrolyte	Product		Notes
	Cathode	Anode	
sodium chloride solution (brine)	hydrogen	chlorine	sodium hydroxide solution is left
molten sodium chloride	sodium	chlorine	manufacture of sodium
molten aluminium oxide	aluminium	oxygen	manufacture of aluminium
a nickel, copper, silver or chromium salt	layer of the metal	metal dissolves	electroplating

■■■■ **QUESTIONS** ■■■

5   What do metal salts and acids all have that makes them electrolytes?
6   What is released at each electrode by electrolysis of hydrochloric acid?
7   Name another metal extracted by electrolysis, besides those given above.
8   Suggest how to electroplate a spoon with silver.

WOW FACTOR!

Over 70 million tonnes of salt per year are electrolysed across the world to produce chlorine and sodium hydroxide.

Carrying the current

Metals conduct electricity by passing electrons from one atom to the next. The current is a flow of electrons. In electrolytes, the current is carried by moving ions.

■ Positive **cations** of a metal or hydrogen move towards the cathode. Here they pick up electrons from the circuit.
■ Negative non-metal ions, or **anions**, move towards the anode, where they give up electrons into the circuit.
■ Alternatively, with a metal anode, metal atoms give up electrons to form positive cations that move away towards the cathode as above.

The ions carry electric charge through the liquid electrolyte. Cations carry positive charge from anode to cathode. Anions carry negative charge (electrons) from cathode to anode. Figure 4 illustrates the flows of electrons and ions.

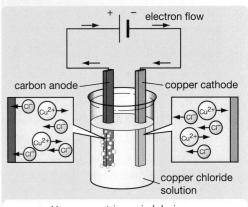

FIGURE 4: How current is carried during electrolysis.

■■■■■ **QUESTIONS** ■■■■■

9   Suggest what makes the ions move, and why they move in opposite directions.
10 What happens to the anions if the anode is metal?

...electrolysis ...electrolyte ...ion ...oxidation ...reduction

Electricity from chemicals

You will find out:

- About the different types of cells used in electrical appliances
- How redox reactions are used to generate electricity in cells and batteries
- That recharging involves electrolysis

Portable power

Imagine life without batteries – no mobile phone, iPod, lap-top or remote controls. And how would people start their cars? We rely on batteries – from tiny cells in watches to 1 tonne monsters for milk floats and fork-lift trucks. Some we throw away when 'flat'; others we recharge. There's some clever chemistry going on, and it's getting cleverer. New types, such as nickel metal hydride and lithium ion cells, arise from military and space research.

Cells and batteries

Most things that we call batteries are actually cells.

- A cell is a packet of chemicals that produce electricity when they react. The most common type contains zinc, carbon and other chemicals.
- The clever thing is that cells react only when connected in a circuit.
- Cells of the same type give the same **voltage**. Whether AAA, AA or larger, zinc–carbon cells all give 1.5 volts.
- A battery contains several cells joined together to give a higher voltage. The square, blue 6 V battery on the left in Figure 2 contains four 1.5 V cells. The smaller rectangular one in front of it has six cells, giving 9 V.
- Smaller cells hold less chemicals, so produce less electricity. But the reaction still produces the same voltage.

Types of cell

- Zinc–carbon cells and batteries are the commonest and cheapest.
- 1.5 V alkaline cells are similar, but last longer.
- Zinc–air button cells for watches and hearing-aids use oxygen from the air.
- Coin-shaped lithium cells give 3 V. Long life makes them useful for heart pacemakers, watches and battery back-up for computer memory.
- Nickel–cadmium (NiCd) cells, nickel metal hydride (NiMH) phone batteries and lead–acid car batteries are all **rechargeable**.

FIGURE 1: Lithium ion battery developed for military communications. The cells inside are triangular, so fit together without gaps. Cylindrical cells waste space.

Watch Out Voltage depends on the type of cell, not its size. Larger cells give more electricity, but at the same voltage.

WOW FACTOR!

The world's biggest battery weighs 1300 tonnes. Its 13 760 cells give 40 megawatts of power – but for only 7 minutes.

FIGURE 2: Eight single cells and six batteries. Can you tell which are which?

QUESTIONS

1. What's the difference between a cell and a battery?
2. A zinc–carbon battery gives 4.5 volts. How many cells does it contain?
3. What does NiMH stand for?
4. Why are car batteries so heavy?

There's some clever chemistry going on in cells and batteries

How do chemicals produce electricity?

Current in an electric wire is a flow of electrons. Electrons can be made to move using chemical reactions, e.g. reacting zinc with copper sulphate solution. A **redox** reaction occurs and electrons pass from zinc atoms onto copper ions.

Suppose we separate the zinc and copper sulphate. Electrons can't jump the gap, but they can travel along a connecting wire.

- Zinc loses electrons, which pass into the wire.
- At the other end, electrons pass out of the wire onto copper ions.

Electrons flow along the wire. Hey presto, you've got an electric current! You need a complete circuit, though. Figure 3 shows how it's done.

- A zinc strip is dipped in zinc sulphate solution and a copper strip in copper sulphate solution.
- When the strips are joined in a circuit, electricity flows along the wire and back through the 'bridge' – filter paper soaked in a conducting solution.
- The digital meter isn't necessary. It just shows the voltage produced.

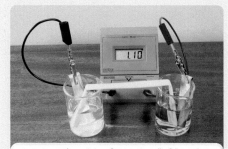

FIGURE 3: Electricity from zinc (left) and copper (right). This simple cell produces 1.10 volts.

Rechargeable cells

A cell like that above but using zinc, carbon and ammonium chloride solution gives 1.5 V. It's cheaper too, but not very convenient for powering your iPod! The zinc–carbon cells you can buy contain a damp paste or gel instead of a solution. However, they have another problem.

- They're non-rechargeable **primary cells**. When all the chemicals have reacted, you have to buy a new one.
- Alkaline, button and some lithium cells are also primary cells.
- Rechargeable cells, or secondary cells, can be used over and over again. You put electricity back in, but it's not like pouring water into a bottle. Charging is actually a chemical reaction.

How charging works

Secondary cells such as NiCd, NiMH and lead–acid batteries are rechargeable.

- Cells produce electricity from a chemical reaction. If this reaction can be reversed, the chemicals can be regenerated.
- We use **electrolysis**. Passing electricity through the cell converts the products back into the original reactants. These can now generate electricity again.

Figure 4 shows the reactions that take place in a nickel metal hydride phone battery. The cycle can be repeated many times.

Primary cells can't be recharged because their reactions aren't reversible.

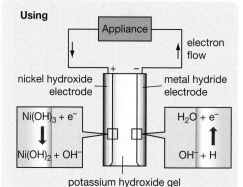

FIGURE 4: Opposite reactions when using and charging a phone battery.

▦▦▦ QUESTIONS ▦▦▦

5 In a zinc–copper cell, in which beaker does oxidation take place?

6 How do electrons get from the zinc atoms to the copper ions?

7 Why doesn't it work if you put the zinc and copper in the same beaker?

8 Name **three** types of secondary cell.

▦▦▦ QUESTIONS ▦▦▦

9 What is a metal hydride?

10 Which element is produced by charging, and is stored in the metal hydride electrode?

Organic families

You will find out:

- How to recognise alcohols, carboxylic acids and esters
- How these three families of compounds are related to each other
- Some of their important everyday uses

The smell of Grasse

No, that's not a spelling error. Grasse, in southern France, is 'the perfume capital of the world'. Here, people with well-trained noses spend their days mixing precise amounts of smelly liquids. Their aim is to produce a 'scentsational' new perfume. The liquids are mainly fragrant oils extracted from plants. They contain complex mixtures of organic compounds, including many esters. To make perfume, the oils are dissolved in alcohol.

Family names and relationships

Like yours, an organic chemical's name shows which family it belongs to.
- Methan<u>ol</u>, ethan<u>ol</u> and propan<u>ol</u> are all members of the **alcohol** family. The ending '-ol' is like a surname.
- Each family name has its own ending. Methan<u>oic acid</u> and ethan<u>oic acid</u> belong to the **carboxylic acid** family.
- Likewise, methyl ethan<u>oate</u> and ethyl benz<u>oate</u> are both **esters**.
- Many compounds from different families have the same 'first' name, e.g. <u>eth</u>ane and <u>eth</u>anol. These have the same number of carbon atoms.

The alcohol, acid and ester families are related to each other. Oxidising an alcohol gives an acid. Reacting an alcohol with an acid gives an ester. All three families have many everyday uses. Here are some common uses of the three types of organic compounds.

FIGURE 1: A perfumer at her 'organ' blending liquid extracts. Her nose can recognise up to 3000 smells.

FIGURE 2: Citrus fruits contain citric acid, ascorbic acid (vitamin C) and various esters.

Alcohols	Carboxylic acids	Esters
making other chemicals, e.g. esters and plastics	making esters	making polyester plastics and fibres
solvents, e.g. perfumes, medicines and inks	making plastics, e.g. polyesters and 'Perspex'	perfumes and other **cosmetics**
fuels (methylated spirits and gasohol)	making synthetic fibres for clothing	solvents used in making medicines
alcoholic drinks (ethanol) car antifreeze	in foods, e.g. citric acid, vinegar and vitamin C	natural esters in foods, as fats, oils and **flavourings**

WOW FACTOR!

For about £25 you can spend two hours at a perfume 'organ' in Grasse, composing your own unique fragrance.

WOW FACTOR!

Make sure you know the difference between 'alkalis'. It's what the –OH is attached to that matters.

QUESTIONS

1 To which chemical family does ethanol belong?
2 What do molecules of methanol and methanoic acid have in common?
3 There are many different alcohols. Which one is in beer, wines and spirits?
4 Find out what the fuel 'gasohol' contains.

...alcohol   ...carboxylic acid   ...cosmetics   ...esters   ...flavourings   ...immiscible

Not just for drinking

To most people, 'alcohol' means the substance that makes people drunk. But there are many other alcohols. They are colourless, flammable liquids. Those below are **miscible** (they can be mixed) with water, giving neutral solutions.

- The alcohol in drinks is ethanol, C_2H_5OH, made by fermenting sugar, e.g. from grape juice. It's heavily taxed.
- Industrial ethanol is made from petroleum. Poisonous methanol, CH_3OH, is added to make it undrinkable.
- Propanol, C_3H_7OH, is the **solvent** in many perfumes and after-shaves.

FIGURE 3: This Brazilian plane uses ethanol as its fuel.

Like these, the formula of any alcohol ends in –OH. It's their family signature.

Sour grapes

Wine left open to the air goes sour. The 'vin' becomes vinegar because the ethanol, CH_3CH_2OH, gets oxidised to ethanoic acid, CH_3COOH. It loses hydrogen and gains oxygen.

- All alcohols oxidise, giving acids with formulae ending in –COOH, the signature of the carboxylic acid family. They are colourless, sharp-smelling liquids, miscible with water. The solutions are only weakly acidic; **pH** 4–7. Many exist naturally.
- Ant bites, wasp and nettle stings all contain methanoic acid, HCOOH.
- Lactic acid is in yoghurt, and forms in your muscles when you exercise hard.
- Fruits contain various acids, not just citric. Vitamin C is ascorbic acid. The formulae of fruit acids are complex, but all have the –COOH group.

Making scents of esters

Complex mixtures of natural esters give fruits their 'fruity' smells. Synthetic esters also smell pleasant, so we use them to produce artificial odours and flavours. Esters are **immiscible** with water.

- Perfumes are created by blending mixtures of natural esters.
- The fruit flavour in sweets and manufactured foods is often a synthetic ester.
- Other 'smelly' uses include cosmetics and air-fresheners.

WANT TO KNOW MORE?

Read page 117 to find out how 'organic acids' are used in soaps and detergents.

> *Complex mixtures of natural esters give fruits their 'fruity' smells*

QUESTIONS

5 What do we mean by a 'family' of organic compounds?

6 How could you distinguish between methanol and methanoic acid?

7 Why don't fruit-flavoured sweets taste quite like the fruit itself?

8 What does 'Esters are immiscible with water' mean?

Pick-and-mix esters

Chemists make esters by reacting acids with alcohols. The general equation is:

$$RCOOH + R'OH \rightarrow RCOOR' + H_2O$$

$$acid + alcohol \rightarrow ester + water$$

R and R′ stand for alkyl (hydrocarbon) groups, such as CH_3, C_2H_5 or C_4H_9.

- R and R' may be the same or different. This gives lots of combinations.
- Two acids and three alcohols can give 2×3 different esters. For example:

	HCOOH	**CH₃COOH**
CH₃OH	HCOOCH₃	CH₃COOCH₃
C₂H₅OH	HCOOC₂H₅	CH₃COOC₂H₅
C₄H₉OH	HCOOC₄H₉	CH₃COOC₄H₉

- So, a few dozen acids and alcohols give hundreds of esters, which can be mixed to make customised aromas and flavours.

Esters are also useful solvents. One of the most important is ethyl ethanoate, used for paints, varnishes, inks and for decaffeinating tea and coffee.

FIGURE 4: Nail varnish hardens quickly because the solvent, ethyl ethanoate, evaporates easily.

QUESTIONS

9 Which is the formula for ethyl ethanoate?

10 Why is ethyl ethanoate found in vinegar made from wine?

11 Why is ethyl ethanoate a 'handy' solvent for ladies to use?

Colour me a rainbow

SELF-CHECK ACTIVITY

CONTEXT

Anna has some Chemistry homework to do and is finding it difficult. She goes round to see her Uncle Nick, who likes working on cars.

'We're doing some work on transition elements,' she tells him. 'Each group has been given an element to research and we're doing chromium, but I don't know anything about it. I mean, I know it's a metal, but all the transition elements are metals.'

They were sat in the garage drinking tea. Nick was working on a 1967 Ford Anglia. Anna didn't know much about cars but she did recognise this one.

'Isn't this like the one in the   film?' she asked.

'Yes,' said Nick, 'and here's the chromium.' He pointed at the front bumper. She guessed it had once been shiny but now was pitted and dull.

'Will it polish up again?' she asked.

'Not really,' he said, 'it'll need re-plating. Unlike this,' and he held up the teaspoon from the mug of tea. She took it and read 'Stainless steel'.

'That's not chromium, it's steel. An alloy. Iron and carbon.'

'And chromium – stops it from rusting' said Nick.

Later that evening Anna sent a text to Zoe, who was in her group, about chromium. Zoe replied that there was a paint called Chrome Yellow that her Mum, who was an artist, used to use. Apparently it had lead in it, so she stopped using it.

Then Anna phoned George. He said he'd been searching on the Internet and had come up with something about chromium hydroxide being a mordant, which he said was something that fixes a dye to material. Finally she tried Joe, who had found out that chromium oxide was a seriously good paint and always came in shades of green.

It seemed to Anna that most of the uses of chromium were as compounds with other elements and quite a lot were to do with bright colours. Apart from the front bumper of a Ford Anglia.

CHALLENGE

STEP 1

Is lead a transition element? Explain your answer.

STEP 2

Anna is right – there are similarities between the transition elements. Suggest what they are, referring to conduction, density and melting point in your answer.

STEP 3

The car bumper was steel, plated with chromium, and is now in need of re-plating. How was the teaspoon different in the way it was made? Why do you think the car bumpers weren't made the same way as the teaspoon?

STEP 4

Draw a simple diagram to show how the bumper could be re-plated. Suggest a suitable electrolyte for the plating bath.

STEP 5

The chemical name for Chrome Yellow is lead chromate. It is barely soluble in water, so how can it be used as a paint? Which elements are present in it?

STEP 6

The following day Anna's group agreed that they would present their findings in the form of a concept map, starting with the element in the centre and working outwards to show alloys and compounds. Draw this, and make it clear:

- Which is an alloy and which is a compound
- Which other elements are involved
- What use the various materials are put to

Maximise your grade

These sentences show what you need to include in your work to achieve each grade. Use them to improve your work and be more successful.

Grade	Answer includes...
	Can find lead on the periodic table.
F	Can identify which elements on the periodic table are transition elements and whether lead is one.
	Can identify a common characteristic of transition elements.
	Can identify common characteristic of transition elements with respect to conduction, density and melting point.
C	Can explain the difference between plating and alloying, why the spoon is an alloy and why the bumper was plated.
	Can identify all the elements present in lead chromate and suggest how it can be used as a paint.
A	Can arrange the information in a concept map.
	Can arrange the information in a concept map in a way that is particularly clear and accessible.

First get some salt

You will find out:
- Why alkali metals top the reactivity series
- The importance of chemicals made from salt
- About household products made from alkalis

Mining brine

Dotted around the fields near Northwich, Cheshire, are little brick huts. Deep below each hut is a huge hole, as big as a cathedral. They're salt mines, but nobody digs them. The salt is dissolved in water and pumped up as brine. It's called solution mining. About two million tonnes of salt a year is extracted. Some is sold as salt, but most is converted into other chemicals – about 14 000 of them.

FIGURE 1: A brine well in rural Cheshire. The brick hut houses a pump. Water goes down one pipe; brine comes back up another.

Dangerous when wet (or dry)

Salt is sodium chloride, NaCl. You need 4 g of salt each day to stay alive. Yet it's made up of chlorine, which is a poisonous gas, and sodium, which is a dangerous metal.

- Sodium, with potassium and lithium, is in Group 1 of the periodic table. They're called **alkali metals**, but they don't behave like most other metals.
- Alkali metals are the most reactive of all – top of the reactivity series.
- They're soft enough to cut with a knife. The metals inside are silvery, but quickly go dull, as they react with oxygen in the air.
- They melt very easily – sodium and potassium melt below 100 °C.
- They also catch fire easily. Sodium burns with a yellow flame, potassium pinky purple, lithium red.
- Metals normally sink in water, but alkali metals float. They don't just lie there but react with the water and melt, forming silvery balls, fizzing and scooting around the surface. During reaction, potassium may burst into flame and explode (so too may sodium).
- The gas given off during the reaction burns with a pop. It's hydrogen!
- When the metal has finished reacting, test the water with indicator paper. Purple! It's strongly alkaline – a solution of the metal's hydroxide.

FIGURE 2: A silver ball of molten potassium reacting with water. Notice the trail of hydrogen bubbles in its wake.

sodium + hydrogen hydroxide → hydrogen + sodium hydroxide

$$2Na + 2HOH \rightarrow H_2 + 2NaOH$$

EXAM HINTS AND TIPS

To write equations for the reaction of potassium or lithium with water, just write K or Li instead of Na.

Watch Out 'Alkali metals' are so-named because they were discovered by electrolysing alkalis, not because they react with water to form alkalis.

QUESTIONS

1 State **three** ways in which alkali metals differ from most other metals.
2 How can you tell that alkali metals have low density?
3 Suggest why alkali metals are stored in bottles of oil.
4 Write the word equation for the reaction of potassium with water.

WOW FACTOR!

About 1% of UK electricity is used to electrolyse sodium chloride solution to make sodium hydroxide and chlorine.

From salt...

We make thousands of chemical products from salt. A few main products are manufactured first, then used to make others.

Sodium carbonate and sodium hydroxide are important **alkalis**, used to make a wide range of everyday products and specialist chemicals.

'Soda' is a general name for several alkalis.

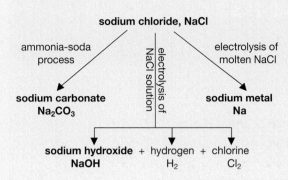

sodium chloride, NaCl

ammonia-soda process → sodium carbonate Na_2CO_3

electrolysis of NaCl solution

electrolysis of molten NaCl → sodium metal Na

sodium hydroxide NaOH + hydrogen H_2 + chlorine Cl_2

- Bicarbonate of soda, sodium hydrogencarbonate, $NaHCO_3$, is initial product of the ammonia-soda process and is used in baking as a raising agent (releases carbon dioxide) and in many other foods.
- Soda ash, **anhydrous** sodium carbonate, Na_2CO_3, is made by heating the initial product to decompose it. Glass is made by melting a mixture of soda ash, sand and limestone.
- Washing soda – crystals of hydrated sodium carbonate, $Na_2CO_3 \cdot 10H_2O$ – is made by dissolving soda ash and then crystallising.
- Caustic soda – sodium hydroxide, NaOH – 'caustic' means corrosive. Household uses include cleaning ovens and drains.

FIGURE 3: Love the gloves! This furnace contains molten glass at 1600 °C, so he needs his protective clothing.

...to soap and (artificial) silk

Sodium hydroxide is the most important alkali in terms of the amount used – well over 1 million tonnes a year in the UK.

- Boiling oils or fats with sodium hydroxide solution gives **soap**. It's also needed to make soapless detergents. (See page 117.)
- Wood or cotton fibres dissolve in sodium hydroxide solution. Squirting the solution through small holes into acid produces fibres of 'rayon' for clothes and motor tyres. They're like cotton, but with a shiny surface, so look like silk.

(See page 117.)

Essential electrolysis

Sodium and chlorine are both very reactive elements. Electrolysis is the only way to separate them. The chlor-alkali industry electrolyses vast amounts of brine.

Brine electrolysis gives three products, chlorine, sodium hydroxide and hydrogen. These must be kept apart. Modern cells use a special plastic membrane between the anode and cathode.

- Brine flows through the anode section. Chloride ions are oxidised to chlorine:

$$2Cl^-(aq) \rightarrow Cl_2(g) + 2e^-$$

- The special membrane allows sodium ions, Na^+, to pass into the cathode section, but not chloride ions, Cl^-.
- Water flows into the cathode section. Water is reduced to hydrogen and hydroxide ions:

$$2H_2O(l) + 2e^- \rightarrow H_2(g) + 2OH^-(aq)$$

- So, sodium and hydroxide ions collect in the cathode compartment. Sodium hydroxide is run off at the bottom.

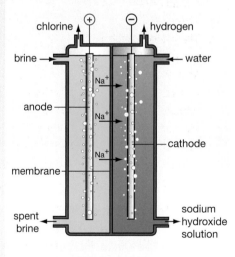

FIGURE 4: A 'membrane cell' for electrolysing brine.

QUESTIONS

5 Which process converts sodium chloride solution into sodium hydroxide?

6 What is the difference between anhydrous and hydrated sodium carbonate?

7 What hazard symbol should containers of caustic soda drain-cleaner show?

QUESTIONS

8 What are the three products of brine electrolysis?

9 Why must they be kept apart?

10 Why can't sodium metal be made by electrolysing brine?

Contact chemistry

You will find out:

- Why sulphuric acid is a vital industrial chemical
- How the Contact process works
- That many household products depend on sulphuric acid

Nasty but necessary

Sulphuric acid sometimes gets a bad press. John Haigh, the infamous 'acid bath murderer', dissolved at least four victims in it. Well, almost. Some body parts remained as proof, and Haigh was hanged. Sulphuric acid in acid rain has also killed many trees. It's nasty stuff, but we couldn't enjoy modern life without it. Though few products actually contain sulphuric acid, almost all rely on it in some way.

FIGURE 1: A mountainside dotted with grey skeletons of trees killed by acid rain.

Anodising to zinc sulphate

Anodising, **b**atteries, **c**atalysts, **d**etergents, **e**xplosives, **f**ertilisers, …

There's a long list of uses for sulphuric(VI) acid, H_2SO_4.

Many affect your everyday life.

- **A**nodising involves electrolysing sulphuric acid. This forms an oxide layer on any aluminium object used as the anode. The object can then be dyed.
- Your car's 'lead–acid' **b**attery contains a litre or two of sulphuric acid.
- The acid is used as a **catalyst** to speed up many chemical reactions. These include making esters (page 107) and biodiesel.
- Washing powders and washing-up liquids are **detergents**. The active part of their molecules often comes from sulphuric acid. (See page 115.)
- We wouldn't have metals or coal without mining and quarrying. Making TNT and dynamite **e**xplosives needs sulphuric acid.
- Ammonium sulphate **f**ertiliser is manufactured by neutralising sulphuric acid. Making phosphate fertilisers (the P in NPK) also needs the acid.
- White paint, plastics, sun-block creams and even paper contain the white **pigment** titanium dioxide. It's extracted from ores using you-know-what.
- Several plastics and synthetic fibres, e.g. Kevlar, need sulphuric acid. It may be used to make the polymer, or to spin the fibre. (See page 115.)
- **Z**inc sulphate is used as the electrolyte for zinc plating, and as a mineral supplement in animal feeds.

FIGURE 2: What do these household products all have in common?

WOW FACTOR!

The atmosphere on Venus is mainly carbon dioxide with clouds of sulphuric acid.

QUESTIONS

1. What is the chemical formula for sulphuric acid?
2. Why are catalysts useful in the chemical industry?
3. Which base neutralises sulphuric acid to make ammonium sulphate?
4. What colour is titanium dioxide?

…catalyst   …Contact process   …detergent

Starting points

Sulphuric acid is widely used because it is relatively cheap to produce. The raw materials are air, water and sulphur dioxide gas, SO_2, from two main sources:

- burning sulphur – obtained by mining, or from sulphur compounds removed from oil and natural gas:

$$S(s) + O_2(g) \rightarrow SO_2(g)$$

FIGURE 3: Sulphur occurs naturally around volcanoes.

- extraction of metals, such as lead, copper and zinc. Roasting sulphide ores (e.g. galena, PbS) in air releases sulphur dioxide as a by-product:

$$2PbS(s) + 3O_2(g) \rightarrow 2PbO(s) + 2SO_2(g)$$

From oxide to acid

Think of sulphuric acid, H_2SO_4, as $H_2O + SO_3$. To make the acid we must oxidise sulphur dioxide, SO_2, to sulphur trioxide, SO_3. We use the **Contact process** – it brings sulphur dioxide and oxygen into contact with a catalyst.

- Sulphur dioxide and air are pumped through the converter – a large vessel in four sections packed with vanadium(V) oxide pellets to catalyse the reaction:

$$2SO_2(g) + O_2(g) \rightleftharpoons 2SO_3(g) + heat$$

Watch Out In a reversible reaction a catalyst speeds up both the forward and reverse reactions. It does not affect the yield.

- Reaction conditions: temperature, 400–450 °C; pressure, slightly above 1 atm to pump the gases through the converter.
- The reaction is reversible, so not all the sulphur dioxide is oxidised. However, each section converts more, giving at least 99.5% conversion overall.
- The reaction is also **exothermic**, so the temperature rises. The gases are cooled between each section.
- To make acid, the sulphur trioxide must react with water:

$$SO_3(g) + H_2O(l) \rightarrow H_2SO_4(l)$$

- The direct reaction is too vigorous. Instead, the sulphur trioxide is dissolved in 98% sulphuric acid. The resulting super-concentrated acid is then diluted back to 98% – but there's now more of it.

FIGURE 4: A Contact process converter. It needs wide pipes to carry the huge volumes of gases.

EXAM HINTS AND TIPS

Sulphuric acid is *not* made by dissolving SO_3 in water. It is dissolved in acid first, then mixed with water.

QUESTIONS

5 Why is it a good idea to use the sulphur dioxide from metal smelting?

6 Which reaction above shows that sulphur is a non-metal?

7 Why is the converter divided into separate sections?

8 What does the $\rightleftharpoons$ sign mean in an equation?

Equilibrium position

The **equilibrium** in the Contact process must be shifted as far to the right as possible:

- for economic reasons
- to minimise the release of unreacted sulphur dioxide into the atmosphere.

Reaction conditions are important.

- The oxidation is exothermic, so lower temperatures shift the equilibrium to the right. This is why the gases are cooled between each catalyst bed.
- High pressure would shift the equilibrium to the right. It isn't used since conversion is over 99.5% anyway.
- Similarly, increasing the concentration of oxygen by using pure oxygen instead of air is also unnecessary.
- Higher percentage conversion is achieved by dissolving out the sulphur trioxide formed in the first three catalysts beds before passing the gases into the fourth bed.

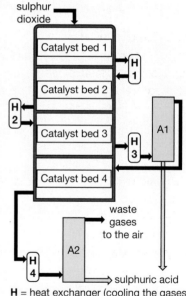

H = heat exchanger (cooling the gases)
A = absorber (dissolving out SO_3)

FIGURE 5: Flow of gases through the Contact process.

QUESTIONS

9 Lower temperatures help. So why use 400–450 °C?

10 Why, theoretically, does high pressure help the equilibrium?

11 Why does removing sulphur trioxide after bed 3 help?

The essential acid

You will find out:
- That many industries rely on sulphuric acid
- What sulphuric acid is used for
- How its uses depend on its chemical properties

Snotty stalactites

Stalactites are usually hard. They're solid limestone. Some caves also contain soft, slimy ones. They're like mucus from your nose, so are called *snottites*. They are bacterial colonies that 'feed' on hydrogen sulphide gas (H_2S), forming sulphuric acid (H_2SO_4), which drips off the end. Over many years this acid has dissolved the rock, forming the caves. Sulphur-loving bacteria may have been the first form of life on Earth, before there was oxygen in the air.

Using neutralisation

The constant drip from snottites forms caves by dissolving the limestone. That's because the drip is sulphuric acid and limestone is a base. They neutralise each other. Many uses of synthetic sulphuric acid also rely on **neutralisation** reactions making salts.

- *Fertilisers*: Gardeners use 'sulphate of ammonia' and 'sulphate of potash'. Their chemical names are ammonium sulphate, $(NH_4)_2SO_4$, and potassium sulphate, K_2SO_4. Both are made by neutralising sulphuric acid.

    ammonia gas + sulphuric acid → ammonium sulphate
    potassium hydroxide + sulphuric acid → potassium sulphate + water

    Farmers use other nitrogen fertilisers more than ammonium sulphate.

- *Pickling steel*: Steel is shaped while hot. It reacts with the air, forming a scale of iron oxide. This must be removed before using the steel. 'Pickling' means dissolving the scale in acid.

    iron oxide + sulphuric acid → iron sulphate + water

- *Making titanium dioxide*: The white **pigment** in 'brilliant white' paint and PVC window frames is titanium dioxide, TiO_2. Titanium ore, $FeTiO_3$, behaves like a mixture of two metal oxides. It dissolves in sulphuric acid, giving two salts.

    oxide ore + sulphuric acid → iron sulphate + titanium sulphate + water

    Further stages convert titanium sulphate into pure titanium oxide.

FIGURE 1: A drop of sulphuric acid hanging from a snottite.

FIGURE 2: Contrasting chemicals. White titanium dioxide extracted from black titanium ore.

Watch Out Unlike other acid–base neutralisations, sulphuric acid and ammonia gas, NH_3, do *not* produce water.

$$2NH_3 + H_2SO_4 \rightarrow (NH_4)_2SO_4$$

WOW FACTOR!

In the UK we use about 1.2 million tonnes of sulphuric acid per year – about 10 litres per person.

WANT TO KNOW MORE?

There is more about detergents on pages 116–117.

⊪ QUESTIONS ⊪

1 What type of reaction turns sulphuric acid into ammonium sulphate?
2 Name a compound that could provide the K in an NPK mixed fertiliser.
3 Why is sulphuric acid used to pickle steel?
4 Why does titanium ore dissolve in sulphuric acid?

...catalyst   ...detergent   ...dyes

Using other properties

Neutralising bases isn't all that sulphuric acid can do. It has many other useful properties. Worldwide we produce more sulphuric acid than any other chemical – about 180 million tonnes a year. That's because so many industries rely on it. Let's look at some important uses.

FIGURE 3: Essential uses of sulphuric acid.

- *Detergents:* Concentrated sulphuric acid reacts with hydrocarbons to add a sulphonate group ($-SO_3H$) onto the carbon chain. This helps to make the 'oily' molecules water-soluble. It produces **detergents**, commonly used in washing powders. Shampoos and shower gels often contain sodium laureth sulphate. This is a different type of detergent, but also made using sulphuric acid.
- *Dyes:* Many **dyes** are also organic compounds containing sulphonate groups. As with detergents, this helps to make the molecules water-soluble, so the dye can soak into the cloth.
- *Explosives:* Name two explosives besides gunpowder. You probably thought of dynamite and TNT (**tri**ni**tro**toluene). Making them needs concentrated nitric acid and an even stronger acid. Guess which – concentrated sulphuric acid.
- *Catalysts:* Many reactions use concentrated sulphuric acid as a **catalyst**. It's usually hydrogen ions, H^+, that catalyse the reaction, so other acids would work. Sulphuric is used because it's cheap, readily available and each molecule of H_2SO_4 gives two H^+ ions.
- *Car batteries:* Lead–acid batteries rely on two properties of sulphuric acid.
  i) It conducts electricity, because it contains H^+ and SO_4^{2-} ions.
  ii) It reacts with the lead and lead dioxide plates inside to produce electricity. These reactions reverse when the battery is recharged, so the acid never needs replacing.

QUESTIONS

5   Why is sulphuric acid economically important in industrialised countries?

6   What is the difference between sulphate and sulphonate groups?

7   Why do industries that involve mining or quarrying rely on sulphuric acid?

8   Does recharging make car battery acid more concentrated, or less? Why?

Making artificial fibres

- Artificial silk fibres and fabrics are soft and comfortable, although they're made from wood. Wood fibres are cellulose, which dissolves in alkali. Squirting the solution through small holes (like a shower head) into sulphuric acid neutralises the alkali. The cellulose solidifies again, but as flexible, thin threads called rayon.
- Kevlar is a polymer chemically similar to nylon. Weight for weight, Kevlar fibres are stronger than steel. Their uses include car tyres, lightweight bikes, golf clubs and bullet-proof vests. Whereas artificial silk is made from an alkaline solution, Kevlar is produced from a solution of the polymer in sulphuric acid.

FIGURE 4: This bullet-proof vest contains several layers of woven Kevlar fibres.

QUESTIONS

9   What is the purpose of sulphuric acid in the manufacture of:
    a rayon   **b** Kevlar?

10 What chemical is rayon?

11 Why is Kevlar used in high-quality sports equipment?

...neutralisation   ...pigment

Chemical cleaners

You will find out:
- The difference between soaps and detergents
- How they remove dirt
- How 'biological' detergents work
- How soaps and detergents are manufactured

Carl's challenge

Children are messy! Blood, biro ink, grass, paint and tomato sauce all stain clothes. Never mind – bung them in the washer. They'll come out clean, thanks to scientists like Carl. His job is to develop new detergents, to make washing powders even better. Carl tests them on cloth soiled with many different types of stain. It's a tough challenge, but he hopes it will turn out all white.

FIGURE 1: Carl's challenge is to make a detergent that will remove all these types of stain.

Getting rid of dirt

Detergents are chemicals that clean things. They remove dirt, stains and grease from clothes, skin and other surfaces. There are two main types:

- **Soaps** – made from animal fats and vegetable oils for over 5000 years.
- Soapless detergents – a 20th century invention, made from petroleum.

Both work in the same way. Strange as it seems, water isn't very good at making things wet. Water can sit on a piece of cloth without soaking in. **Surface tension** keeps the water in round drops, and stops it spreading out.

- Detergents are **surfactants** – substances that reduce surface tension. The water can now spread, soak in and get at the dirt.
- Detergent molecules surround particles of dirt and grease. This makes them break away from the fibres and mix with the water.
- When the water runs away, the dirt goes with it. The clothes are left clean.

FIGURE 2: Surface tension in action: water droplets on woven cloth.

Tackling food stains

Dried-on blood and food can be difficult to wash out. Special 'biological' detergents containing **enzymes** make it easier.

- Enzymes are biological catalysts. They help break down complex protein molecules, so they dissolve in water.
- They digest food stains in the same way as enzymes in your stomach.

Watch Out Soap is a detergent. What we usually call 'detergents' are mostly soapless detergents.

QUESTIONS

1 What do we use detergents for?
2 Detergents reduce surface tension. How does this help?
3 What happens to the dirt during the washing process?
4 What's special about biological detergents?

WOW FACTOR!

Soap operas are so called because when first broadcast, the adverts, aimed at housewives, were mainly for laundry products!

...alkali   ...detergents   ...enzyme   ...ester

Soap for all

Before 1800 soap was a luxury, made only in small amounts. People dissolved potash (an **alkali**) out of wood ash, and boiled it with animal fat. Soap manufacture began in the 1800s, when scientists discovered how to make soda (another alkali) from salt. By 1900 soap was an everyday item.

Modern soap-making uses the same basic process.

- The alkali is sodium hydroxide solution, NaOH, made by electrolysing salt solution.
- Vegetable oils (e.g. palm oil) are used, as well as animal fats. They contain similar chemicals.
- Boiling alkali reacts with oils and fats to produce soap and glycerine.
- Adding hot brine dissolves out glycerine and impurities, leaving molten soap.
- The soap is cooled, coloured, perfumed and made into tablets, powder or flakes.

Hard problem – easy solution

Problem: Water from limestone areas contains calcium salts. We call it **hard water** because it's hard to make a lather with soap. Scum forms instead and gets trapped between the fibres of clothes.

Solution: Most washing powders contain soapless (or non-soap) detergents. These do not form scum.

FIGURE 3: What caused the tide-mark of scum in this wash basin?

They can be made from vegetable oils, but most are manufactured using mineral oil (petroleum). Hydrocarbons react with concentrated sulphuric acid forming sulphonates – compounds containing the $-SO_3H$ group. Neutralisation forms ionic $-SO_3^-$ Na^+ groups, making them soluble in water. Sodium laureth sulphate, $C_{16}H_{33}O_2SO_3Na$, is used in shampoos and shower gels.

Heads and tails

Both soap and soapless detergent molecules have a water-soluble ionic group at one end (the 'head') and an insoluble hydrocarbon 'tail'. To get away from water, the tails bury themselves in dirt or grease. The dirt particle is now surrounded by ionic heads, so it can dissolve.

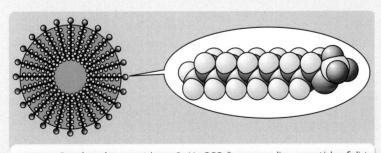

FIGURE 4: Soapless detergent ions, $C_{12}H_{25}OSO_3^-$, surrounding a particle of dirt.

QUESTIONS

5 What do you get by reacting vegetable oil with:
   a) boiling sodium hydroxide solution   **b)** concentrated sulphuric acid?

6 Why do we wash clothes with soapless detergents rather than soap?

7 What are the **two** main features of all detergent molecules?

DID YOU KNOW?

Soap labels show the oil or fat used; e.g. sodium palmate comes from palm oil, tallowate from beef fat (tallow).

The chemistry of soap

Fats and oils are **esters** of **fatty acids**. Their molecules have three RCOO– groups.

- R represents a large group of carbon and hydrogen atoms, such as $C_{17}H_{35}$. The three R groups may be the same or different, depending on the fat or oil.
- Sodium hydroxide splits the esters into glycerine and the sodium salts of the fatty acids, RCOONa. These are soap.
- The size of the R groups varies. Most are 13 to 19 carbon atoms long, forming the molecule's hydrocarbon tail.
- The ionic $-COO^-$ Na^+ group is the molecule's water-soluble head.

Soap forms a scum in hard water because it forms the calcium salt $(RCOO)_2Ca$, which is insoluble in water.

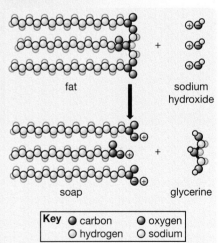

Key ● carbon ● oxygen ○ hydrogen ○ sodium

FIGURE 5: Each molecule of fat makes three molecules of soap.

QUESTIONS

8 What is an ester?

9 Explain why soap is usually a mixture, not a single compound.

10 Suggest why we use sodium salts, rather than fatty acids themselves, to make soap.

Green chemistry

You will find out:
- How hydrogen may replace petrol
- How chemistry helps to reduce our use of finite materials, and control pollution
- What we mean by sustainability

Hydrogen – fuel of the future?

Save our planet! Use hydrogen-powered vehicles instead of petrol and diesel. Burning hydrogen produces only water – no global-warming carbon dioxide. Hydrogen vehicles already exist. Their fuel comes from electrolysis – splitting water into hydrogen and oxygen. Problem! Generating the required electricity by burning fossil fuels produces large amounts of carbon dioxide. Solution? Generate the electricity using **renewable energy** sources that don't burn fuels.

FIGURE 1: This car's engine can burn either hydrogen or petrol.

Zero pollution

Figure 2 shows a driver filling up with liquid hydrogen from the white tank.

- The filling station makes its own hydrogen by electrolysing water.
- The electricity needed is generated by thousands of solar cells. You can see two panels of them at the left.
- Generating the electricity produces no pollution. Neither does electrolysing water; nor burning the hydrogen as fuel.
- At present this technology is expensive and still experimental.
- We already produce hydrogen by electrolysis of brine. (See page 111.) However, most of the electricity for this comes from burning fossil fuels, so is not pollution-free.
- Hydrogen can also power fuel cells to drive electric vehicles.

FIGURE 2: Experimental liquid hydrogen filling station.

Chemistry working for the environment

People often blame the chemical industry for pollution. Yet chemists prevent far more pollution than they cause. It is chemists who develop ways to ...

- use less fuel – by making reactions work at lower temperatures
- use fewer raw materials – by making processes more efficient
- reduce waste – by recycling, and finding uses for waste products
- improve safety – by using less dangerous chemicals wherever possible.

Read on to find out how.

The future will be green, or not at all.
Chairman, UK Sustainable Development Commission.

▪▪ QUESTIONS ▪▪

1 Why does burning hydrogen produce no pollution?
2 How do we make hydrogen without using fuel?
3 What do solar cells do?
4 How does burning less fuel help the environment?

WANT TO KNOW MORE?

Follow links at www.sustain-ed.org/. You can even try a quiz to check how 'green' you are.

...biodegradable

Making the best use of resources

Using less energy and raw materials saves fuels and finite mineral resources. That leaves more oil for making organic chemicals, such as plastics, medicines and detergents. Metal ores and other minerals will last longer.

Let's see how some of the topics in pages 98–117 help the environment. The following save fuel, and reduce carbon dioxide emissions.

- Metals conduct heat. Metal heat exchangers recover heat from exothermic reactions. It may be used to create steam to generate electricity, as in the Contact process (page 113).
- Many transition metals and their compounds are catalysts (page 99). They make reactions go faster at lower temperatures.
- Similarly, enzymes help biochemical reactions. Making ethanol (alcohol) from ethene needs 300 °C, but fermentation works at 30 °C.
- Recycling, e.g. metals and polymers, saves both fuel and raw materials.

Controlling pollution

Chemists take steps to avoid releasing dangerous chemicals into the environment. Here are a few examples.

- Extracting metals from sulphide ores produces sulphur dioxide. Instead of releasing it into the air, it is used to make sulphuric acid. By law, all sulphuric acid plants must convert at least 99.5% of the sulphur dioxide into acid (page 113).
- Some cells and batteries (page 104) contain compounds of toxic metals, e.g. mercury or cadmium. You should not throw away those used batteries. Waste disposal sites collect them for reprocessing.
- Electrolysis of brine used to be done using mercury as the cathode. This method has mostly been replaced by membrane cells (page 111), so avoiding the use of poisonous mercury.
- Some early soapless detergents were not **biodegradable**. This caused problems in rivers and sewage works. Chemists solved the problem by starting with different hydrocarbons.

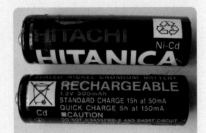

FIGURE 3: 'Recycle' and 'Do not bin' symbols on Ni-Cd cells. What do Ni and Cd stand for?

FIGURE 4: Foam on a river – a common sight 50 years ago when detergents were non-biodegradable.

QUESTIONS

5 Apart from reducing pollution, why is it important to burn less fossil fuel?

6 How does the use of catalysts help to reduce pollution?

7 Why should you be careful about how you dispose of used batteries?

8 Why do non-biodegradable substances cause problems at sewage works?

WOW FACTOR!

Recycling 1 tonne of aluminium saves 8 tonnes of ore and uses only 5% as much energy as making new aluminium.

Sustainability

Reducing our use of materials helps, but we can't go on consuming them for ever. All finite resources will run out sooner or later.

For the sake of future generations we must develop a **sustainable** lifestyle. That is, one that can keep going while using the minimum of finite resources. This means using:

- renewable energy sources
- materials that can be recycled or re-used
- processes that do not damage our environment – locally and globally.

The 'hydrogen economy' outlined opposite is one possible example.

- Hydrogen fuel is made from water using renewable energy.
- When burned, the hydrogen produces the same amount of water as at the start.
- If nothing escaped, this cycle could continue indefinitely.

FIGURE 5: The future of nature is in our hands. What will you do to help?

QUESTIONS

9 What's the difference between recycled and re-used materials?

10 Why is the hydrogen economy not fully sustainable in practice?

11 Finally, think about how you can make your own lifestyle more sustainable.

Unit summary

Transition metals are typical metals. They conduct heat and electricity, and have high melting points and densities. Their uses depend on these properties. Their compounds are used as catalysts and pigments.

Metals are extracted from ores by reduction. This often means removing oxygen, but not always.
Reduction also means adding electrons to change positive metal ions into atoms. Removing electrons is oxidation. Transition metal catalysts work by using redox reactions.

The chemical industry uses and makes a huge range of chemicals. It faces major problems:
- finite resources will eventually run out
- pollution damages the environment
- present methods are not sustainable.

Ways that chemists tackle these problems include:
- using alternative energy sources
- developing more efficient reactions to reduce waste
- controlling pollution
- recycling materials.

Reduction and oxidation also occur when electrons are added and removed electrically. This is electrolysis.
Reduction occurs at the cathode, releasing a metal or hydrogen. Oxidation occurs at the anode, dissolving it away, or releasing a non-metal.
Uses include purifying copper, electroplating and the alkali industry.

Alkali metals can only be extracted by electrolysis. They differ from other metals. They are soft, have low melting points and densities, and react violently with water.
Electrolysis of brine gives chlorine and sodium hydroxide, an important alkali. Its uses include making soap and synthetic fibres. Another alkali, sodium carbonate, is used to make glass.

Alcohols, carboxylic acids and esters are families of organic compounds containing oxygen. Many occur naturally, but we make most from petroleum. Uses include food and drink, detergents, solvents, perfumes and cosmetics.

Cells and batteries produce electricity from chemical reactions – the reverse of electrolysis.
The voltage depends on which chemicals are used.
Secondary cells are rechargeable; primary cells are not.
Charging involves electrolysis.

Sulphuric acid is one of the most widely used chemicals. It is made by the Contact process, using sulphur dioxide from sulphur or metal sulphide ores.
We use sulphuric acid to de-rust steel, and make a huge range of everyday chemicals.

Alkalis and sulphuric acid react with fats and oils to make soaps and soapless detergents.
These clean by reducing surface tension, and reacting with dirt and grease. Soap forms a scum with hard water. Soapless detergents don't.

Unit quiz

1. Tungsten is a transition metal used for light bulb filaments. What properties make it suitable for this use?

2. Match each catalyst with what it is used to make:
   a) iron
   b) nickel
   c) nickel oxide
   d) platinum
   e) vanadium(V) oxide
   i) hydrogen
   ii) ammonia
   iii) sulphuric acid
   iv) margarine
   v) catalytic converters

3. In connection with redox reactions, what does OIL RIG stand for?

4. Explain whether each of the following is reduction, oxidation or neither:
   a) burning sulphur to make sulphur dioxide
   b) reacting sulphur trioxide with water to make sulphuric acid
   c) dissolving away an impure copper anode during purification
   d) depositing pure copper on the cathode
   e) making vinegar by converting ethanol into ethanoic acid

5. What, scientifically, is the difference between a cell and a battery?

6. Name two types of primary cell, and two types of secondary cell.

7. Is each of the following compounds an alcohol, a carboxylic acid or an ester?
   a) ethanoic acid
   b) ethyl propanoate
   c) methanol
   d) C_3H_7OH
   e) $CH_3COOC_2H_5$
   f) C_2H_5COOH

8. Which two of the above three types are used in perfumes? What is the purpose of each?

9. Why are alkali metals stored in jars of oil?

10. a) Complete the following word equation:
    $$lithium + water \rightarrow ? + ?$$
    b) Write the balanced equation for this reaction.

11. What type of substance reacts with sodium hydroxide to make soap?

12. Soap and soapless detergents are *surfactants*. How do surfactants help the washing process?

13. How do *biological* detergents work?

14. Name one fertiliser, one pigment and one synthetic fibre made using sulphuric acid.

15. The Contact process has four main stages. Briefly outline what happens in each of the following:
    a) burner
    b) catalyst beds
    c) heat exchanger
    d) absorber

Numeracy activity

In the UK in 2004, we used 190 000 tonnes of aluminium packaging – 77% of it for drinks cans. Although aluminium can be used over and over again, most aluminium packaging ends up being thrown away. Only a small proportion is recycled.

Government statistics show the amounts of aluminium packaging thrown away in 2004:

	tonnes
Drinks cans at home	57 000
Drinks cans in pubs, restaurants, etc.	30 000
Dishes and foil	25 000
Other cans (e.g. aerosols)	11 000
Composites (e.g. Tetrapacks)	11 000
Unspecified	7 000

QUESTIONS

1. How many tonnes of aluminium were made into drinks cans in 2004?

2. a) How many tonnes of aluminium packaging were thrown away?
   b) Draw a pie chart to show the proportions of each type.

3. From the mass of cans made, and the mass of cans thrown away, calculate the percentage recycled.

4. a) Explain why it is good citizenship to recycle aluminium and other materials.
   b) What should you do before putting cans in a recycling skip – and why?

5. It takes 14 000 kW h of electricity to make 1 tonne of aluminium from bauxite ore – but only 5% of this to recycle 1 tonne. How much electricity would we have saved if we had recycled all aluminium cans in 2004?

Exam practice

1 Put a tick if the property is true for that group of metals. The first one has been done for you.

	Transition metal	Group 1 metal
Good electrical conductor	✓	✓
Good catalyst		
Low melting point		
High boiling point		
Low density		
Used to make pigments		

[5]

2 Draw lines to match each type of organic compound with its use, and with the formulae as an example.

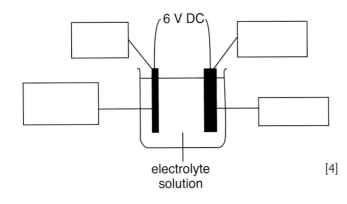

alcohol   used as fruity flavouring

organic acid   used as a solvent in perfumes

ester   used in making detergents   [6]

3 A i Electrolysis can be used to purify copper. The diagram shows how this can be done. Add these labels:

negative electrode   **positive electrode**
pure copper   **impure copper**

6 V DC

electrolyte solution   [4]

ii What electrolyte could be used?

.... [1]

iii Add an arrow to show which direction the electrons move in the external circuit. [1]

B Write half equations to show the reactions at the negative electrode and the positive electrode.

negative: ....

positive: .... [2]

C i What happens to the more reactive impurities?

.... [1]

ii What happens to the less reactive impurities?

.... [1]

(Total 10 marks)

4 A piece of lithium is placed in water containing universal indicator.

A Give three observations that would be made.

....
....
.... [3]

B Write a word equation for this reaction.

.... [2]

C Write a balanced symbol equation for this reaction. Include state symbols.

.... [4]

D If a piece of potassium were placed on water, how would the observations be different?

.... [1]

(Total 10 marks)

5 A Give two uses of sodium carbonate.

.... [2]

B Give two uses of sodium hydroxide.

.... [2]

(Total 4 marks)

6 **A** What advantage does a soapless detergent have over a soap in a hard water area?

.... [1]

B What two substances are needed to make a soap?

.... and .... [2]

C How do biological detergents work?

....

....

.... [2]

(Total 5 marks)

Worked example

Sulphuric acid can be manufactured from sulphur or sulphide ores.

a Zinc sulphide is one such ore. Write a word equation to show the reaction when it is roasted in air. [2]

| sulphur | Burn → in air | sulphur dioxide | Air, V₂O₅ → 450 °C | sulphur trioxide | Dissolve in conc. acid. Then add water → | sulphuric acid |

b In the contact process, sulphur is first burnt in the air to form sulphur dioxide.

  i Write a symbol equation to show this reaction. [2]

The second step of the process is to further oxidise the sulphur dioxide by reacting it with more oxygen in the presence of vanadium(V) oxide to make sulphur trioxide.

  ii What is the purpose of the vanadium(V) oxide? [2]
  iii Write a symbol equation to show this reaction. [2]
  iv Explain the choice of 450 °C as the temperature for carrying out this process. [3]
  v In the final step the sulphur trioxide is dissolved in 98% sulphuric acid to make 99.5% sulphuric acid, which is then watered down. You might think it would be a good deal easier to react the sulphur trioxide with water. Explain why this is not done. [1]

c Give three uses for the sulphuric acid formed. [3]

Overall Grade: B

Good

b iii is not a balanced equation. It should read $2SO_2 + 3O_2 \rightleftharpoons 2SO_3$.
b iv is partly right but, for 3 marks, more was needed. The reaction is reversible and at high temperatures the reverse reaction is favoured so a compromise temperature is used. This gives a reasonable yield at a reasonable rate.

All correct. In addition it is also needed to make fibres, soaps, dyes and fertilisers but these were not needed to get the mark.

a Zinc sulphide + oxygen → zinc oxide + sulphur dioxide

b **i** $SO_2 + O_2 \rightarrow SO_2$
  ii It acts as a catalyst to speed the reaction up.
  iii $SO_2 + O_2 \rightleftharpoons SO_3$.
  iv This is to speed up the reaction.
  v The reaction of sulphur trioxide and water is far too exothermic.

c The sulphuric acid can be used for making detergents, plastics and paints.

How to get an A

Always check to make sure that symbol equations are balanced. The student did not seem to notice that 3 marks were available for **b iv** and this lost her 2 marks. When asked to explain why a particular temperature is used, always discuss rate but if the reaction is reversible you should also consider the yield. For an exothermic reaction an increase in temperature will always decrease the yield.

PARTICLES IN ACTION

The tracks are in a bubble chamber. This device was used to first identify many of the particles discovered during the 20th century.

The tracks are made by particles moving through a liquid such as liquid hydrogen which is kept as a liquid under pressure. The pressure is reduced to allow the tracks to form.

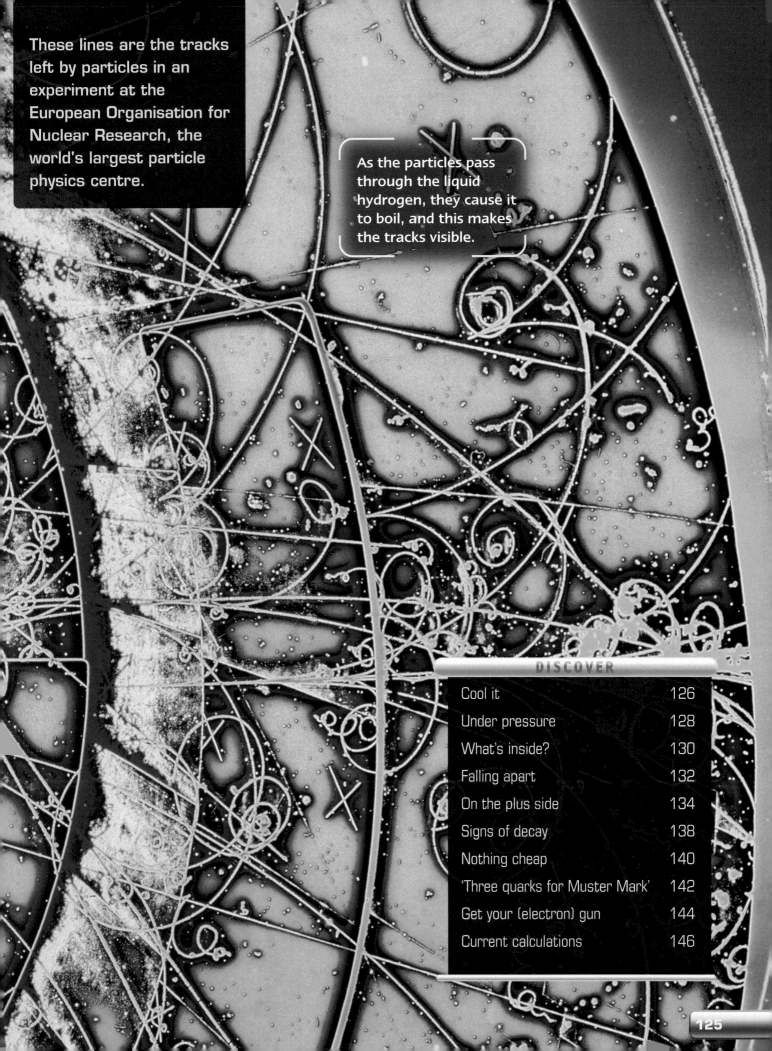

These lines are the tracks left by particles in an experiment at the European Organisation for Nuclear Research, the world's largest particle physics centre.

As the particles pass through the liquid hydrogen, they cause it to boil, and this makes the tracks visible.

Cool it

You will find out:

- How to measure temperature on the Kelvin scale

- How a change in temperature affects the motion of particles in a gas

- What you are really measuring when you measure temperature

Absolute zero

Where's the coldest place? The lowest **temperature** recorded on Earth is –89 °C (degrees **Celsius**) in Antarctica. Outer space has a temperature of about –270 °C. Scientists believe that the coldest temperature possible is –273.15 °C. This temperature is called **absolute zero** and forms the basis of a scale of temperature measurement called the **Kelvin** scale. Small amounts of material have been cooled in laboratories to less than one-thousandth of a degree above absolute zero.

FIGURE 1: How cold is it here?

A difference in scale

Absolute zero is the lowest possible temperature, so it is a sensible place to start a scale of temperature measurement. The scale was first developed by William Thomson (Lord Kelvin) a British physicist who lived and worked during the nineteenth century.

- Absolute zero is written as 0 K. We read this as 'nought k' or 'nought Kelvin'. Notice that we don't say 'nought degrees k' or 'nought degrees Kelvin'.
- 0 K is taken to be the same temperature as –273 °C.
- A temperature change of 1 K is the same size temperature change as 1 °C.
- To go from a temperature in °C to one in K, you add 273.
- To go from a temperature in K to one in °C, you take away 273.

For example: What is the value on the Kelvin scale for a temperature of 37 °C (the average temperature of the human body)?

$$37 + 273 = 310 \text{ K}$$

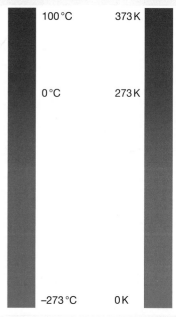

FIGURE 2: Temperature scales.

WOW FACTOR!

The coldest place people actually live is Oymyakon, in eastern Siberia. Lowest temperature is below –70 °C!

▪▪ QUESTIONS ▪▪

1 What value on the Kelvin scale is equal to 50 °C?
2 What value on the Kelvin scale is equal to –10 °C?
3 What value on the Celsius scale is equal to 100 K?
4 What value on the Celsius scale is equal to 300 K?

DID YOU KNOW?

The Celsius scale is named after its inventor, Anders Celsius, a Swedish scientish of the 18th century.

...*absolute zero*   ...*Celsius*   ...*Kelvin*

Get moving

Heat is a form of energy. When heat energy is put into any substance, the particles in the substance gain extra energy. This results in their moving faster than they were before. The heat energy supplied has increased the **kinetic energy** of the particles in the material.

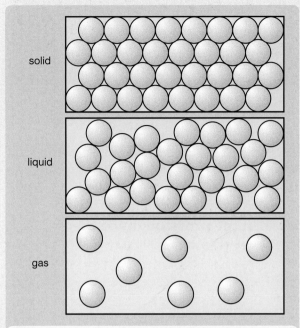

FIGURE 3: How the molecules are arranged in solids, liquids and gases.

- In a solid, this increases the vibration of the particles in their fixed positions. This causes them to occupy more space and the solid will expand. If enough energy is supplied some of the particles break free and the solid begins to melt.
- In a liquid, the particles are close together and moving slowly. Heating will cause them to move more quickly and spread out a little, causing the liquid to expand. Some particles will gain enough energy to leave the liquid altogether and evaporate.
- In a gas the particles are moving quickly and colliding with each other and the sides of the container. As the gas is heated the particles increase their speed. If it can, the gas will expand.
- The volume of a sample of gas (at constant **pressure**) is directly proportional to its Kelvin temperature:

$$V \propto T$$

- This can also be written as

$$V/T = \text{constant}$$

- This rule is known as Charles' Law, named for its discoverer the French physicist Jacques Charles. Charles is also famous for the fact that he made the first hydrogen balloon flight in 1783.

Watch Out The particles in a material don't get bigger when it expands, but the spaces between them do.

QUESTIONS

5 What effect does heating generally have on any material?

6 Evaporation and boiling are both ways that a liquid turns into a gas. List some of the differences between these two processes.

7 Describe what happens to the particles as a gas expands.

8 How does heating a gas cause it to expand?

Heat and temperature

Lord Kelvin built on the work of James Joule and the French physicist, Sadi Carnot, to describe the temperature of an object as a measure of its kinetic energy.

FIGURE 4: Lord Kelvin.

- Heating a gas raises its temperature and increases the speed of movement and kinetic energy of its particles.
- The Kelvin scale relates temperature to the average kinetic energy of the particles.
- The relationship could be written as

$$\tfrac{1}{2}mv^2 = \tfrac{3}{2}kT$$

where $\tfrac{1}{2}mv^2$ is the average kinetic energy per particle, T is the Kelvin temperature and k is a constant called the Boltzmann constant.
- What the equation tells us is that average kinetic energy is directly proportional to Kelvin temperature.

QUESTIONS

9 Why is it not always true, for a liquid or solid, that heating it raises its temperature?

10 Why can we only know the average kinetic energy of particles in a gas.

11 What will be the average speed of the particles at 0 K?

12 Why is 0 K the lowest possible temperature?

Under pressure

You will find out:

- How the particles of a gas exert pressure
- How pressure depends on temperature
- What the general gas equation is and how it is used

Bang, bang

This old photograph is a picture of the remains of a boiler that blew up in April 1862 at the Millfields Ironworks in Wolverhampton. The explosion hurled about 8 tonnes of molten metal high into the air, caused many deaths and injuries and destroyed many of the surrounding buildings. Boilers explode when the **pressure** inside them becomes too much for the walls of the boiler to contain.

FIGURE 1: The explosion of this boiler caused many deaths.

Crash, bang, wallop

You are being constantly bombarded by objects travelling at hundreds of metres per second, much faster than an express train or a Formula 1 racing car, so why don't you notice?

- The objects bombarding you are the molecules in the air.
- Air molecules are very small and have very little mass. The mass of a carbon dioxide molecule (one of the heavier ones) is about 0.000 000 000 000 000 000 000 000 073 kg.
- However, millions of these molecules are hitting every part of you every second and this causes a continuous pressure to be applied to every part of you. We call this atmospheric pressure.
- Pressure is the force per unit area. The units of pressure are newtons per square metre (N/m^2) which can be called pascals (Pa).
- We calculate pressure from the equation

$$\text{Pressure} = \text{Force/Area or } P = F/A$$

- Atmospheric pressure is about 100 000 Pa. This means that there is a force of 100 000 N pushing on every square metre of your skin or about 10 N pushing on every square centimetre.
- Our bodies are developed to exist under this pressure and death soon results if this pressure is removed by, for example, an accident in space.

FIGURE 2: This pressure gauge will tell you if the pressure is becoming dangerous.

▪▪ QUESTIONS ▪▪

1 A box of icing sugar weighs about 10 N. The area of its base is 50 cm². What pressure (in pascals) does the box exert on the surface below?

2 A horse weighs 5000 N. She stands on four horseshoes, each of area 25 cm². What pressure (in pascals) does the horse exert on the ground?

3 How would atmospheric pressure change if the air molecules were more densely packed, but moving at the same speed?

4 How would atmospheric pressure change if the air molecules were moving more quickly but with the same average spacing?

DID YOU KNOW?

Pressure gauges are called Bourdon gauges after Eugene Bourdon, the French engineer who invented them.

...Kelvin   ...kinetic energy   ...particle

Hotting up

When a gas is heated, the thermal energy supplied increases the **kinetic energy** of the **particles** in the gas as the average speed of the particles increases.

- The pressure exerted by a gas is caused by the collisions of the gas particles with the sides of the container.
- If the sample of gas is trapped in a container of fixed volume then it cannot expand.
- Increasing the speed of the particles means that they will collide with the sides of the container more often.
- Increasing the speed of the particles means that they will collide with the sides of the container harder.
- Both of these effects increase the average force being applied to each part of the container and the pressure (force per unit area) will increase.
- This pressure is directly proportional to the square of the average speed of the particles and therefore directly proportional to the average kinetic energy of the particles.
- As average kinetic energy is proportional to **Kelvin temperature**, the pressure in a sample of gas (at constant volume) is directly proportional to its Kelvin temperature:

$$P \propto T$$

- This can also be written as

$$P/T = \text{constant}$$

- This rule is known as the Pressure law and can be demonstrated using apparatus as shown in the diagram.

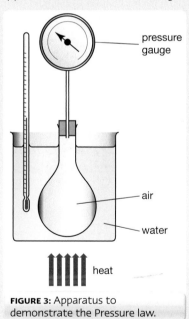

pressure gauge

air

water

heat

FIGURE 3: Apparatus to demonstrate the Pressure law.

Watch Out In the gas laws, the temperature is always the Kelvin temperature.

QUESTIONS

5   What will be the pressure in a sample of gas at 0 K?
6   Why does the pressure have this value at 0 K?
7   Sketch a graph to show the relationship between pressure and temperature on the Kelvin scale.
8   Sketch a graph to show the relationship between pressure and temperature on the Celsius scale.

Pressure, temperature, volume

Charles' law and the Pressure law are two of the three rules known as the gas laws.

- The third gas law is called Boyle's law and deals with how the pressure and volume of a fixed mass of gas at constant temperature are related.
- Boyle's law is named in honour of the 17th century Irish physicist Robert Boyle.
- Pressure is inversely proportional to volume:

$$P \propto 1/V$$

- This can be written as

$$P \times V = \text{constant}$$

- The three gas laws can be combined in the general or ideal gas equation:

$$\frac{P_1 V_1}{T_1} = \frac{P_2 V_2}{T_2}$$

- This means that for a fixed mass of gas, pressure multiplied by volume and then divided by Kelvin temperature always gives the same number.

QUESTIONS

9   Sketch a graph of pressure against volume for a sample of gas at constant temperature.
10 A 1000 cm³ sample of gas has a pressure of 100 000 Pa. If it is compressed to a volume of 500 cm³ at constant temperature, what will be the pressure?
11 Complete this table.

	Before	After
Pressure (Pa)	100 000	?
Volume (cm³)	100	200
Temperature (K)	400	500

What's inside?

You will find out:

- About the different particles that are in atoms or given out by them
- About the properties of different types of radiation

Power for the future? Problems from the past?

Governments faced with trying to reduce the use of fossil fuels are considering building new nuclear power stations. In 2006 the world remembered the explosion at the Chernobyl nuclear power station in the Ukraine in 1986. This explosion continues to cause problems 20 years later. The use of **radioactive** materials to produce power remains a controversial subject.

FIGURE 1: Sheep are still affected by the fallout from the explosion at Chernobyl.

Going in

When you think about how the particles are arranged in solids, liquids or gases or about how a gas causes pressure, you don't need to worry about what the particles themselves are like. For these explanations you can think of atoms and molecules as little round balls. However, molecules are made up of atoms, and atoms themselves are made up of smaller particles.

- Atoms contain a very small **nucleus** which is surrounded by **electrons**.
- Electrons are negatively charged.
- The nucleus contains most of the mass of the atom but takes up less than about 1/1 000 000 000 000th of the volume of the atom.
- The nucleus contains **neutrons** and **protons**.
- Protons are positively charged and neutrons have no charge.
- The number of protons defines which element the atom is.
- A neutral atom contains the same number of protons and electrons.
- The number of protons is called the proton number or atomic number and given the symbol Z.
- The number of protons added to the number of neutrons is called the mass number or nucleon number or atomic mass and given the symbol A.
- The number of neutrons N can be quite different from the proton number Z.
- Atoms of the same element can have different numbers of neutrons.
- Atoms of a particular element which have different numbers of neutrons are called **isotopes**.

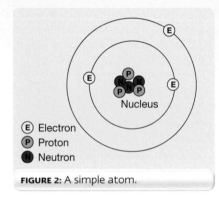

- (E) Electron
- (P) Proton
- (N) Neutron

FIGURE 2: A simple atom.

▥ QUESTIONS ▥

1   A carbon atom has 6 protons and 6 neutrons in its nucleus.

   a How many electrons will it have?
   b What is its proton number?
   c What is its mass number?

2   Another carbon atom has 8 neutrons in the nucleus.

   a How many protons will it have?
   b What is its mass number?
   c What name is given to these different carbon atoms?

...alpha particle   ...beta particle   ...electrons   ...gamma radiation   ...isotopes

Coming out

An isotope is described in terms of its mass number. For example: carbon-14 means the isotope of carbon with mass number 14 (6 protons and 8 neutrons). Some isotopes of common elements are radioactive. This means that they will emit **radiation**. Isotopes which don't emit radiation are stable.

- Radiation is emitted spontaneously. This means that nothing needs to happen to the atom to trigger it into giving out the radiation.
- Radioactivity is a random process: the emission of radiation can happen at any time for a particular atom and there is no way to predict when this will be.
- The radiation can remove electrons from atoms in surrounding material: it is said to be ionising radiation.
- There are three common types of radiation emitted by naturally occurring radioactive materials: alpha, beta and gamma radiation.

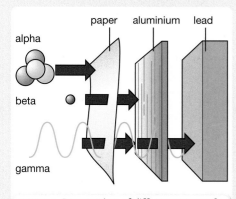

FIGURE 3: Penetration of different types of radiation.

- Alpha radiation: an **alpha particle** consists of two protons and two neutrons. It has a double positive charge and a relatively large mass. Alpha particles are easily stopped but cause a lot of ionisation on the way.
- Beta radiation: a **beta particle** consists of an electron. It is more penetrating than alpha radiation and causes less ionisation.
- **Gamma radiation**: gamma rays consist of high-energy electromagnetic rays. They are very difficult to stop even with thick lead or concrete and cause least ionisation.

Watch Out: Beta particles may be the same as electrons but they come from the nucleus, not the electrons around the nucleus.

Alpha, beta and gamma are not the only types of radiation

Other emissions

Alpha, beta and gamma are not the only types of radiation that can be emitted by nuclei.

- Neutrons can be ejected from the nucleus either spontaneously or when the nucleus is disturbed by some other event.
- Neutrons have no charge and do not directly ionise, but their interactions with atoms generally cause ionisation by some other process.
- Neutrons also stimulate radioactive behaviour in atoms including those which make up the human body, and are considered as dangerous as alpha, beta or gamma radiation.
- Because of their weak interaction with matter, neutrons are difficult to detect.
- Some nuclei emit **positrons**.
- Positrons have the same mass as electrons but a positive charge.

QUESTIONS

7 Neutrons can be more penetrating than gamma rays. Why?

8 How would a positron emission affect the nucleus compared to a beta emission?

9 Positrons have a medical use. Find out about positron emission tomography PET.

QUESTIONS

3 What charge does a beta particle have?
4 Which types of emission would affect the charge on the nucleus?
5 How would this affect the element the atom belonged to?
6 Which type of radiation would be the most dangerous if
   a it was given out by some radioactive material inside you?
   b it was coming from a source in the next room?

...neutron   ...nucleus   ...positron   ...proton   ...radiation   ...radioactive

Falling apart

You will find out:

- Which atoms give out alpha particles
- Which atoms give out beta particles
- What happens in the nucleus when these radiations are emitted

How big?

The heaviest naturally occurring atom is the uranium atom with a proton number of 92. The most common **isotope** of uranium is uranium-238 which has 92 **protons**, 92 **electrons** and 146 **neutrons**. The heaviest element generally accepted to have been created in the laboratory is ununhexium (symbol Uuh), with proton number 116. Credit for this element goes to the Joint Institute of Nuclear Research (JINR) at Dubna in Russia. Both these elements are unstable.

FIGURE 1: On the job at JINR.

Off track

Figure 2 is a graph showing neutron number against proton number for stable atoms.

- Stable atoms are atoms which do not **decay**: they do not emit radiation, they are not radioactive.
- The graph has been drawn up to the element with a proton number of 82 (after this, elements only have unstable isotopes).
- For small atoms, the stable isotopes have the same or nearly the same number of neutrons as protons and the graph is a straight line.
- For larger nuclei, stable isotopes have more neutrons than protons and the line curves upwards.
- The curve is broad in places because many elements have more than one stable isotope.
- Nuclei that do not lie on the curve are unstable. Nuclei that lie below the curve have too few neutrons to be stable. Nuclei that lie above the curve have too many neutrons to be stable.

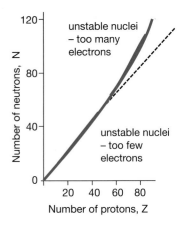

FIGURE 2: How the number of neutrons varies with the number of protons.

QUESTIONS

1. Use a periodic table to find the element with a proton number of 82.
2. Use the periodic table to list **three** elements that have no stable isotopes.
3. Carbon has two stable isotopes, Carbon-12 and Carbon-13. Carbon-14 is also relatively common.
   a. Find out how many protons and neutrons are there in each of these isotopes of carbon.
   b. Carbon-14 is radioactive. Why?
4. Suggest an isotope of carbon that would be unstable because it has too few neutrons.

...alpha particle ...beta particle ...decay ...electrons

Alpha decay

The nuclei of atoms heavier than lead (Z = 82) are all unstable.

- These atoms generally emit an **alpha particle**.
- Alpha particles contain two protons and two neutrons.
- Emitting an alpha particle reduces the proton number by 2:

$$Z \rightarrow Z - 2$$

- This means that the **nucleus** has changed into that of another element.
- Emitting an alpha particle reduces the mass number by 4:

$$A \rightarrow A - 4$$

Example

The isotope of uranium U-238 contains 92 protons and 146 neutrons.

- It emits an alpha particle.
- This changes it into the element with proton number 90, which is thorium.
- It also has lost two neutrons so the mass number reduces to 234.
- Uranium-238 becomes thorium-234.

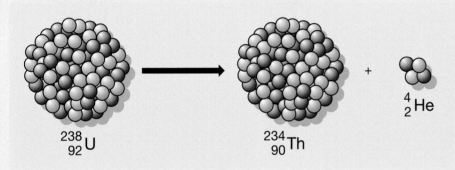

FIGURE 3: How uranium changes to thorium.

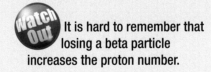 It is hard to remember that losing a beta particle increases the proton number.

The nuclei of atoms heavier than lead (Z = 82) are all unstable

Beta decay

Isotopes with proton numbers less than 82 may also be unstable and decay.

- Nuclei above the stability curve have too many neutrons to be stable.
- These nuclei will decay and emit a **beta particle**.
- A beta particle carries a negative charge.
- Emission of a beta particle increases the proton number by 1:

$$Z \rightarrow Z + 1$$

- This also causes the nucleus to become the nucleus of a different element.
- The mass number of the nucleus does not change.

Example

Iodine-131 emits a beta particle. The proton number goes up by one and the new nucleus is a nucleus of xenon.

QUESTIONS

5 Use a periodic table to find out what each of these isotopes will turn into when they emit an alpha particle:

  a Uranium-235

  b Polonium-215

  c Radon-220

  d Thorium-229

6 The following isotopes are produced by alpha particle emission. Use a periodic table to find out which isotopes they come from.

  a Uranium-235

  b Polonium-215

  c Radon-220

  d Thorium-229

QUESTIONS

7 Use the periodic table to find the proton number for iodine.

8 Use the periodic table to find the proton number for xenon.

9 What will be the mass number of the new nucleus?

...*isotope* ...*neutrons* ...*nucleus* ...*protons*

On the plus side

You will find out:

- What happens to nuclei below the stability curve
- What changes in the nucleus during positron decay
- More about positrons

Total annihilation

Positrons are antimatter particles. They are the antimatter equivalent of **electrons**. If a positron and electron collide, they will annihilate each other and their energy will be converted into electromagnetic radiation in the form of gamma rays. This is not just their kinetic energy, but the energy that made up their mass: $E = mc^2$. It also happens in reverse: a gamma ray may cause the production of an electron positron pair.

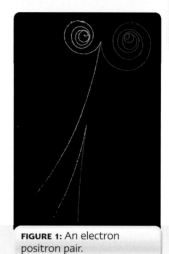

FIGURE 1: An electron positron pair.

Under the curve

The area under the stability curve contains the **isotopes** that have too few neutrons to be stable. Protons all have a positive charge and like charges repel so protons will not stay together unless they are held together. The presence of neutrons provides the 'glue' that holds these protons together, and if there are not enough neutrons, the nucleus will **decay**.

- For small atoms this happens when there are fewer neutrons than protons.
- For larger atoms there may be more neutrons than protons but not enough for the nucleus to be stable.
- Nuclei under the curve will decay and give out a positron.
- A positron is sometimes referred to as a beta plus (β+) particle and the **beta particle** is referred to as a beta minus (β−) particle.

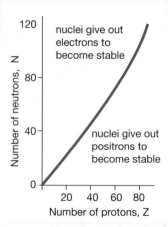

FIGURE 2: How the number of neutrons varies with the number of protons.

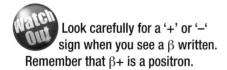 Look carefully for a '+' or '−' sign when you see a β written. Remember that β+ is a positron.

■■ QUESTIONS ■■

1 Which of these atoms would be likely to decay and emit a positron?

   a Sodium-22 (sodium-23 is stable)
   b Beryllium-10 (beryllium-9 is stable)
   c Cobalt-58 (cobalt-59 is stable)

2 What happens to the charge on the nucleus when a positron is emitted?

3 Use the periodic table to find out what one of the nuclei in question **1** changes into.

...beta particle   ...decay   ...electron

What's left?

A nucleus that has emitted a positron is changed by this process.

- A proton changes into a neutron.
- The proton number Z goes down by 1.

$$Z \rightarrow Z - 1$$

- This creates a different element.
- The neutron number N goes up by 1.
- The mass number A is unchanged.

Example

Potassium-40 has a nucleus with 19 protons and 21 neutrons. It can decay by emitting a positron.

- A positron carries a positive charge.
- Emission of a positron reduces the proton number by 1.

$$Z \rightarrow Z - 1, 19 \rightarrow 18$$

- This causes the nucleus to become the nucleus of a different element: the element with $Z = 18$ is argon.
- The mass number of the nucleus does not change so the isotope of argon is argon-40.
- This transition from potassium to argon is useful to geologists in dating rocks.

WOW FACTOR!

Carl Anderson, who discovered the positron, was only 31 when he received the Nobel Prize. The youngest ever winner was also a physicist: William Lawrence Bragg in 1915 at age 25.

Positively useful

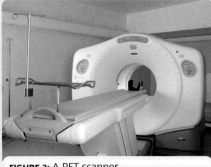

FIGURE 3: A PET scanner.

Positrons have an important application in medical imaging: Positron Emission Tomography or PET.

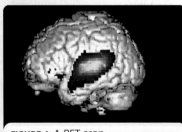

FIGURE 4: A PET scan.

- **PET scans** are used to diagnose and monitor cancers, study brain activity and to investigate blood flow to the heart muscle to look for signs of heart disease.
- Isotopes such as carbon-11, nitrogen-13, oxygen-15 and fluorine-18 have to be made in an instrument called a cyclotron near to where the scan will take place because of their very short half-lives.
- The radioactive material is incorporated into compounds used by the body such as water and glucose and injected into the patient.
- The distribution of the radioactive material in the body is detected by a scanner and can be analysed by the doctors.

QUESTIONS

4. Other isotopes that emit positrons include carbon-11, nitrogen-13, oxygen-15 and fluorine-18. Use the periodic table to write down what each of these will become.

5. Figure 1 shows an electron and positron moving in a magnetic field. They move in opposite directions. What fact about them could explain this difference?

6. Potassium-40 can also decay and emit an electron (β–). Use a periodic table to find out what it would then become.

QUESTIONS

7. What does 'very short half-lives' mean?

8. Why is having a short half-life a good thing for radioactive tracers?

9. Find out about the discovery of positrons.

SELF-CHECK ACTIVITY   CHALLENGE

CONTEXT

Jules Verne, a French author, wrote a book called *Journey to the Centre of the Earth*. It was translated into English in 1871 and tells the story of an expedition by three men to the Centre of the Earth. Before they embark on this they discuss their trip and they talk about temperature. The group leader, The Professor, argues against the notion that travelling deeper into the Earth necessarily means getting hotter.

At the time, there was a lot of speculation about the internal structure of the Earth, including the view that it was hollow (supported by Edmund Halley, whose name was given to the famous comet).

The core of the Earth is now known to be solid and fantastically hot – about 5500 °C. This isn't completely surprising, bearing in mind that the process that formed the Earth would have transferred a lot of energy into it. However, it took scientists a long time to work out why it should be so hot. The core is cooling down, but very slowly.

Some scientists argued that the Earth couldn't be very old, as the core was still so hot. At the same time, Charles Darwin was arguing the case for evolution and argued that the Earth had to be much older to allow for the gradual evolution of the huge range of animals, plants and protozoa that exist.

It is thought now that around half of the energy in the core is left from the formation of the Earth, some 4.6 billion years ago, and the other half is from radioactive materials. These are mainly uranium and thorium, which are releasing radioactive emissions. These emissions are then absorbed by surrounding rocks, a process which releases heat.

The uranium is composed of three major isotopes, ^{238}U, ^{235}U and ^{234}U. ^{238}U is the most abundant, has a half-life of 4.5×10^9 years and is an α emitter. Naturally-occurring thorium is composed of one isotope, ^{232}Th, with a half-life of 14×10^{10} billion years. It is a beta source.

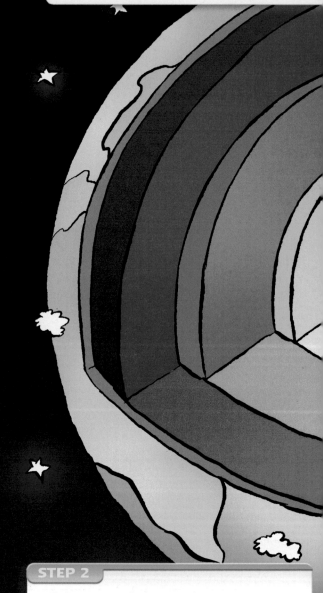

STEP 1

If the core of the Earth is so hot, why is it there are parts of the Earth's surface that are bitterly cold? With a hot core, why isn't it hot everywhere on the surface of the Earth?

STEP 2

If the core of the Earth is so radioactive, why is life on Earth still possible? Why hasn't the radioactivity killed all life forms?

STEP 3

What does the article mean when it says that uranium has three isotopes? If they were safe to handle, how could you tell which one was which?

STEP 4

^{238}U has a half-life of 4.5×10^9 years'. What does this mean? What has happened to the uranium at the end of that period?

STEP 5

How does the rate of emission compare between samples of ^{238}U and ^{232}Th which contain the same numbers of atoms?

Maximise your grade

These sentences show what you need to include in your work to achieve each grade. Use them to improve your work and be more successful.

Grade	Answer includes...
	Offer ideas as to why the hot core hasn't warmed up all of the surface.
F	Offer ideas as to why there are significant variations in the temperature of the surface of the crust despite the core being hot.
	Explain why the hot core hasn't warmed up all of the surface.
C	Explain why there are significant variations in the temperature of the surface of the crust despite the core being hot.
	Explain why radioactivity from the core hasn't made life on earth impossible.
A	Draw and label diagram to show emissions from uranium heating up neighbouring rocks.
	Explain concept of half-life and what it shows about the source.
	Compare half-life and emissions of thorium and uranium.

Signs of decay

You will find out:

- When gamma emission takes place and how it affects the nucleus
- A short-hand way of representing changes in a nucleus
- How to write nuclear equations

Looking inside

Gamma radiation is very penetrating and so can easily escape from inside the body. This is useful in medicine for diagnosing a variety of medical problems. The patient takes in a substance containing a radioactive isotope that emits gamma radiation. A gamma camera spots where the radiation is coming out of the body, enabling the doctors to see what is going on.

FIGURE 1: A gamma camera is a great help to doctors.

Gamma getting out

When a **nucleus** emits an **electron** (β- **decay**) or a **positron** (β+ decay) there may also be other changes in that nucleus.

- There may be a rearrangement within the nucleus: a 'settling down' into a lower-energy arrangement.
- This will result in energy being given out from the nucleus.
- This energy is released as a gamma ray.
- The emission of a gamma ray does not change the proton number or mass number of the nucleus.
- So the emission of a gamma ray does not cause a different element to be formed.
- Gamma radiation is the highest-frequency, shortest-wavelength, highest-energy electromagnetic radiation.
- There is an overlap in wavelength and frequency between gamma rays and X-rays, and there is no physical difference between gamma rays and X-rays of the same wavelength.
- The difference between gamma rays and X-rays is that gamma rays are emitted from the nuclei of atoms and X-rays are not.

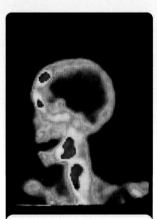

FIGURE 2: Images such as this can help doctors make a diagnosis.

QUESTIONS

1. What is one thing that will be the same for all gamma rays and X-rays?
2. Why are gamma rays considered to be the most dangerous part of the electromagnetic spectrum?
3. How is gamma emission different from alpha, beta plus or beta minus emission?
4. A nucleus emits a β-particle and a gamma ray. How will the new nucleus be different from the original one?

Watch Out Gamma rays are the most ionising radiation of the electromagnetic spectrum, but are less ionising than alpha and beta radiation.

Results of decay

The different forms of radioactive decay have different effects on the nuclei of the atoms involved. A radioactive nucleus (radionuclide) can be represented as follows:

$$^A_Z X$$

where X (or another letter which is not actually an element symbol) represents the symbol for the element. The different types of radioactive emission can be represented as follows:

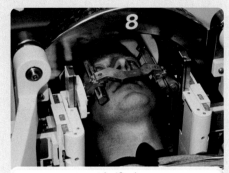

FIGURE 3: Gamma knife therapy.

- Alpha decay removes two **neutrons** and two **protons**, meaning that the proton number, Z, goes down by 2 and the mass number, A, goes down by 4. This change in the nucleus can be written as

$$^A_Z D \rightarrow ^{A-4}_{Z-2} E$$

  where D is the original or 'parent' nucleus and 'E' is the new or 'daughter' nucleus.

- Beta minus decay removes one neutron and adds one proton, meaning that the proton number, Z, goes up by 1 and the mass number, A, is unchanged. This change can be written as

$$^A_Z D \rightarrow ^A_{Z+1} E$$

- Beta plus decay adds one neutron and removes one proton, meaning that the proton number, Z, goes down 1 and the mass number, A, is unchanged. This change can be written as

$$^A_Z D \rightarrow ^A_{Z-1} E$$

- Gamma decay does not change the number of protons or neutrons meaning that the proton number, Z, and the mass number, A, are unchanged. This can be written as

$$^A_Z E \rightarrow ^A_Z E$$

Example:

A carbon-14 can emit a beta minus **particle** to become a nitrogen-14 nucleus:

$$^{14}_6 C \rightarrow ^{14}_7 N$$

DID YOU KNOW?

Technetium-99 exists in two forms. The most useful is technetium-99m which emits gamma to become technetium-99 (a beta and gamma emitter).

QUESTIONS

Use the periodic table to help you to write down the nuclear transition in each of these examples.

5 Sodium-22 emits a positron (β+).

6 Radon-220 emits an alpha particle.

7 Technetium-99 emits a gamma ray.

8 Phosphorus-32 emits an electron (β–).

Nuclear equations

Nuclear equations represent the transitions that occur during radioactive decay. They include all the particles involved and like chemical equations need to be balanced.

- The radiations emitted are represented as follows:
  Alpha: $^4_2 He$ which represents the fact that an alpha particle is identical to the nucleus of a helium atom.
  Beta minus: $^0_{-1} e$ which represent the fact that a β– is an electron.
  Beta plus: $^0_1 e$ which represent the fact that a β+ is a positron.
  Gamma: $^0_0 \gamma$
- The nuclear equation for alpha decay is as follows:

$$^A_Z D \rightarrow ^{A-4}_{Z-2} E + ^4_2 He$$

  The nuclear equation comes from including the symbol for the radiation as shown above to the change in the nucleus shown in 'Results of decay'.
- Notice that the totals for the mass number and proton number are the same on both sides of the equation: it is balanced.

QUESTIONS

9 Write the nuclear equation for beta minus emission.

10 Write the nuclear equation for beta plus emission.

11 Write the nuclear equation for gamma emission.

12 Write the nuclear equation for alpha decay of uranium-238.

...particle   ...positron   ...protons

Nothing cheap

You will find out:

- What is meant by the term 'fundamental particles'
- How scientists create particles that do not exist in normal matter
- How and why scientists from many countries work together in this research

CERN

This picture shows part of CERN, the European Organisation for Nuclear Research The name CERN comes from the French version of its original name '**C**onseil **E**uropéen pour la **R**echerche **N**ucléaire'. CERN is situated near Lake Geneva on the border between France and Switzerland.

FIGURE 1: The large circle marks the path of the one piece of apparatus at CERN.

The basics

CERN and other similar institutes around the world study subatomic particles. These make up everything we see.

Some of these particles are described by scientists as being 'fundamental'.

- **Fundamental particles** are not made up of other particles.
- Electrons and positrons are fundamental particles.
- Protons and neutrons are not fundamental particles because they are made up of even smaller particles.
- The structure and behaviour of particles can be investigated by accelerating them to high speeds and colliding them into each other.
- The particles are accelerated in machines called **particle accelerators**.
- A particle accelerator uses **electric fields** or **magnetic fields**, or both, to accelerate charged particles.
- One type of accelerator is the linear accelerator which is straight. The longest, at over 3 km, is the Stanford Linear Accelerator (SLAC) in California.
- Other accelerators are circular. A circular accelerator has the advantage that the particles can go round many times continuously accelerating, whereas in a linear accelerator they can only be accelerated once.
- The detectors that record the particles produced in collisions are as important as the accelerators themselves.

FIGURE 2: The Stanford Linear Accelerator.

QUESTIONS

1. Are alpha particles fundamental particles? Explain how you know.
2. What evidence do you have that neutrons and protons are not fundamental?
3. What type of accelerator is used at CERN?

...electric fields   ...fundamental particle

The Large Hadron Collider

The particle accelerators at CERN and other nuclear research facilities around the world accelerate particles to very high velocities and create very high-energy collisions. In these collisions many different particles are produced.

- The large circular tunnel at CERN currently houses the Large Electron Positron Collider (LEP).
- A new instrument is being built in the same tunnel, the Large Hadron Collider (LHC).

FIGURE 3: The Large Hadron Collider.

- The LHC will collide protons and ions at higher energies than has been possible before.
- The frequency of revolution of the particles in the LHC is about 11 kHz (11 000 revolutions per second).
- It is hoped that LHC will answer some of the remaining questions about the structure of matter, the events just after the Big Bang at the start of the universe and why particles have mass.
- To produce the very strong magnetic fields needed to accelerate these particles, superconducting electromagnets will be used.
- This requires the magnets to be kept close to absolute zero using helium to cool them.
- The LHC is the largest superconducting application in the world.

WOW FACTOR!

The length of the tunnel housing the LHC is nearly 27 km.

Time to share

CERN is intended to do pure science research: research for its own sake that may never have a commercial value. As the founding constitution states:

'The Organisation shall provide for collaboration among European States in nuclear research of a pure scientific and fundamental character, and in research essentially related thereto. The Organisation shall have no concern with work for military requirements and the results of its experimental and theoretical work shall be published or otherwise made generally available.'

QUESTIONS

7   Use the CERN website to find out answers to one of these questions:

    a How much does CERN cost to run?

    b How many countries are involved in the research?

    c How do scientists from different countries share the use of the equipment?

8   Find out about other facilities where particle research is carried out.

9   What do you think about scientific research for its own sake?

QUESTIONS

4   The LHC will be extremely expensive. What is one thing that has been done to save money in the construction process?

5   What is one aspect that will make the LHC very expensive to run even when construction is complete?

6   Use the information on this page to work out how fast the particles in the LHC will be travelling.

'Three quarks for Muster Mark'

You will find out:

- Why protons and neutrons are not described as fundamental particles
- How protons and neutrons are made up
- More about β– and β+ decay

What's in a name?

James Joyce was an Irish author who lived and worked during the first half of the twentieth century. Murray Gell-Mann is a physicist who won the Nobel Prize in 1969 for his theoretical work on **fundamental particles**. The connection? Gell-Mann used the word '**quark**' from Joyce's novel *Finnegan's Wake* to name the fundamental particle he described.

FIGURE 1: James Joyce.

Now't so strange as quarks

In the 1950s and 1960s experiments in **particle accelerators** were producing many new particles. There was a need to explain how all these particles fitted together and were related to each other. It was a very similar problem to explaining how all the different elements exist, a problem that was solved by the theory of atoms and the periodic table.

- Two scientists, Murray Gell-Mann and Yuval Ne'eman, independently organised all the known particles into families, depending on their properties.
- A pattern emerged which could be explained by assuming that particles such as **protons** and **neutrons** were made up of even smaller particles with a charge of –1/3 or +2/3 of the charge on an electron. Gell-Mann called these particles 'quarks'.
- A third scientist, George Zweig, came up with the same idea independently but did not publish his idea because a charge of less than that on the electron was thought to be impossible.
- In normal matter there are two types of quark: the 'up' quark and the 'down' quark.
- Neutrons each consist of two 'down' quarks (each charge –1/3) and one 'up' quark (charge +2/3).
- Protons each consist of two 'up' quarks (each charge +2/3) and one 'down' quark (charge –1/3).

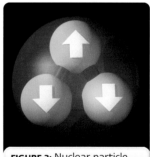

FIGURE 2: Murray Gell-Mann

FIGURE 3: Nuclear particle quark diagram.

QUESTIONS

1 What is a 'particle accelerator?
2 Which particle from the nucleus of an atom is represented by Figure 3?
3 Draw a diagram like Figure 3 for the other particle in the nucleus.

DID YOU KNOW?

George Zweig called his particles 'aces', but all scientists now refer to these particles as 'quarks'.

...*decay*   ...*fundamental particles*   ...*neutrons*   ...*nucleus*

Quarks and beta decay

Beta **decay** of both sorts causes changes in neutron and proton numbers in the **nucleus**. Beta decay can be described in terms of changes to quarks in the nucleus.

- β- decay changes a neutron into a proton.

- Two 'down' quarks and one 'up' quark become two 'up' quarks and one 'down' quark.

- This means that one 'down' quark has changed into an 'up' quark.

- β+ decay changes a proton into a neutron.

- Two 'up' quarks and one 'down' quark become two 'down' quarks and one 'up' quark.

- This means that one 'up' quark has changed into an 'down' quark.

- The 'down' quark has a larger mass than the 'up' quark.

- This means that neutrons have a larger mass than protons.

- This difference in mass is one reason why β− decay is more common than β+ decay. It is easier to make a proton out of a neutron than the other way round.

- It is possible to make a neutron out of a proton in the nucleus because mass and energy are really the same thing ($E = mc^2$) and energy in the nucleus can be changed into mass.

- A proton on its own will not decay to release a **positron**, but a neutron on its own can decay to release an electron. The half-life of free neutron decay is about 10 minutes.

> ### DID YOU KNOW?
> Some physicists believe that protons do decay: with a half-life of 10^{32} years.

Many other matters

The term 'normal matter' refers to atoms made up of protons, neutrons and electrons.

- Neutrons and protons are made from two types of quark.

- It follows that normal atoms seem to consist of two types of quark and electrons.

- There is however a third type of particle found in normal matter. This is called a neutrino.

- Neutrinos, like electrons, are fundamental particles and have little or no mass.

- As we have already seen, quarks are also fundamental particles. There are two types of quark that appear in normal matter, but there are several other types that appear in anti-matter.

QUESTIONS

4 Use quarks to explain why a neutron has no overall charge.

5 What is meant by a 'free' neutron or proton?

6 Protons in the nucleus behave differently from free protons. Give an example of this difference.

7 Neutrons in the nucleus behave differently from free neutrons. Give an example of this difference.

QUESTIONS

8 Find out about the 'standard model' of particle physics.

9 To anybody at all familiar with particle physics, the name of Gell-Mann is associated with 'quarks'. Do you think this is because his name for them caught on rather than Zweig's 'aces'?

You will find out:

- One way in which electrons can be removed from atoms
- About electron guns
- Some ways that an electron gun can be used

Early days

Electrons were discovered in 1897 by the English physicist J. J. Thomson. In fact as is often the case, Thomson built on the work of other physicists, many of whom had been experimenting with the 'cathode rays' as they were then called. It was Thomson's experiments, though, that provided the deciding evidence that electrons are negatively charged particles and that they are a fundamental building block of all atoms.

FIGURE 1: J. J. Thomson.

Load

Thomson used a 'cathode ray tube' during his experiments.

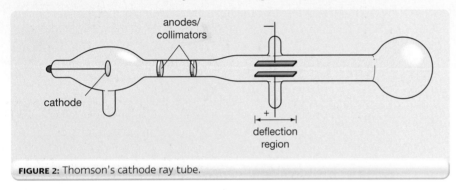

FIGURE 2: Thomson's cathode ray tube.

- This device produces electrons and makes them move through the tube.
- The electrons are removed from metal atoms in the **cathode** by heating the metal.
- This process is called '**thermionic emission**'.
- When a current passes through a metal, some electrical energy is transformed into heat energy.
- This raises the temperature of the metal.
- A high enough temperature allows some electrons to escape from the metal.
- We say that electrons have been 'boiled off' from the metal.
- To make this useful it is important that the electrons produced are able to reach the other end of the tube. To do this most of the air has to be removed from the tube.

▪▪ QUESTIONS ▪▪

1. What happens to the particles in a substance when it is heated?
2. Why is 'boiling off' a good description of what happens to the electrons?
3. Why would air in the tube stop the electrons from reaching the other end?

DID YOU KNOW?

Thomson originally called the particles corpuscles, only later using the name electrons.

Shoot

Normally, electrons produced from the metal will stay near the metal from which they are produced, falling back into the metal as other electrons are emitted. An electron gun is designed to move the electrons away from the metal and make them into a beam of electrons.

- The electrons can be repelled from the metal by connecting it to a negative voltage.

- The negatively charged metal is called a 'cathode'.

- The electrons can be accelerated by having a positive electrode nearby which will attract the electrons. This electrode is referred to as the '**accelerating anode**'.

- If electrons simply hit the anode, then a current flows across the vacuum but no **electron beam** is created.

- If the anode has a hole in it, the accelerated electrons will pass through the hole, forming a beam.

- Even Thomson's cathode ray tube has more than just a simple anode and many electron guns have quite a complicated structure for the anode to improve the beam produced.

- The beam can be aimed using charged plates. The beam will bend towards the positive plate and away from the negative plate.

- Increasing the voltage across the plates will increase the deflection of the beam.

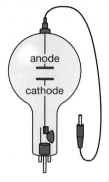

FIGURE 3: Thermionic diode.

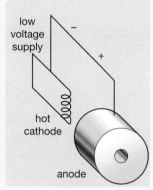

FIGURE 4: An electron gun.

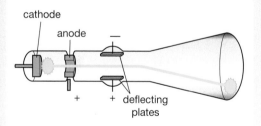

FIGURE 5: Electron gun with plates.

...oscilloscopes   ...thermionic emission

On target

Traditionally, devices with a screen such as a television, computer monitor and cathode ray **oscilloscopes** (CRO) have used an electron gun to create the image required.

Another important application of the electron gun is in the production of X-rays.

- The X-ray tube is similar to the thermionic diode in that the electrons hit the anode rather than pass through it.

- The anode is made of tungsten.

- The electrons are accelerated by a very high voltage, typically 100 000 V.

- The intensity of the X-rays can be increased by increasing the temperature of the cathode to produce more electrons.

- The energy of the X-rays can be increased by increasing the accelerating voltage.

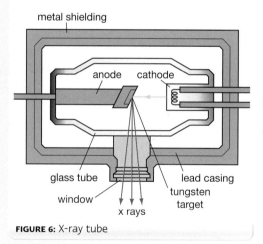

FIGURE 6: X-ray tube

QUESTIONS

4   If electrons leave a metal surface, what effect will that have on the surface?

5   If the electrons stay near the surface what will happen to them?

6   What is meant by the terms 'anode' and 'cathode'?

7   In what ways could an electron beam be improved?

QUESTIONS

8   How do **a** the frequency and **b** the wavelength of X-rays relate to their energy?

9   Find out how an electron gun is used in a traditional television set.

10 Find out about the technologies that are replacing television tubes.

Current calculations

You will find out:

- How a cathode ray oscilloscope works
- How to calculate electron speed
- How to calculate the current flowing in an electron beam

Go with the flow

Electrons in an **electron beam** are moving charges. An electric current is defined as a flow of electric charge. This means that an electron beam is an example of an electric current even though it is not flowing through wires. The electrons in the beam may be moving very quickly but it takes a very large number of electrons to make up a coulomb of charge and beam currents are usually small.

FIGURE 1: A beam of electrons.

Cathode ray oscilloscope

The **cathode ray oscilloscope** uses an electron beam to represent electrical signals in a visual way.

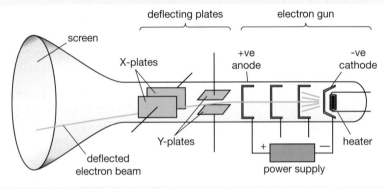

FIGURE 2: The structure of a cathode ray oscilloscope.

- The electron gun produces the electron beam which makes a bright spot on the phosphorescent screen (Figure 3a).
- The structure of the gun allows the beam to be focused and the brightness adjusted.
- The electrical signal being studied is connected across the Y plates. This means that as the voltage in the signal changes, the beam will move up and down and so will the spot on the screen.
- This would just produce a vertical line if the X plates are not used (Figure 3b).
- The X plates are controlled by the 'time-base' of the oscilloscope. An increasing voltage is repeatedly applied to these plates, switched off and then applied again.
- This makes the spot move repeatedly across the screen from one side to the other, giving a picture of the signal (Figure 3c).

(a)

(b)

(c)

FIGURE 3: Oscilloscope images.

QUESTIONS

1 What part of the beam are you looking at when you see the spot on an oscilloscope screen?

2 If the electric signal makes the top Y plate positive and the bottom Y plate negative, what will the beam do?

3 Why does an A.C. signal make a vertical line on the screen?

4 Why does switching the time-base on change a vertical line into a wave pattern?

...cathode ray oscilloscope   ...electron beam

Electrons on the move

Voltage or potential difference measures the amount of energy changed per unit charge. This may be the amount of energy transformed into electrical energy in a battery or the amount of energy transformed into light and heat in a bulb.

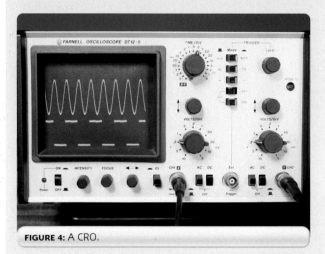

FIGURE 4: A CRO.

DID YOU KNOW?

J. J. Thomson measured the value of charge to mass ratio for electrons during his experiments at the end of the 19th century.

- We write $E = q \times V$
  where E is the energy changed in joules (J), V is the voltage in volts (V) and q is the charge in coulombs (C).
- The charge on a single electron is represented by the symbol e, so for one electron the energy gained as it passes through a potential difference of V volts is given by

$$E = e \times V$$

- This energy is transformed into the **kinetic energy** of the electron and we can write this as

$$KE = e \times V$$

Electric current is the rate of flow of electric charge:

$$I = q/t$$

where I is the current in amperes (A), q is the charge in coulombs (C) and t is the time in seconds (s) for that charge to pass.

- For an electron beam the total charge on a number of electrons is given by

$$q = ne$$

where n is the number of electrons and e is the charge on each electron.

- Current will then be found from

$$I = ne/t$$

- The quantity n/t is the rate of flow of electrons, the number of electrons passing per second.

QUESTIONS

5 The charge on an electron is 1.6×10^{-19} C. How many electrons are there in 1 C of charge?

6 How much energy in joules is given to an electron as it is accelerated by a voltage of 1 V?

7 There are 625 000 000 000 electrons hitting the anode in a vacuum diode every 10 seconds.
  a What is the rate of electron flow?
  b What current is flowing?

How fast?

This equation $KE = e \times V$ can be used to calculate the speed of electrons using the principle of conservation of energy and the equation for kinetic energy.

- $KE = \frac{1}{2}mv^2$ where v is the electron speed in metres per second (m/s) and m is its mass in kilograms (kg).

- Therefore

$$\frac{1}{2}mv^2 = e \times V$$

- This can be rearranged to get

$$v^2 = 2eV/m$$

- To calculate v you need to know the mass and charge of an electron or at least the value of e/m, the charge to mass ratio.

QUESTIONS

8 What are the units for charge/mass?

9 Calculate the value of charge/mass for an electron if its mass is 9.1×10^{-31} kg.

10 An electron is accelerated through a voltage of 5000 V.
  Calculate
  a the kinetic energy of the electron
  b its velocity.

...*kinetic energy*

Unit summary

Concept map

Atomic nuclei contain protons and neutrons.
Some nuclei are unstable and decay, giving out alpha, beta or gamma radiation.

At absolute zero particle movement ceases.
Increasing the temperature increases the speed of particle movement.
In a gas the Kelvin temperature is directly proportional to the average kinetic energy of its particles.

Temperature can be measured on the Kelvin scale.
$0\,K = -273\,°C$
$273\,K = 0\,°C$

Neutrons and positrons are other types of radiation that can be emitted.

A positron is a positively charged particle with the same mass as the electron.

$$\frac{\text{Pressure}}{\text{Temperature (Kelvin)}} = constant$$

$$\frac{P}{T} = constant$$

$$\frac{\text{Volume}}{\text{Temperature (Kelvin)}} = constant$$

$$\frac{P_1 V_1}{T_1} = \frac{P_2 V_2}{T_2}$$

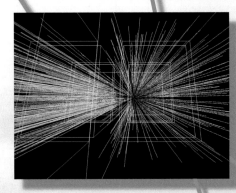

The number of neutrons (N) in nucleus can plotted against the number of protons (Z) for stable isotopes.
An isotope that does not lie on this curve it will be unstable and radioactive.
An isotope that lies above the curve has too many neutrons to be stable and will undergo β– decay.
An isotope that lies below the curve has too few neutrons to be stable and will undergo β+ decay.

In β– decay, a neutron becomes a proton plus an electron.
In β+ decay, a proton becomes a neutron plus a positron.

Beams of electrons can be produced using an electron gun.

Electron guns have been used in televisions, cathode ray oscilloscopes and X-ray tubes.

Alpha decay changes the proton and mass number, forming a new element.
β– or β+ decay changes the proton number, forming a new element.
Gamma decay does not change proton or mass number or form a new element.

As a result of β– or β+ decay nuclei often undergo rearrangement with energy emitted as gamma radiation.

Some particles are fundamental and some are not.
Electrons are fundamental. Neutrons and protons are made of quarks and are not fundamental.

The nature of particles is investigated using particle accelerators. This is a very expensive process and physicists from different universities and different countries work together in shared facilities.

Beta (+ and –) decay can be explained in terms of quarks.

Unit quiz

1 What is meant by the term absolute zero?

2 Why can there not be a lower temperature than 0 K?

3 Complete this table by writing in the equivalent measurement

Temperature in Kelvin	Temperature in °C
0 K	
100 K	
273 K	
300 K	
	0 °C
	37 °C
	50 °C
	100 °C

4 Sketch a graph to show how pressure varies with Kelvin temperature for a sample of gas.

5 Explain why pressure increases with temperature in terms of the motion of particles in the gas.

6 Sketch graphs to show **a)** how volume changes with Kelvin temperature for a gas and **b)** how pressure varies with volume for a gas at constant temperature.

7 State the general (ideal) gas equation and explain what each symbol stands for.

8 Describe what makes up each of these types of radiation: alpha (α) beta minus ($\beta-$), gamma (γ), beta plus ($\beta+$).

9 Describe how the nucleus of an atom is changed by emitting each type of radiation in question 8.

10 What types of nuclei will emit
   a) a beta plus particle ($\beta+$)?
   b) a beta minus particle ($\beta-$)?

11 Complete the following nuclear equations:
   $$^{14}_{6}C \rightarrow\ ^{?}_{?}N +\ ^{0}_{-1}e$$
   $$^{226}_{?}Ra \rightarrow\ ^{?}_{86}Rn +\ ^{4}_{2}\alpha$$

12 Explain what a particle accelerator is.

13 Explain why facilities for research into nuclear physics are used by scientists from many different universities and different countries.

14 **a)** What is meant by the term 'fundamental particle'?
   b) Give three examples of fundamental particles.
   c) Give three examples of particles which are not fundamental particles.

15 Describe in terms of quarks
   a) the difference between protons and neutrons
   b) $\beta-$ emission
   c) $\beta+$ emission.

16 In an electron gun how are electrons produced from a metal?

17 List three applications of electron guns.

18 State the equation relating kinetic energy of an electron to accelerating voltage.

19 How are X-rays different from gamma rays?

20 In an X-ray tube what controls the frequency of X-rays produced?

Numeracy activity

This table shows the pressure and volume of a sample of gas which is compressed at constant temperature.

Pressure (kPa)	100	112	125	143	166	201	248
Volume (cm^3)	50	45	40	35	30	25	20

QUESTIONS

1 Draw a graph of pressure against volume for this sample of gas.

2 Use your graph to find and compare the pressures for volumes of 24 cm^3 and 48 cm^3.

3 What is the relationship between pressure and volume as shown from your graph?

4 What graph could you plot using the results from this experiment to get a straight line through the origin (a graph showing direct proportionality)?

Exam practice

Exam practice questions

1 The graph shows how the stability of a nucleus varies as the proportion of neutrons and protons vary.

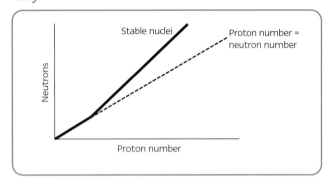

A Nuclei with fewer than 20 protons are stable if the proton : neutron ratio is 1 : 1.

Explain why oxygen $^{18}O_8$ is unstable. [1]

B $^{18}O_8$ can change to a stable nucleus by emitting a beta particle. Explain how this happens. [2]

C Mark on the graph where you would expect alpha decay to occur. [1]

D State how excess energy from the nucleus can be released during β decay. [1]

2 **A** Explain what is meant by a fundamental particle, giving an example. [3]

B Neutrons can undergo β- decay. Describe the changes that occur inside the neutron as a result. [2]

C What are the particles that result from β- decay? [2]

3 **A** The diagram shows an electron gun. Indicate on the diagram where thermionic emission takes place. [1]

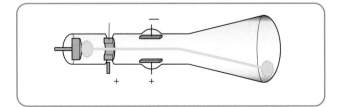

B Describe how the gun can be used to produce a beam of electrons. [3]

C Explain how electron guns are used to produce X-rays. [3]

D Calculate the kinetic energy gained by an electron which is accelerated by a potential difference of 5000 V.

The electronic charge is 1.6×10^{-19} C. [2]

4 The table shows five different types of nuclear radiation.

A Explain what is meant by nuclear radiation. [2]

B Complete the table to show the properties of the nuclear radiation. [5]

Type of radiation	Mass	Charge
alpha	4	
beta	negligible	
gamma		0
positron		+1
neutron	1	

(Total 28 marks)

The diagram shows a balloon that has been inflated.

a Explain why the air in the balloon would be absolute zero. [2]

b Use the idea of particles to explain why the pressure inside the balloon increases when it is blown up. [1]

c The volume of the balloon is 2000 cm³ when the temperature is 300 K and the pressure is 80 kPa.

Calculate the new volume if the temperature is changed to 330 K and the pressure stays constant. [4]

Not correct. The molecules have no kinetic energy at absolute zero and take up a negligible volume. It is their constant movement when heated that causes the gas to have a measurable volume.

a *It would be zero because the gas would have escaped.*

b *There are more particles inside the balloon.*

Correct for 1 mark.

c $\dfrac{P_1 V_1}{T_1} = \dfrac{P_2 V_2}{T_2}$

P stays the same so $\dfrac{V_1}{T_1} = \dfrac{V_2}{T_2}$

$V_2 = \dfrac{V_1 T_2}{T_1}$

$= 2 \times \dfrac{280}{300}$

$= 1.87$

Correct working and laid out well. The student forgot to include units, however, and so loses 1 mark.

Overall Grade: C

How to get an A

Always remember to get the details correct. Include units as often as necessary, and show detailed working. It will help you to focus on the answer as well as giving the examiner a chance to award marks even if you make a mistake at the end of the calculation.

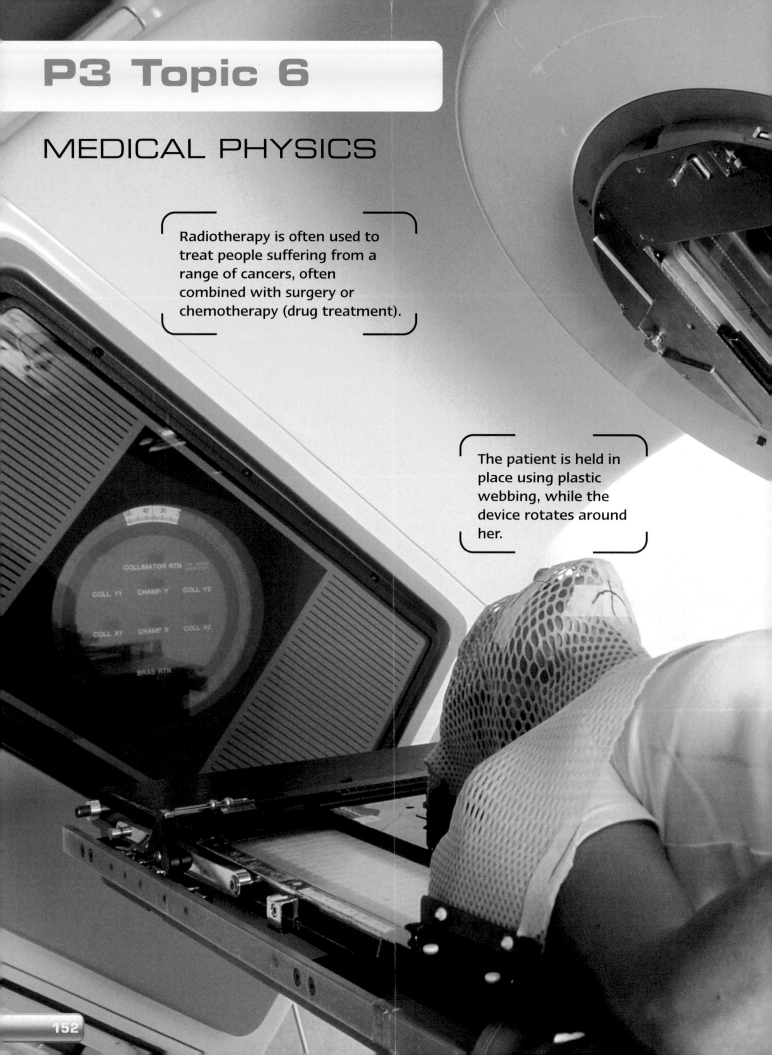

P3 Topic 6

MEDICAL PHYSICS

Radiotherapy is often used to treat people suffering from a range of cancers, often combined with surgery or chemotherapy (drug treatment).

The patient is held in place using plastic webbing, while the device rotates around her.

COLLIMATOR RTN

COLL Y1   CHAMP Y   COLL Y2

COLL X1   CHAMP X   COLL X2

BRAS RTN

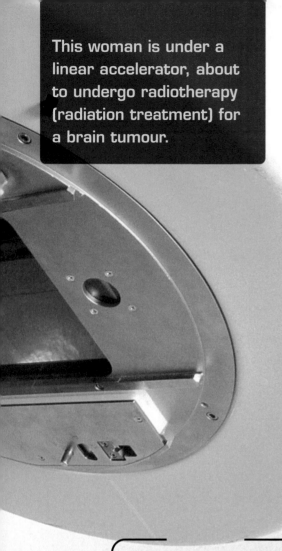

This woman is under a linear accelerator, about to undergo radiotherapy (radiation treatment) for a brain tumour.

Linear accelerators are used as a source of high-voltage X-rays, which can penetrate the body to a great depth and deliver a precisely targeted dose of radiation.

Laser beams (red lines) are used to identify the area to be treated.

Bend it

You will find out:

- The meaning of refraction
- That total internal reflection allows light to be transmitted along an optical fibre
- How optic fibres are used in endoscopes

Looking inside you

This doctor is looking down an **endoscope** to see inside a patient's stomach without needing to carry out surgery. It uses an **optical fibre**.

Optical fibres have revolutionised medicine. Without them, keyhole surgery (surgery without large incisions) would not be possible.

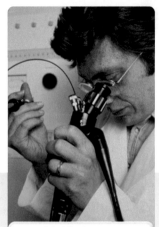

FIGURE 1: Why is an endoscope so useful?

Refraction

The speed of a ray of light will change when it enters a substance of different optical density.

This change in speed may cause a change in the direction of the ray of light. This change in direction is called **refraction**.

Trapped light

Light can stay inside materials such as glass, Perspex or water. These materials are denser than air.

Light is reflected at the boundary between the material and the air. This is known as **total internal reflection**.

Light, infrared radiation or a laser beam can travel along a very thin piece of solid glass called an optical fibre. Every time the light meets the boundary with air, it is reflected back into the fibre.

Optical fibres are very flexible, even though they are made of glass, as they are so thin.

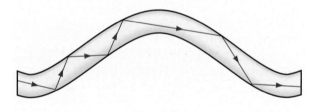

FIGURE 2: Total internal reflection allows the light to travel round the bend

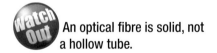 An optical fibre is solid, not a hollow tube.

▉▉ QUESTIONS ▉▉

1 What is the relationship between the angle of incidence and the angle of reflection?

2 Why does an optical fibre need to be flexible to be used in an endoscope?

...critical angle   ...endoscope   ...optical fibre

Critical angle

When light is passing from a more dense material, such as glass, into a less dense material, such as air, the angle of refraction is greater than the angle of incidence.

If the angle of incidence is increased, it is possible for the angle of refraction to be a right angle (90°). When this happens, the angle of incidence is called the **critical angle**.

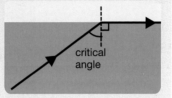

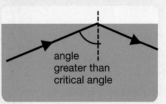

Total internal reflection

If the angle of incidence is increased even more, *all* the light is reflected back inside the more dense material. This is total internal reflection.

This allows light to travel along an optical fibre by a series of reflections.

An optical fibre consists of a glass core (a diameter of about 0.01 mm is typical) surrounded by a coating, called the cladding, to improve reflection.

Total internal reflection will occur only if the angle of incidence is greater than the critical angle. As optical fibres are very thin, the angle of incidence is bound to be large (over 80°). This means total internal reflection occurs repeatedly as light travels along the optical fibre.

Endoscopes

An endoscope contains optical fibres to enable a doctor to look inside the body. Light passes along the outer fibres and lights up the inside of the patient. The reflected light passes back along the inner fibres and the image is viewed through an eyepiece which collects and magnifies it. A camera is often attached to the eyepiece.

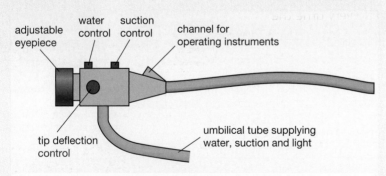

FIGURE 3: An endoscope uses optical fibres to look inside the body. It is about 10 mm in diameter and can be up to 2 m long.

QUESTIONS

3   What is meant by 'critical angle'?

4   Why cannot total internal reflection occur when light passes from air to glass?

5   Why does an endoscope require a powerful light source?

More about optical fibres

The bundle of optical fibres that carries light from the area under examination to form an image must be coherent. This means the fibres are in the same relative positions at each end of the bundle. This is essential for transmitting images. The bundle of optic fibres illuminating the inside of the patient is not coherent.

Uses of endoscopes

Endoscopes allow doctors to view inaccessible parts of the body. They can be equipped with tiny scalpels and other instruments to carry out surgical procedures – keyhole surgery. Uses include:

- carrying out biopsies, i.e. removing suspect tissue to test for malignancy
- providing visual evidence of the presence of ulcers, tumours and internal bleeding
- removing gallstones.

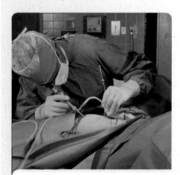

FIGURE 4: Surgeon using a laparoscope to examine the inside of a patient's abdomen.

QUESTIONS

6   Why must some bundles of optical fibres in an endoscope be coherent while others are not coherent?

7   Endoscopes usually have many thin fibres rather than just one thick fibre. Suggest why.

8   Give **two** advantages of keyhole surgery compared with traditional methods.

Checking on you

You will find out:
- That a 'pulse oximeter' measures the pulse and the oxygen saturation level in arterial blood
- About the principles and use of pulse oximetry

Monitoring patients

When a person is very ill or undergoing surgery it is important to monitor them closely at all times. A **pulse oximeter** can be attached to a finger and connected to a microprocessor that gives up-to-date information on the patient's cardio-respiratory system.

Most pulse oximeters give out an audible tone, the pitch of which depends on the oxygen level in the blood in the arteries. This gives nurses an instant warning if all is not well.

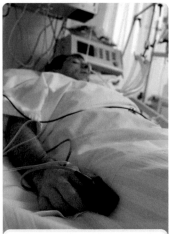

FIGURE 1: Pulse oximeter on the finger of a patient in a hospital's intensive care ward.

What are 'normal' pulse rates?

- The average resting heart rate for an adult is between 60 and 100 beats per minute. Well-conditioned athletes can achieve between 40 and 60 beats per minute.
- The maximum pulse rate is 220 minus your age. The target for a healthy pulse rate during, or just after, exercise, is 60–80% of this.

Pulse oximetry

A pulse oximeter is worn on the finger. As well as the pulse rate, it tells the doctor how well the blood is getting oxygen.

Pulse oximeters are now used routinely

- in intensive care
- during anaesthesia
- in the recovery room.

There are also portable versions as shown here. These are ideal for overnight sleep screening and making measurements when walking.

FIGURE 2: What is the advantage of this version of a pulse oximeter?

QUESTIONS

1 Calculate your maximum pulse rate.
2 Why do some pulse oximeters emit a sound of varying pitch?

...artery   ...haemoglobin   ...light-emitting diode (LED)

What does a pulse oximeter measure?

A pulse oximeter:

- measures the pulse rate, in beats per minute
- indirectly measures the amount of oxygen in a patient's blood.

It is often attached to a monitor so staff can directly note the readings at all times.

How does it work?

- The coloured substance in blood (**haemoglobin**) is also its carrier of oxygen.
- The absorption of visible light by haemoglobin varies with its oxygenation.
- Light from a **light-emitting diode (LED)** is directed at a patient's finger or ear lobe and a **photodetector** (light detector) placed on the other side to receive the light that is **transmitted** through it.
- By comparing the intensity of the light before, I_{in}, and after, I_{out}, passing through an **artery** the degree of oxygenation can be found.

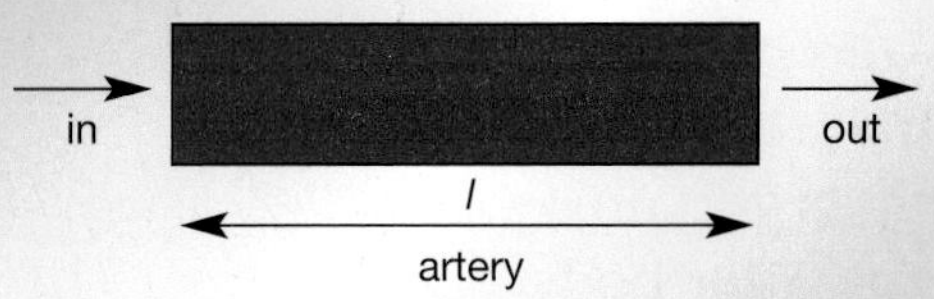

FIGURE 3: The intensity of the light coming out of an artery is not the same as the intensity going in.

Intensity, I, is the power of radiation falling on unit area of surface:

$$I = \text{power} / \text{area}$$

The unit of intensity is W/m^2.
Under normal conditions arterial blood is 97% saturated.

A standardisation graph is obtained by getting volunteers to breathe in gases which give reduced levels of oxygen. As it is unethical to go below 70% **saturation**, results below this level are unreliable.

Uses of pulse oximetry

In addition to the routine use of pulse oximetry during surgery and in intensive care units, pulse oximetry is also used:

- in cases of respiratory failure to monitor how well the arterial blood is oxygenated
- in neonatal intensive care since many premature babies require a ventilator to help them to breathe
- when investigating sleep disorders.

Watch Out A pulse oximeter does not actually measure the oxygen content of the blood.

QUESTIONS

3 Suggest why a pulse oximeter is usually attached to a fingertip or earlobe.

4 Explain why a pulse oximeter is better than frequent monitoring of a patient's pulse rate by a nurse.

5 **a** What is a light-emitting diode?

b Calculate the intensity when a LED of power 6 W is shone on an area of 2 mm².

More about pulse oximeters

Oxygen is carried in the blood stream mainly bound to haemoglobin. One molecule of haemoglobin can carry up to four molecules of oxygen. It would then be described as saturated. The average percentage saturation of haemoglobin molecules in a blood sample is the oxygen saturation of the blood. This is what is actually measured by a pulse oximeter.

How it works

- The light signal through the tissues varies because of the changing volume of blood in the arteries with each pulse beat. This is separated by the microprocessor from the steady light absorption by other tissues.
- The absorption of light at two different wavelengths by haemoglobin differs depending on its degree of oxygenation. This is because the two common forms of the molecule, oxidised haemoglobin (HbO_2) and reduced haemoglobin (Hb), have very different optical spectra in the range 500–1000 nm.

The probe contains two LEDs, one in the visible red (660 nm) and the other in the **infrared** (940 nm) region and a photodetector to detect the light or infrared that has passed through the patient's tissues.

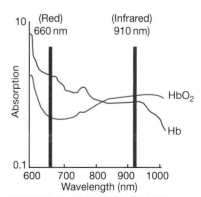

FIGURE 4: How the spectra of oxidised haemoglobin and reduced haemoglobin differ.

QUESTIONS

6 Why do pulse oximeters not use radiation of wavelength 800 nm?

Using energy

You will find out:
- That work done is equal to energy transferred
- How to calculate work done
- How to calculate power
- About basal metabolic rate

Exercise

We all need to exercise to keep fit and healthy. This may be gentle or strenuous, competitive or just for fun, such as trampolining, attending aerobics classes, swimming, playing football or squash. It doesn't matter what you choose to do as long as you enjoy it! Strenuous work-outs use lots of energy. Your body also needs energy when you are asleep just to keep you alive.

FIGURE 1: Playing football is good for you, as well as fun!

Work, energy and power

Work is done whenever a force moves. The amount of work done depends on:

- the size of the force
- the distance moved in the direction in which the force acts.

When we climb stairs or jump in the air, the force moved is our weight. Weight is due to gravitational attraction so acts towards the centre of the Earth.

We need **energy** to do work. We get our energy from the food we eat.

The more work we do the more energy we need.

Work done = energy transferred

Work and energy are measured in **joules** (J).

Power is the rate of doing work or transferring energy.

Power is measured in **watts** (W) or kilowatts (kW). 1 kW = 1000 W.

FIGURE 2: The jumping clown does work to raise his weight. Where does he get the energy from to jump?

EXAM HINTS AND TIPS

Always check units when doing calculations on work, power and energy.

DID YOU KNOW?

The daily energy requirement of an adult is usually in the range 1.0 to 1.6 MJ.

QUESTIONS

1. What units are used to measure **a** weight, **b** work, **c** energy and **d** power?
2. Write down **two** things that affect the amount of work done by a force.
3. Sam is walking on the level. Explain why he does no work to move his weight.

...basal metabolic rate (BMR)   ...energy   ...joules

Calculating work done and power

Work done = force × distance moved (in the direction of the force)

$$W = F \times s$$

$$\text{Power} = \frac{\text{Work done}}{\text{Time taken}} \qquad P = \frac{W}{t}$$

Emma runs up a flight of 16 stairs, each 0.2 m high, in 5 s. She weighs 500 N.

The vertical height she rises = 16 × 0.2 = 3.2 m.

Work done = force x distance moved in the direction of the force

Work done = 500 × 3.2 = 1600 J

$$\text{Power} = \frac{\text{work done}}{\text{time}} = \frac{1600}{5} = 320\,\text{W}$$

If Emma walks up the stairs she takes 8 s.

Her power then is

$$\frac{1600}{8} = 200\,\text{W}$$

FIGURE 3: Going up stairs needs power.

Basal metabolic rate (BMR)

Your body needs a regular intake of energy to perform all the tasks you do. Emma needed 1600 J of energy to run up the stairs.

You get this energy from the food that you eat – carbohydrates, fats and proteins. The rate at which the body uses this energy is called the metabolic rate.

The body uses energy even when resting. For example, it needs to

- keep the heart beating and keep the brain and nerves functioning
- sustain breathing
- repair tissues.

The **basal metabolic rate (BMR)** is the rate at which the body uses energy when it is at rest. It depends on a person's height, weight, age, sex and activity.

In general it is

- greater for children than for adults, as children need extra energy for growing
- greater for men than for women, as men have less body fat so use more energy to maintain body temperature
- greater for people with a large surface area.

BMR values can be given in
- kilojoules per hour per square metre of body surface (kJ/h/m^2)
- calories per day, where 1 calorie = 4200 J.

QUESTIONS

4   Ashna has a mass of 60 kg. She runs up a 20 m slope, rising 4 m vertically, in 8 s. Calculate her power. [Take $g = 10\,\text{N/kg}$.]

5   Use your knowledge of physics to explain why the BMR is **a** greater for men than for women, and **b** greater for people with a large surface area.

6   Tom is found to be using energy at a rate of 80 W. Tables show that, with his height and weight, his surface area is about $2\,\text{m}^2$. Estimate his BMR in kJ/h/m^2.

The energy balance

The rate at which the body

- produces energy depends on its volume
- loses energy depends on its surface area.

This means that the surface area : volume ratio of the body affects the amount of food a person needs to maintain a healthy balance.

Our daily energy requirement depends not only on our BMR but on our lifestyle and surroundings:

- the amount of clothes we wear
- the temperature of our surroundings
- the amount of exercise we do.

We use energy to maintain normal body temperature – to keep warm when cold and to keep cool when hot.

Activity	Typical rate of energy consumption in W
resting	80
walking	250
swimming	450
playing football	600
running fast	1000

Getting the energy balance right between exercise and good food is an essential part of staying fit and healthy.

DID YOU KNOW?

Thyroxin is a hormone that controls the metabolic activity within the body.

QUESTIONS

7   Explain why babies are at greater risk of hypothermia than adults.

8   Dean expends 1.5 MJ (1.5×10^6 J) of energy during a 30 minute run. His muscles are 30% efficient. Calculate his rate of production of thermal energy during his run. What happens to this energy?

Heartbeat

You will find out:

- About the link between frequency and time period for oscillatory motion
- How muscle cells can generate potential differences
- How action potentials can be measured and used to monitor heart action
- About an electrocardiogram (ECG)

Heart monitoring

The **electrocardiogram (ECG)** is an important diagnostic tool in medicine, recording the electrical activity of the heart. Electrocardiography electrodes are placed at specific points on the chest.

The heart is a hollow muscular organ that pumps blood around the body. The muscular activity is produced by a rhythmic electrical activity, which is being recorded by these electrodes. Many cardiac diseases show characteristic alterations to a normal ECG trace.

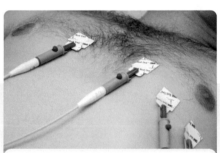

FIGURE 1: Four of the six chest electrodes used in an ECG examination are seen here.

Oscillations

Frequency (f) is the number of complete waves, or **oscillations**, in a second.

Frequency is measured in **hertz** (Hz).

A frequency of 50 Hz means there are 50 oscillations in a second.

The time period (T) is the time for one complete oscillation. If there are 50 complete oscillations in a second the time for one oscillation is 1/50 = 0.02 s.

$$\text{Frequency} = \frac{1}{\text{Time period}}$$

$$f = \frac{1}{T}$$

A normal heart beats regularly as it pumps blood around the body. An electrocardiogram (ECG) measures the electrical activity of the heart. Any abnormalities can be seen and identified.

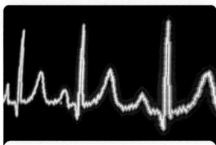

FIGURE 2: An ECG of a healthy heart.

DID YOU KNOW?

There are about 268 000 heart attacks a year in the UK, which equates to one every two minutes.

▥ QUESTIONS ▥

1   Middle C has a frequency of 256 Hz. What does this mean?
2   Dushi shakes one end of a rope, making 8 waves in 2 s.
    a   What is the frequency of the wave?
    b   What is the time period of the wave?

WOW FACTOR!

The first ECG was carried out in 1903.

...*action potential* ...*electrocardiogram (ECG)* ...*electrodes*

How the heart works

The heart is a double pump. It has four chambers – the right and left atria and the right and left ventricles.

The regular pumping action of the heart is controlled by special muscle cells. These are activated by changes in electrical potentials. This is the **action potential** of the heart.

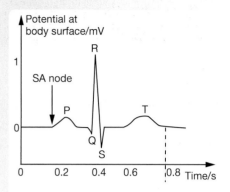

FIGURE 3: Model of heart function.

This electrical stimulus makes the heart muscle contract.

- Right-hand chambers take blood *from* the body, which is low in oxygen, and pass it *to* the lungs.
- Left-hand chambers take oxygen-rich blood *from* the lungs and pass it *to* the body.

Contraction of heart

- The sino-atrial (SA) node, or pacemaker, in the right atrium produces an electrical pulse about 70 times a minute. This makes the left and right atria contract and pump blood into the left and right ventricles.
- The pulse passes to the atrio-ventricular (AV) node. The two ventricles contract and force blood into the arteries and round the body.
- Two one-way valves, the bicuspid and tricuspid, prevent the blood returning to the atria.

Relaxation of heart

- The ventricle nerves and muscles relax and the cycle starts again.
- Two one-way valves in the arteries, the semilunar valves, prevent blood being forced back into the ventricles.

This cycle represents one heartbeat.

Measuring the ECG

- Six electrodes (usually silver) are taped to the chest and others to two limbs. (The right leg is not used as it is too far from the heart.)
- The skin is smeared with a conductive gel and hair and dead skin are removed from contact areas.
- **Potential differences** between the chest and limb electrodes are recorded.
- A computer produces a trace of potential difference against time on the screen. This is an electrocardiogram, or ECG. (The waveform depends on the patient as well as on the placing of the electrodes.)

QUESTIONS

3 The SA node in a patient produces an electrical pulse 72 times a minute. Calculate **a** its frequency in hertz and **b** its time period.

4 Suggest why the walls of the left ventricle are much stronger than the others.

5 Why are hairs and dead skin removed before attaching the ECG electrodes?

6 Why are the valves in the heart all one-way?

Looking at a normal ECG

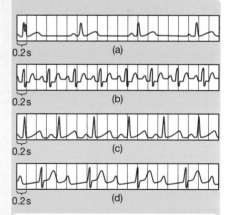

FIGURE 4: An ECG of a single heartbeat.

The action potential links with the graph:

- P: contraction of the atria
- QRS: contraction of the ventricles
- T: relaxation of the ventricles.

The time period for a cycle depends on the body's demands, increasing during strenuous physical activity.

An ECG can be taken when the patient is resting or active, for instance on a treadmill or exercise bike.

Irregular ECG traces

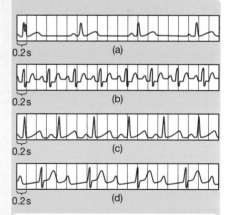

FIGURE 5: (a) Bradycardia (slow heart rate); (b) tachycardia (high heart rate); (c) arrhythmia (uneven heart rate) and (d) partial block (a gap between the P and QRS contractions).

QUESTIONS

7 Estimate the pulse rates per minute from the traces (a) to (d) above.

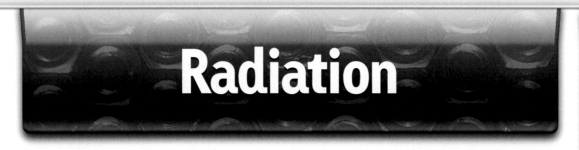

Radiation

You will find out:

- More about the intensity of radiation
- What affects the intensity of radiation received
- The effects of radiation on living matter

Radiation

For many young people the mobile phone is the most brilliant invention of the last century. The advent of the camera phone has made it an even more prized possession. We have become users of an ever-growing range of technologies, but we are constantly faced with media-led frenzies about the dangers associated with various forms of radiation. We know about the dangers of X-rays and gamma radiation, but the evidence on microwave radiation from mobile phones or the radiation from overhead power lines is still inconclusive.

FIGURE 1: Are mobile phones a health hazard?

What is radiation?

Radiation is used to describe any form of **energy** that spreads out from a source. Examples are:

- microwave radiation from a mobile phone
- ultraviolet radiation from the sun
- light and infrared radiation from a lamp
- gamma radiation from the nucleus of an atom.

These are all part of the **electromagnetic spectrum**.

X-rays and gamma rays are very penetrating and can ionise body cells, increasing the risk of cancer. An ion is an atom that has become charged by gaining or losing **electrons**.

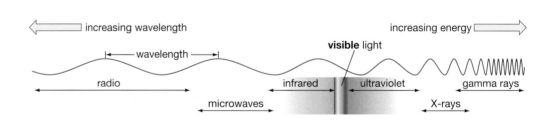

increasing wavelength

increasing energy

visible light

wavelength

radio

infrared

ultraviolet

gamma rays

microwaves

X-rays

FIGURE 2: The smaller the wavelength of the radiation, the more harmful it is.

▪▪ QUESTIONS ▪▪

1 Which has the greater frequency, microwaves or X-rays?

2 If an atom loses an electron, does it become a positive or a negative ion?

WOW FACTOR!

The adult human body is composed of approximately 55–60% water. The brain is composed of 70% water.

Intensity of radiation

The intensity of radiation received at a point some distance from the source depends on:

- the distance from the source
- the medium through which the radiation passes.

Intensity = **power** of incident radiation/area, or $I = P/A$.

If waves spread out uniformly in all directions from a point source the power of the source, P, is spread over a sphere of radius r. This means $A = 4\pi r^2$.

Example: Find the intensity 2 m from a 60 W lamp.

$$I = \frac{P}{A}$$
$$= \frac{P}{4\pi r^2}$$
$$= \frac{60}{4 \times \pi \times 2^2}$$
$$= 1.2\,W/m^2$$

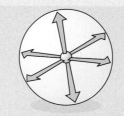

FIGURE 3: The light spreads out over a sphere.

When the radiation passes through an optically denser medium it loses energy. This reduces the power of the incident radiation, and hence the intensity.

Effect of radiation on living matter

Radiation can be divided into non-ionising and ionising radiation.

Non-ionising radiation has no proven effect on living matter but some people are concerned about possible health risks including:

- childhood leukaemia caused by living near high-voltage power lines
- brain tumours caused by the use of mobile phones.

Ionising radiation – X-rays and gamma radiation – are known to affect body cells. The cells may

- mutate
- die
- fail to reproduce themselves.

Effects of radiation damage include:

- skin burns
- nausea
- destruction of bone marrow
- hair loss
- changes in genetic material
- sterility
- cancers.

Very high doses can cause death within days.

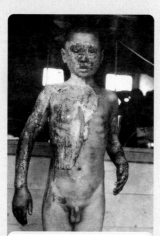

FIGURE 4: Radiation burns caused by the atomic bomb that exploded above Nagasaki in 1945.

QUESTIONS

3 Calculate the intensity 3 m from a 24 W radiation source in air.

4 Name **two** types of non-ionising radiation.

5 Which type of radiation, α, β, γ or X-rays, is most likely to cause skin burns?

6 Suggest why cancer cells are particularly susceptible to ionising radiation.

More about ionising radiation

Cell damage can be:

- stochastic (random) - having no threshold dose. The probability of damage occurring is proportional to the dose received but if it occurs the size of dose has no effect, e.g. cancer – due to cells mutating
- non-stochastic effects only occur above a threshold dose and increase in severity with increased dose, e.g. skin burns – due to cells being killed or unable to reproduce themselves
- somatic (stochastic or non-stockastic) – affect only the person exposed to the radiation
- hereditary (stockastic)– affect reproductive cells, passing any effects on to future generations.

The *extent* of the damage depends on

- the dose received
- the part of the body exposed – rapidly dividing cells are most susceptible
- the time over which the dose is received – a given dose over a long time is less harmful than the same dose in a short time
- the nature of the radiation – α, β, γ or X-rays. α-particles are absorbed by the skin so do not present a serious hazard unless their source gets inside the body. Other forms of ionising radiation are much more penetrating and so can cause much damage.

Radiation damages cells through

- direct action – ionising molecules such as DNA
- indirect action – causing chemical changes in the water content of cells which can then damage important molecules such as DNA.

QUESTIONS

7 Discuss why the hereditary effects of ionising radiation are of greater concern than somatic effects.

8 Suggest, with a reason, which type of action, direct or indirect, is the main cause of cell damage.

Finding a pulse

SELF-CHECK ACTIVITY

CONTEXT

Will is in his school's cross-country team and was about two-thirds of the way round the course in his last race when he blacked out and fell to the ground. He wasn't really hurt, but dropped out of the race. The team coach wanted to make sure things were OK and insisted he went to see his doctor, who arranged for him to have a chest X-ray and an ECG.

He had the chest X-ray at the local hospital. He stripped to the waist and stood in front of a large metal plate. The X-ray tube was pointed at his back, the radiographer went behind a protective screen, 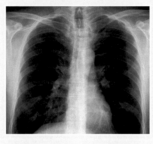 and after a few seconds it was all done. The image would be sent straight to his doctor.

The ECG also involved a trip to the local hospital. Once more it was time to strip to the waist and a nurse attached a number of electrodes to his chest by 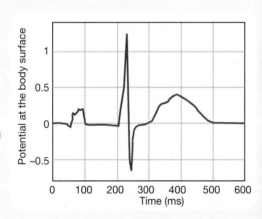 means of sticky pads. The electrodes measure the electrical impulses across the chest, and therefore the heart, in different directions.

The first, quite small, peak shown is the P-wave, as the atria contract. The second, much larger one, is QRS, as the ventricles contract. The third one is the T-wave, which is, in effect, the resetting of the ventricles. The doctor told Will that the distance between the first and second peaks, second and third peaks and width of the second peak should all be pretty short.

CHALLENGE

STEP 1

What can you see in the chest X-ray?

STEP 2

Why are some parts of the X-ray pale and others dark?

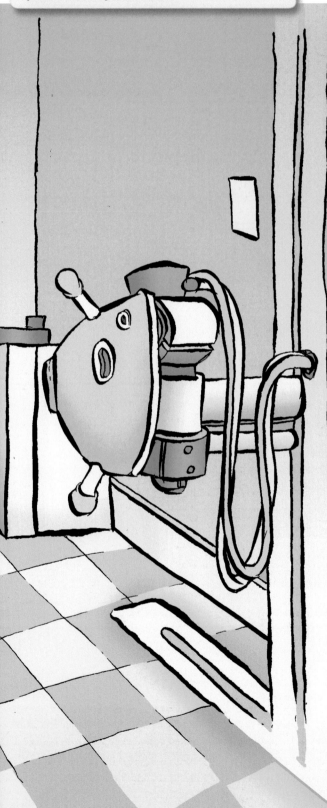

STEP 3

Why did the radiographer go behind a screen when the X-ray machine was turned on?
Why was it OK for Will not to be protected by a screen?

STEP 4

What does the ECG show?

STEP 5

What is meant by 'action potential'?

STEP 6

What can you say about the ECG trace?

STEP 7

What do you think Will's doctor will say when the results of the tests get back to him?

Maximise your grade

These sentences show what you need to include in your work to achieve each grade. Use them to improve your work and be more successful.

Grade	Answer includes...
	Interpret some features of a chest X-ray.
F	Explain what causes some parts of an X-ray image to be darker than others.
	Give comprehensive explanation of chest X-ray.
	Explain about risk from repeated exposure to X-ray.
C	Explain what an ECG is.
	Interpret Will's ECG trace.
A	Explain what is meant by action potential.
	Draw together information from both images to suggest an overall diagnosis.

Slow neutrons

You will find out:

- What is meant by a thermal neutron
- How to write nuclear equations using thermal neutrons
- About momentum conservation
- How to do calculations on momentum

Thermal neutrons

Thermal neutrons are neutrons that have been slowed down to a speed of about 2 mm/s. Such thermal neutrons cause uranium fission in a nuclear power station.

They are also used in an advanced cancer treatment called boron neutron capture therapy. Thermal neutrons are used to 'activate' boron implanted inside a cancerous **tumour**. Alpha radiation is emitted, giving a high-radiation dose to the tumour while reducing the radiation exposure in the surrounding healthy tissues.

FIGURE 1: Sizewell B nuclear power station uses thermal neutrons.

Nuclear fission

Fission is the splitting up of a large nucleus, such as uranium, to form smaller daughter products with the release of energy.

Fission is started by a slow-moving neutron – a **thermal neutron**.

The neutron is slowed down so that it has the same average thermal energy as the atoms or molecules through which it is passing.

The thermal neutron is absorbed by the nucleus of a uranium-235 atom. The nucleus is now less stable than before. It splits into two parts, releasing energy.

Several neutrons are also produced. These may go on to strike the nuclei of other atoms, causing further fission. This is called a **chain reaction**.

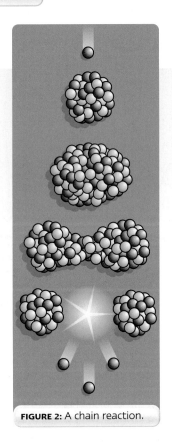

FIGURE 2: A chain reaction.

░ QUESTIONS ░

1   What is a thermal neutron?
2   What is needed to create a chain reaction?

DID YOU KNOW?

The existence of the neutron was predicted in 1920 but it was not until 1932 that Chadwick demonstrated its existence.

...alpha particle   ...bombarding   ...chain reaction   ...gamma radiation   ...half-life

Momentum

$$\text{Momentum} = \text{mass } (m) \times \text{velocity } (v)$$

It is measured in kilogram metre per second (kg m/s).

Momentum is a vector quantity, therefore direction is important.

Example: Find the momentum of a car of mass 1000 kg travelling due north at 20 m/s.

Momentum = mv = 1000 × 20 = 20 000 kg m/s due north.

Conservation of momentum

In any collision, if no external forces act, the total momentum before the collision is equal to the total momentum after the collision.

Example: Two trolleys collide and stick together. Find their common velocity.

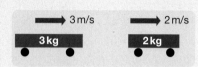

Momentum before = (3 × 3) + (2 × 2) = 13 kg m/s

Momentum after = (3 + 2) × v, where v = common velocity after collision

$$13 = 5v$$
$$v = 13/5 = 2.6 \text{ m/s to the right}$$

The idea of **momentum conservation** can be used to find out what happens when a neutron collides with a nucleus.

Boron neutron capture therapy

This is used to treat brain tumours as boron is picked up more easily by tumour cells than by normal brain tissue.

- A boron compound is injected into the bloodstream and absorbed by the tumour.
- A single dose of thermal neutron radiation is given; this targets the boron in the tumour cells.
- High-energy **alpha particles** are emitted. These have a very short range and kill the tumour cells.

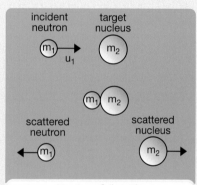

FIGURE 3: Neutron fails to be absorbed and bounces off nucleus.

Artificial radioactivity

Radioisotopes can be made artificially by **bombarding** some nuclei with radiation.

The first nuclear transformation was carried out by Rutherford in 1919. It can be described in terms of a nuclear equation:

$$^{14}_{7}\text{N} + ^{4}_{2}\text{He} \rightarrow ^{17}_{8}\text{O} + ^{1}_{1}\text{H}$$

Note that for each side of the equation

- the nucleon numbers are equal
  14 + 4 = 17 + 1
- the proton numbers are equal
  7 + 2 = 8 + 1

Now radioisotopes for specific purposes are produced. For example:

$$^{130}_{52}\text{Te} + ^{1}_{0}\text{n} \rightarrow ^{131}_{52}\text{Te} \rightarrow ^{131}_{53}\text{I} + ^{0}_{-1}\text{e}$$
(A neutrino is also emitted.)

$^{131}_{53}\text{I}$ is used as a **tracer** to investigate and to treat thyroid problems. $^{123}_{53}\text{I}$ is now preferred for diagnosis as it only emits **gamma radiation**, reducing the dose to the patient.

A gamma camera is placed next to the thyroid and monitors the uptake of iodine by the thyroid gland.

Radioisotopes produced especially for medical purposes need to have a short **half-life** because radiation could damage the patient and the patient could expose others to radiation.

Nuclear equation for fission

A possible nuclear equation for fission is

$$^{235}_{92}\text{U} + ^{1}_{0}\text{n} \rightarrow ^{90}_{36}\text{Kr} + ^{143}_{56}\text{Ba} + 3(^{1}_{0}\text{n}) + \gamma\text{-rays}$$

The extra neutrons emitted cause a chain reaction so a large amount of energy can be produced.

Uranium-235 nuclei do not always split in the same way but extra neutrons are always emitted.

QUESTIONS

3 Sam has a mass of 50 kg. Find her momentum when she is running at 6 m/s.

4 A car of mass 1200 kg travelling at 30 m/s runs into the back of a stationary lorry. Find the mass of the lorry if they both move at 4 m/s after the impact.

5 How does a moderator such as graphite slow down neutrons?

6 Give **two** advantages of boron neutron capture therapy.

QUESTIONS

7 Find a, b, c and d in the nuclear equations:

$$^{216}_{84}\text{Po} \rightarrow ^{a}_{b}\text{Pb} + ^{4}_{2}\text{He}$$

$$^{9}_{c}\text{Be} \rightarrow ^{d}_{3}\text{Li} + ^{1}_{1}\text{H}$$

Positrons and PET scans

You will find out:

- About positron emitters
- What happens when a positron meets an electron
- About momentum and mass-energy conservation
- About positron emission tomography (PET) scanning

PET scanning

Positron Emission Tomography (PET) scans are different from other medical scans because they do not actually look at the human body itself. They look at the decay products from radioactive tracers injected into the body. PET scans show how your body uses substances such as glucose, ammonia, water and oxygen. Seeing how these molecules move through your body, and where they are being used, allows your doctor to check for anything unusual that might suggest the presence of disease.

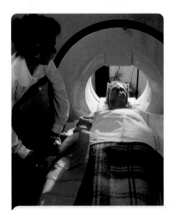

FIGURE 1: PET brain scanning, showing a radiographer about to inject a radioisotope into a vein and the patient's head surrounded by the detector.

What is a positron?

A **positron** is a positively charged **electron**. It has the same mass and amount of charge as an electron, but its charge is positive rather than negative.

When some stable elements, such as fluorine-18 and oxygen-15, are bombarded with proton radiation they create radioactive isotopes that emit positrons.

This is the basis of Positron Emission Tomography (PET) scanners.

PET scans are used to

- look for cancerous tumours
- image brain activity
- look at blood flow in the heart.

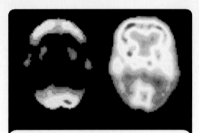

FIGURE 2: PET scans of normal (right) and Alzheimer-afflicted (left) human brains.

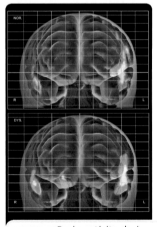

FIGURE 3: Brain activity during reading aloud in a normal (top) and dyslexic subject. The most active areas are in the left cerebral hemisphere (right), site of the brain's language centres.

QUESTIONS

1 What is a proton?
2 Give **one** similarity and **one** difference between a proton and a positron.

...annihilate ...conservation of energy ...electron ...gamma rays ...half-life ...momentum

e = mc²

Einstein showed that

- mass can be converted into energy
- energy can be converted into mass,

according to the equation $E = mc^2$ where

E = energy equivalent of a mass, m;

c = velocity of electromagnetic radiation (e.g. light) = 3×10^8 m/s.

Example: Find the energy equivalent of a 1 kg mass.

$$E = mc^2$$
$$= 1 \times (3 \times 10^8)^2$$
$$= 9 \times 10^{16} \text{ J}$$

This link between mass and energy must be accepted for the principle of **conservation of energy** to hold.

Positrons and electrons

When a positron (e⁺) and an electron (e⁻) meet:

- they **annihilate** each other (neither exists any more)
- their mass is converted into energy
- two **gamma rays** are emitted in opposite directions because **momentum** is conserved.

How a PET scan works

- The patient is injected with a radioactive **tracer** such as fluorine-18 that emits positrons.
- These positrons meet electrons present in the body and annihilate each other, producing two gamma rays in opposite directions.
- The scanner detects the resulting gamma rays.
- A computer produces an image.

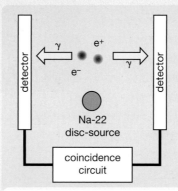

FIGURE 4: Sodium-22 (Na-22) emits a position, which hits an electron and annihilates by emitting two gamma rays.

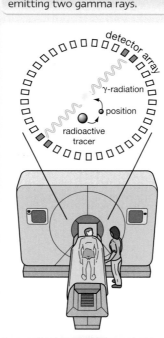

FIGURE 5: How a PET scan works.

WOW FACTOR!

A positron is an anti-matter electron – yes, there is such a thing as anti-matter!

Making positron emitters

- A suitable target material is bombarded with protons, creating an unstable nucleus, e.g.

$$^{18}_{8}\text{O} + ^{1}_{1}\text{H} \rightarrow ^{18}_{9}\text{F} + ^{1}_{0}\text{n}$$

- The new nucleus decays by emitting a positron with a **half-life** that can vary from a split second to thousands of years. (A neutrino, υ, is also emitted.)

$$^{18}_{9}\text{F} \rightarrow ^{18}_{8}\text{O} + ^{0}_{1}\text{e} (+ \upsilon)$$

Other target materials are chosen depending on the reason for the PET scan.

- Oxygen is used as the tracking molecule to image brain activity or to look at blood flow to the heart to detect coronary heart disease.
- Tracking how the body uses glucose produces images of cancerous tumours as cancerous tissue absorbs more glucose than normal tissues.

DID YOU KNOW?

A neutrino is a particle with no mass or charge that travels at near the speed of light.

QUESTIONS

3 An electron has a mass of 9.11×10^{-31} kg.

   a How much energy is released when an electron and positron annihilate?
   b How much energy does each gamma ray acquire?

4 How much mass is equivalent to 1 J of energy?

5 Why should the radioactive tracer used in PET scans have a short half-life?

QUESTIONS

6 List the differences between the normal and diseased PET scans shown in Figures 2 and 3.

Treatment

Treating cancers

Nuclear radiation and high-energy X-rays are often used to treat cancers. The photograph shows a patient undergoing gamma knife radiotherapy to treat a brain tumour. The patient receives a dose of gamma radiation. The head is held in place by a metal frame. Radiation is targeted at a specific area of the brain and has a minimal effect on surrounding areas. It is non-invasive and provides access to areas of the brain that cannot be reached by other techniques.

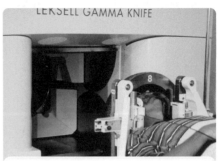

FIGURE 1: A patient receiving a dose of gamma radiation.

Radiotherapy

Not all cancers are the same. Different **tumours** need different treatments.

The three main forms of treatment are:

- surgery
- chemotherapy (using drugs)
- radiotherapy (using radiation).

Many patients receive a combination of these treatments.

Radiotherapy directs beams of high-energy radiation (**X-rays** or **gamma rays**) at a tumour to damage its cells. This means they are unable to reproduce or spread.

A radiographer carries out procedures using X-rays and gamma rays. Figure 2 shows a woman being treated for skin cancer. She has a lead block on her eye and cheek to protect the healthy cells from the radiation. The lead is covered in cling film because it is toxic on contact with the skin.

FIGURE 2: Radiographers position an X-ray generator over a woman's cheek.

when radiation is effect.

QUESTIONS

1 What are X-rays?
2 Why is lead used to shield healthy tissue from radiation?

DID YOU KNOW?

A linear accelerator produces X-rays with about ten times the energy of the gamma rays emitted by the decay of cobalt-60.

...*brachytherapy* ...*gamma rays* ...*neutrons*

Using gamma radiation

Gamma radiation is used to treat cancer because it can damage and destroy cancerous cells. Large doses of radiation from a high-energy source such as cobalt-60 can be used in place of surgery or, more usually, after surgery, to try to make sure *all* the cancerous cells are removed or destroyed.

If any cancerous cells are left behind they can multiply and cause further problems, such as the development of secondary cancers elsewhere in the body. The side effects of the treatment can be unpleasant but it can slow down or completely cure the cancer.

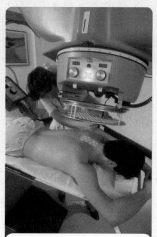
FIGURE 3: A 'cobalt bomb' being set up to treat a patient.

Brachytherapy

Internal radiation, or **brachytherapy**, works by implanting radioactive 'seeds' directly into a tumour where they remain for a period of time. This targets cancer cells directly, making the tumour unstable. It can be used to treat a number of types of tumours including those in the mouth, lip and breast. Very thin radioactive needles, caesium or iridium wires or tubes are inserted.

They are left in place for a period between 24 hours and a week.   Iridium-192 emits β-particles and low-energy gamma rays. It deposits most of its energy close to the cancer and so does little damage to the healthy tissue around it.

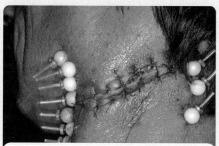
FIGURE 4: Radioactive iridium wires implanted into a man's neck to treat a lymphatic cancer.

DID YOU KNOW?

Brachytherapy is the name given to the implanting of radioactive 'seeds' directly into tumours.

Comparing X-rays and gamma rays

- X-rays and gamma rays are exactly the same; they differ only in their origin.
- An X-ray machine allows the rate of production and energy of the X-rays to be controlled, but you cannot change the gamma radiation emitted from a particular radioactive source.
- X-rays can have a much higher energy than gamma rays.

Using radiation

High-energy, fast **neutrons** can penetrate target atoms and interact with their nuclei easily because they are uncharged. They collide with several nuclei, producing considerable ionisation, before losing their energy.

FIGURE 5: Neutron therapy.

Laser cross-hairs (red) are aimed onto the site of the patient's tumour. Once targeted, a beam of high-energy neutrons is fired at the tumour. The neutron beam is formed by bombarding a beryllium target with protons which are deflected by a linear accelerator (at right of picture). The neutron beam will stop the tumour's growth and could destroy it. The patient is wearing a mask to hold the head still while the treatment takes place.

QUESTIONS

3 Why is gamma radiation used for most cancer treatments using radiotherapy?

4 Suggest why the treatment using cobalt-60 is called a 'cobalt bomb'.

5 Why is radiotherapy often used after surgery to remove a tumour?

6 What are the advantages of brachytherapy to treat a localised tumour?

QUESTIONS

7 Give **one** advantage of using X-rays rather than gamma rays as a source of radiation.

8 Write a possible nuclear equation for producing neutrons by bombarding beryllium ($^{9}_{4}$Be) with protons.

Radiation – friend or foe?

You will find out:

- About the importance of limiting exposure to radiation
- About palliative care
- About social and ethical issues of new medical techniques

Nuclear radiation

Granite rocks contain small amounts of uranium so are radioactive. When uranium decays it emits radon gas which is also radioactive. In areas such as Devon and Cornwall, where houses were traditionally built from granite, there is concern about the health risks associated with breathing in radon gas. More worrying to many people is the radiation caused by human activities, such as nuclear power stations and the use of ionising radiation in medicine.

FIGURE 1: Is it safe to live here?

Background radiation

Background radiation is always around us. It comes from many sources, most of them naturally occurring. Radon gas emitted by granite rocks makes a large contribution to background radiation. Medical procedures contribute about 10%.

Radiation knows no boundaries. After the Chernobyl accident at a nuclear power station in the Ukraine in 1986, prevailing winds blew radiation over much of Europe. Welsh farmers could not sell their lambs for several years because of the risk of radiation contamination.

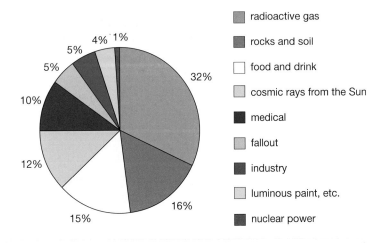

radioactive gas
rocks and soil
food and drink
cosmic rays from the Sun
medical
fallout
industry
luminous paint, etc.
nuclear power

4% 1%
5%
5%
10%
12%
15%
16%
32%

FIGURE 2: Radiation from background sources.

⊪ QUESTIONS ⊪

1 Suggest how Welsh lamb became contaminated by radiation.

2 Louis measures background radiation in Devon. It is 50 counts per minute. Ann measures it in London. It is only 30 counts per minute. Suggest why there is such a big difference.

WOW FACTOR!

Radium is the most powerful radioactive substance known: it emits radiation a million times more intensely than uranium!

Limiting exposure to radiation

When using radiation for medical purposes steps must be taken to protect

- the patient
- hospital staff
- the general public.

A film badge is worn by people who work with radioactive substances to determine their exposure to radiation. The badge contains a piece of photographic film.

Radiation affects the film in a similar way to light. The badge's exterior is of differing thicknesses because the various types of radiation penetrate to different depths. Thus the depth of penetration provides a measure of exposure to the various types of radiation.

FIGURE 3: A film badge.

The **thermoluminescent dosimeter (TLD)** is more accurate and sensitive than a film badge. It contains lithium fluoride, which emits light when ionising radiation falls on it.

Treating cancer

Whenever radiation is used, for diagnosis or therapy, steps must be taken to minimise damage to healthy tissue.

High-powered gamma radiation, from a radioisotope such as cobalt-60, can be used to destroy a tumour inside the body, such as a brain tumour. But a large enough dose to destroy the tumour would also destroy the healthy tissue it passed through. This problem is solved in one of two ways:

- Three **sources** of radiation, each providing one third of the required dose, are arranged as shown. Each source is focused on the tumour, but healthy tissue only receives a third of the dose.
- A single source of radiation is slowly rotated around the patient, with the tumour at the centre of the circle. The tumour constantly receives radiation but healthy tissue for only a small fraction of the time.

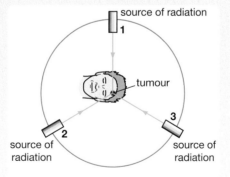

FIGURE 4: Three sources of radiation are used.

Lead wedges are also used to stop radiation reaching healthy tissue. It is particularly important to shield vulnerable organs.

General safety rules

When using radioactive sources:

- keep your distance from the source as large as possible
- reduce your exposure time to a minimum
- use shielding when appropriate
- with open sources, avoid or contain any contamination.

Social and ethical issues

Modern medical techniques allow doctors to prolong life.

We need to consider several important points:

- Some treatments can be very painful. Should they be carried out to extend life if there is no possibility of a cure? Does it depend on the extra life expectancy offered?
- Some treatments are expensive. Should they be offered to a patient to ease their suffering (**palliative care**) although there is no possibility of a cure?
- It is now possible to transplant various organs. Recently a patient in France underwent the world's first face transplant. Do you agree with organ transplants?
- The postcode lottery. New drugs are sometimes only available to residents of some Health Authorities.

There are several medical issues that have received wide publicity:

- cloning
- embryo research
- designer babies
- voluntary euthanasia.

QUESTIONS

3 Why is a syringe used to inject technetium-99m surrounded by lead?

4 Debbie has an iridium implant to treat breast cancer. Why should she not cuddle her baby?

5 Distinguish between diagnosis and therapy.

QUESTIONS

6 Choose **one** of the medical issues above and write a paragraph for or against it.

Unit summary

Concept map

Refraction
Refraction is a change in speed of a ray of light which may give rise to a change in direction

Optical fibres
Total internal reflection occurs in optical fibres. Optical fibres are used in endoscopes to see inside the body.

Total internal reflection (TIR)
TIR happens when light passes from a dense to a less dense medium, e.g. glass to air.
The critical angle is the angle of incidence for which the angle of refraction is 90°.
If the angle of incidence is greater than the critical angle, all the light is reflected.

Heartbeat
The heart beats regularly as it pumps blood around the body.

$$\text{frequency} = \frac{1}{\text{time period}}. \quad f = \frac{1}{T}$$

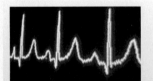

An electrocardiogram (ECG) measures the action potential, or electrical activity, of the heart.

Using energy
Work done = energy transferred = force × distance moved in direction of force. $W = F \times s$

Power = work done/time. $P = W/t$

Basal metabolic rate (BMR) is the rate at which the body uses energy when completely at rest.

Thermal neutrons are slow-moving neutrons.

Thermal neutrons cause fission of uranium nuclei. Extra neutrons are emitted, causing a chain reaction.

Radiation
Radiation describes energy that spreads out from a source. Ionising radiation – X-rays and gamma rays – can affect body cells and can cause cancers.

Artificial radioisotopes are made by bombarding nuclei with radiation. For example:

$$^{14}_{7}N + ^{4}_{2}He \rightarrow ^{17}_{8}O + ^{1}_{1}H$$

Treatment
High-powered radiation, such as X-rays, gamma rays or neutron radiation, is used to treat cancers.

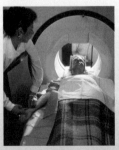

Positrons and PETs
A positron is a positively charged electron. Some artificial radioisotopes emit positrons when they decay. This is the basis of Positron Emission Tomography (PET) scanners.

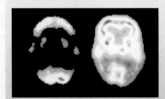

Radiation – friend or foe?
It is important to limit exposure to radiation. Background radiation is low level and always around us, but high levels due to, for example, medical uses and nuclear accidents can be damaging.
Precautions must be taken when using radiation to treat cancers. It is sometimes used to ease suffering (palliative care) if no cure is possible.

Unit quiz

1 What is meant by the 'critical angle'?

2 How does light travel along an optical fibre?

3 What do we call an instrument that uses optical fibres to enable a doctor to see inside the body?

4 What two things does a pulse oximeter tell you about a patient?

5 What is meant by the intensity of light falling on a surface?

6 How much energy does Jack need to lift a 25 kg bag of potatoes onto a shelf 0.5 m above the ground?

7 What is meant by 'basal metabolic rate'?

8 What do the letters ECG stand for?

9 What does an ECG measure?

10 Give one similarity and one difference between X-rays and gamma rays.

11 Give one effect of ionising radiation on body cells.

12 What is meant by a radioisotope?

13 What is a *thermal* neutron?

14 What is meant by nuclear fission?

15 Calculate the momentum of a car of mass 1500 kg travelling at 20 m/s.

16 What is a positron?

17 What happens when a positron and electron meet?

18 What type of radiation is emitted by a radioactive tracer?

19 What is the difference between therapy and diagnosis?

20 Why may three radioactive sources be used to treat a brain tumour?

Literacy activity

Thyroid cancer

The following passage is taken from an information leaflet given to Sam's Dad before he has radiation treatment for thyroid cancer.

The treatment uses a radioactive form of iodine called iodine-131. The radioactive iodine circulates throughout your body in your bloodstream. Thyroid cancer cells will pick up the iodine wherever they are in your body. The radiation in the iodine will then kill the cancer cells. The treatment will make you slightly radioactive for a few days, so the time that the staff and your visitors spend with you will be limited.

You will have to stay in your hospital room for a few days until your radiation levels have fallen. A radiation monitor may be used to monitor you or test anything that is taken out of your room. After a few days, you will have a scan to see if the radiation has dropped to a safer level. Once it has, you will be able to go home. You may be told that you shouldn't be in contact with children or breastfeeding mothers for a day or two when you get home.

QUESTIONS

1 Why is radioactive iodine used to treat thyroid cancer?

2 What type of radiation is given out by iodine-131?

3 How do you know that iodine-131 has a short half-life?

4 Why will Sam's Dad's visitors be allowed to stay for only a short time?

5 What instrument could be used to monitor the CD he has been listening to?

6 Why may Sam's Dad be told not to go near his children for a day or two when he gets home?

Exam practice

Exam practice questions

1
  A   Explain what is meant by the basal metabolic rate (BMR).   [2]

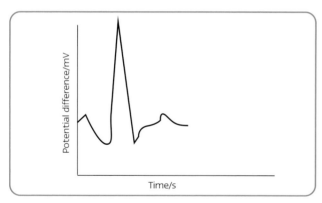

6 m

  B   The diagram shows a cross-section of a climbing wall. A climber climbs 8 m up the wall. If his weight is 750 N, calculate the work done.   [4]

  C   If the climber took 4 minutes to complete his climb, calculate the power he achieved.   [4]

2   The graph shows a typical electrocardiogram (ECG) trace.

Potential difference/mV

Time/s

  A   Mark on the graph the point at which the ventricles are contracting.   [1]

  B   Continue the line to show the trace caused by the next heartbeat.   [2]

  C   In a healthy adult, the heart beats approximately 70 times per minute. Draw on a suitable time scale to the graph.   [1]

  D   One person's pulse rate is measured as 75 beats per minute. What is the frequency of their pulse? Include units.   [4]

  E   Describe how an ECG trace can be used to identify whether a person has had a heart attack.   [2]

3   A person diagnosed with a cancerous tumour may be offered radiotherapy as a possible treatment.

  A   Explain what is meant by radiotherapy.   [2]

  B   Describe how the risks of radiotherapy can be reduced for the patient.   [3]

  C   Radiotherapy does not always cure cancer. What other purpose may radiotherapy be used for when treating cancer?   [1]

(Total: 26 marks)

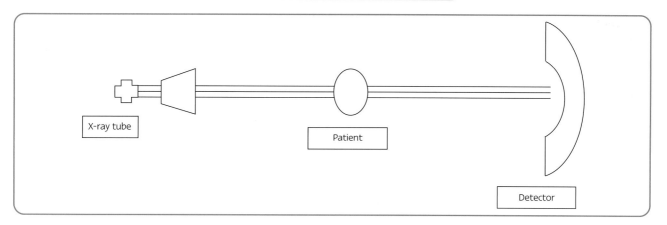

The diagram shows how a positron emission detector can be used to scan a section of the body.

a Explain how the scanner uses positrons to create gamma rays. [2]

b Describe how the PET scanner produces a scan. [4]

c State what physical quantities are conserved when a positron collides with an electron. [3]

d State one use of a PET scanner. [1]

Good. This answer gains 2 marks.

a *The positron meets with an electron and they destroy each other, releasing gamma rays.*

This is enough for 3 marks. Also state that the positrons collide with electrons to create X-rays, which are detected by the scanner.

b *The patient is injected with a radioactive material. This collects in certain tissues. Positrons are emitted and can be detected.*

Correct for 2 marks but the mark scheme allows for 3 marks. Momentum is also conserved.

c *Mass and charge.*

d *To detect brain tumours.*

Correct. Also to locate the site of epileptic activity.

Overall Grade: A

How to get an A

If you need to write a longer answer, take a little time to plan what you will write. Think about the sequence and you will be less likely to miss out facts.

Databank

The periodic table

Key:
- Atomic Number
- Symbol
- Name
- Molar mass in g mol^{-1}

Period	Group 1	Group 2												Group 3	Group 4	Group 5	Group 6	Group 7	Group 8
1	1 **H** Hydrogen 1																		2 **He** Helium 4
2	3 **Li** Lithium 7	4 **Be** Beryllium 9												5 **B** Boron 11	6 **C** Carbon 12	7 **N** Nitrogen 14	8 **O** Oxygen 16	9 **F** Fluorine 19	10 **Ne** Neon 20
3	11 **Na** Sodium 23	12 **Mg** Magnesium 24												13 **Al** Aluminium 27	14 **Si** Silicon 28	15 **P** Phosphorus 31	16 **S** Sulphur 32	17 **Cl** Chlorine 35.5	18 **Ar** Argon 40
4	19 **K** Potassium 39	20 **Ca** Calcium 40	21 **Sc** Scandium 45	22 **Ti** Titanium 48	23 **V** Vanadium 51	24 **Cr** Chromium 52	25 **Mn** Manganese 55	26 **Fe** Iron 56	27 **Co** Cobalt 59	28 **Ni** Nickel 59	29 **Cu** Copper 63.5	30 **Zn** Zinc 65.4		31 **Ga** Gallium 70	32 **Ge** Germanium 73	33 **As** Arsenic 75	34 **Se** Selenium 79	35 **Br** Bromine 80	36 **Kr** Krypton 84
5	37 **Rb** Rubidium 85	38 **Sr** Strontium 88	39 **Y** Yttrium 89	40 **Zr** Zirconium 91	41 **Nb** Niobium 93	42 **Mo** Molybdenum 96	43 **Tc** Technetium (99)	44 **Ru** Ruthenium 101	45 **Rh** Rhodium 103	46 **Pd** Palladium 106	47 **Ag** Silver 108	48 **Cd** Cadmium 112		49 **In** Indium 115	50 **Sn** Tin 119	51 **Sb** Antimony 122	52 **Te** Tellurium 128	53 **I** Iodine 127	54 **Xe** Xenon 131
6	55 **Cs** Caesium 133	56 **Ba** Barium 137	57 **La** Lanthanum 139	72 **Hf** Hafnium 178	73 **Ta** Tantalum 181	74 **W** Tungsten 184	75 **Re** Rhenium 186	76 **Os** Osmium 190	77 **Ir** Iridium 192	78 **Pt** Platinum 195	79 **Au** Gold 197	80 **Hg** Mercury 201		81 **Tl** Thallium 204	82 **Pb** Lead 207	83 **Bi** Bismuth 209	84 **Po** Polonium (210)	85 **At** Astatine (210)	86 **Rn** Radon (222)
7	87 **Fr** Francium (223)	88 **Ra** Radium (226)	89 **Ac** Actinium (227)	104 **Unq** Unnilquadium (261)	105 **Unp** Unnilpentium (262)	106 **Uuh** Unnilhexium (263)													

Lanthanides:

58 **Ce** Cerium 140	59 **Pr** Praseodymium 141	60 **Nd** Neodymium 144	61 **Pm** Promethium (147)	62 **Sm** Samarium 150	63 **Eu** Europium 152	64 **Gd** Gadolinium 157	65 **Tb** Terbium 159	66 **Dy** Dysprosium 163	67 **Ho** Holmium 165	68 **Er** Erbium 167	69 **Tm** Thulium 169	70 **Yb** Ytterbium 173	71 **Lu** Lutetium 175

Actinides:

90 **Th** Thorium 232	91 **Pa** Protactinium (231)	92 **U** Uranium 238	93 **Np** Neptunium (237)	94 **Pu** Plutonium (242)	95 **Am** Americium (243)	96 **Cm** Curium (247)	97 **Bk** Berkelium (245)	98 **Cf** Californium (251)	99 **Es** Einsteinium (254)	100 **Fm** Fermium (253)	101 **Md** Mendelevium (256)	102 **No** Nobelium (254)	103 **Lr** Lawrencium (257)

Some useful formulae

pressure = $\dfrac{\text{force}}{\text{area}}$ or $P = \dfrac{F}{A}$

Charles' law = $\dfrac{V}{T}$ = constant

Pressure law = $\dfrac{P}{T}$ = constant

Boyle's law = PV = constant

ideal gas equation = $\dfrac{P_1 V_1}{T_1} = \dfrac{P_2 V_2}{T_2}$

kinetic energy gained by electron = charge on electron $\times$ potential difference through which it is accelerated

$KE = eV$

number of moles = $\dfrac{\text{mass of substance}}{\text{mass of one mole}}$

Keyword	Definition	Page
absolute zero	A scale linked to an external value, for example the absolute scale of temperature uses the value of –273 °C as zero.	126–127
accelerating anode	Positive electrode which will attract electrons in electron gun.	144–145
acid(s)	A chemical that turns litmus paper red – it can often dissolve things that water cannot.	74–75, 88–89, 106–107
active ingredient	Ingredient in medicine that makes it work.	32–33
action potential	A rapid change in the electrical conditions in a nerve cell that helps to carry messages along nerves.	160–161
alcohol	Group of compounds containing carbon, hydrogen and oxygen, with a formula ending in –OH. Usually made by fermentation.	16–17, 106–107
alkali(s)	A substance which makes a solution that turns red litmus paper blue.	74–75, 110–111, 116–117
alkali metals	Metals in group 1 of the periodic table.	110–111
alloys	A mixture of two or more metals.	98–99
alpha particle	The charged nucleus of a helium atom with a charge of +2 and a mass of 4.	130–131, 132–133, 166–167
altruistic behaviour	When members of species take turns at social activity that is good for whole group.	50–51
amino acid	The sub-units making up protein molecules. There are over 20 different amino acids used by living things.	18–19
amount	Quantity.	78–79
anhydrous	Without water.	110–111
anion	A negatively-charged ion.	102–103
annihilate	Destroy.	168–169
anode	The positive electrode in a circuit or battery.	102–103
anthropomorphism	Interpreting animal behaviour in terms of human behaviour.	60–61
antibiotic	A substance produced by a microbe which kills other microbes. Some antibiotics can be purified and used to treat infections.	14–15
artery	A blood vessel carrying blood away from the heart under high pressure.	156–157
Avogadro constant	Number of atoms in exactly 12 g of carbon, 6×10^{23}.	78–79
Avogadro's law	Avogadro's law states that equal volumes of all gases under identical conditions of pressure and temperature contain the same number of molecules.	84–85
background radiation	Radiation present at all times in an area due to natural causes.	172–173
bacteria	Microscopic single-celled living things that have no nucleus.	14–15
balancing	Making both sides of a chemical equation have equal numbers of each element, either as the element itself or in compounds.	70–71
basal metabolic rate (BMR)	A measure of the average rate of reactions in the body.	158–159
base	Substance with pH greater than 7.	88–89
behaviour	Set of actions.	42–43
beta particle	A fast-moving electron not captured by an atom, mass is negligible, charge is –1.	130–131, 132–133, 134–135
biodegradable	A substance which can be broken down by biological action in the environment.	118–119
biotechnology	Technology that uses biological materials, for example enzymes, in an industrial context. It is also used to describe the range of genetic engineering techniques in use today.	14–15, 22–23
birds	Feathered animals.	58–59
blood sugar	The level of glucose present in the blood.	30–31
bombarding	Targeting continuously.	166–167
brachytherapy	A form of radiotherapy that places small radioactive objects as near to the tumour as possible – often inserted into the body or into body cavities.	170–171
breeding	Production of young.	14–15
Bunsen burner	Small source of gas used in laboratory.	84–85
carbonates	Compounds containing the carbonate group of atoms. The carbonate group formula is CO_3.	76–77
carboxylic acid	An organic acid that contains one or more carboxyl groups.	106–107
carnivores	Meat eaters.	54–55
catalyst(s)	Catalysts speed up a reaction but are not changed by or used up by it.	98–99, 100–101, 112–113, 114–115
cathode	The negative electrode in a circuit or a battery.	102–103, 144–145
cathode ray oscilloscope	A device that uses a moving electron beam on a phosphor screen to display moving representations of phenomena such as sound or rapidly changing electrical signals.	146–147
cation	A positively-charged ion.	102–103
Celsius	A temperature scale where water freezes at 0 °C and boils at 100 °C.	126–127
chain reaction	A reaction which, once started, propagates itself.	166–167
chemical formula	Shorthand for chemical elements or compounds.	70–71
cholesterol	A chemical found particularly in animal fats and foods made from them. The body uses cholesterol to make nerve tissue and some hormones. High levels of cholesterol may make heart attacks more likely.	20–21
chymosin	An enzyme that coagulates milk. It is used in the manufacture of some cheeses.	18–19
citric acid	A colourless acid found in citrus fruits like oranges and lemons.	18–19
combustion	Combustion is the reaction between a fuel and oxygen to form carbon dioxide and water, and release energy as light and heat.	82–83

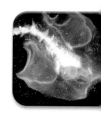

Glossary

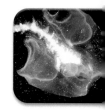

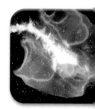